Cultivating Critical Conversations in Art Education

Cultivating Critical Conversations in Art Education

Honoring Student Voice, Identity, and Agency

Connie Stewart
Eli Burke
Lisa Hochtritt
Toya Northington

EDITORS

Foreword by James Haywood Rolling Jr.

TEACHERS COLLEGE PRESS
TEACHERS COLLEGE | COLUMBIA UNIVERSITY
NEW YORK AND LONDON

Published by Teachers College Press,® 1234 Amsterdam Avenue, New York, NY 10027

Front cover illustration by Val_Iva / Shutterstock.

Library of Congress Cataloging-in-Publication Data is available at loc.gov

ISBN 978-0-8077-6898-3 (paper)
ISBN 978-0-8077-6899-0 (hardcover)
ISBN 978-0-8077-8203-3 (ebook)

Printed on acid-free paper
Manufactured in the United States of America

Contents

Foreword

It has been my privilege to have previously encountered many of the educators assembled in the pages of this new book either in my current role as the president of the National Art Education Association, or during my past service as the senior editor of the *Art Education* journal from 2015 to 2017. Whether their primary pedagogical space has been in K–12 and university classrooms, museums, or community-based settings, each of the authors presented in this volume has been engaged in the essential work of creating space for *others* to find their voices.

Why does voice matter? Because at the heart of our professional work is the understanding that art is a meaning-making activity (Rolling, 2016). One of the purposes of the arts is to maintain a rich and diverse stock of narratives about what it means to be human and to experience the world, while communicating and conserving shared meanings across cultures (Gudmundsdottir, 1995). However, in 2023, the work of art has never been more difficult. In the preface of this important new book, the coeditors remind us that artists and arts learners are engaged in the very difficult practice of making, deriving, and communicating a working sense of the world during polemic times. Polemics—a term originating from a Greek word meaning "war"—has mired our ability to dialogue and make sense of one another within a ceaseless scrum of contested meanings disputed across a muddy field of partisan echo chambers, distorting sound bites, media spin, and increasing accusations of "fake news" intended to sabotage dialogue and preselect a set of winners and losers that advantages a select few over others. Playing this zero-sum game of polemics in order to preempt any possibility of mutually beneficial exchange is the very opposite of the work of art, which has historically been a primary agency for generating, modeling, and adapting new cultural patterns and achievements—the stuff our civilizations are made of.

This book offers its readers a much-needed resource for dialogical interventions capable of dampening the contemporary uproar of outrage and insensitivity. Many years ago, I wrote an article recounting a political cartooning project I developed as the visual arts teacher for my 4th-grade classes at a New York City elementary school—part of my effort to reconceptualize a problematic assumption that children have little to contribute to the dialogues charging our current events. On the contrary, like all arts learners, children are full of opinions and perspectives. They also see the world and have something meaningful to say about a *lot* of things, if simply given the opportunity.

When the 4th-grade-level teaching team at the last elementary school I taught at agreed on a third-trimester theme of Social Justice one year, I became interested in viewing the opinions of my students both on matters we had been talking about in our classrooms and also on matters important to them that were invisible to me. Since we were then in the wake of the 2004 presidential election and the buzz of conversation about the candidates among the children and families at home and at school, I proposed the idea of having each student create his or her own political cartoon. I explained a political cartoon to be a commentary on current events that expresses an opinion and serves to persuade others by its appearance in the public conversation. I further explained that political cartoons are drawings representing current public figures or important social issues symbolically and often satirically, and that art was very much about the ideas my students thought were important. My conception of this political cartooning project depended a great deal on my conception of my job as a teacher—to open the pedagogical space for students to be as critical, as perspicacious, and as opinionated as they choose to be.

I introduced my article about that unique project with the argument that "To be critical is to be political" (Rolling, 2008). Politics is simply an aggregate of people engaged in a complicated conversation to preserve the things that work to hold them together and reshape the things that don't. Critical voices (Rolling, 2013) are the sharpest tools we have to engage in this ongoing dialogue. This new book understands the enduring role of an educator to create space for such voices just as well as I did, and I heartily applaud the coeditors for successfully assembling these chapters for its audiences. A critical voice makes itself heard. A critical voice validates new stories to live by. A critical voice becomes an agent for change. A critical voice helps us all to chart our best course toward our next creative leap.

—Dr. James Haywood Rolling Jr.
Dual Professor of Arts Education and Teaching & Leadership and the Co-Director of the Lender Center for Social Justice at Syracuse University

REFERENCES

Gudmundsdottir, S. (1995). The narrative nature of pedagogical content knowledge. In H. McEwan & K. Egan (Eds.), *Narrative in teaching, learning, and research* (pp. 24–38). Teachers College Press.

Rolling, J. H. Jr. (2008). Sites of contention and critical thinking in the elementary art classroom: A political cartooning project. *International Journal of Education & the Arts, 9*(4), 1–26. http://www.ijea.org/v9n7/

Rolling, J. H. (2013). Art as social response and responsibility: Reframing critical thinking in art education as a basis for altruistic intent. *Art Education, 66*(2), 6–12.

Rolling, J. H. Jr. (2016). Sacred structures: Assembling meaning, constructing self. In M. J. Narey (Ed.), *Multimodal perspectives of language, literacy, and learning in early childhood: The creative and critical "art" of making meaning* (pp. 47–68). Springer.

Preface

Art education by its very nature evolves as artists, including the young, find visual expressions for the changing context of their lives. I have found that teaching is as much a process of definition and redefinition of content and practices as it is a process of conveying established skills and techniques. The powerful place art has in our culture also engenders a struggle for its definition as a discipline within educational systems. Comments from political leaders similar to "Why can't art just be pretty?" and "Why do art standards need to talk about culture? Leave that to Social Studies" imply a definition of art that is vastly different than the healing force artmaking is in my life.

Toni Morrison (1988) states in her novel *Beloved* that "definitions belong to the definers, not to the defined" (p. 190). This much-quoted phrase from a story based within the horrors of slavery now challenges all of us to look at who has the power to define and who is defined. Recently, our local school board meeting was noisily disrupted as a community member demanded the removal of certain books from school libraries, including *Beloved*. We teach in a time when many voices compete to define what teachers should be teaching, what students should be reading and thinking, what role art has within educational systems, and, in the end, what we value as true.

Ta-Nahesi Coates (2015) describes his school years and concludes, "Schools did not reveal truths, they concealed them" (p. 26). I thought of this when I recently visited a high school, walking through a group of students being actively recruited for the military. I reached the art room to observe a well-taught lesson based on the color wheel. I wondered if the same students learning about tints and shades were also thinking about the life choices they soon would have to make. The lesson, like many others, was intended to prepare students for making art later. But I wondered if art would continue to serve the students after they graduated and entered "the real world." I had to question what truths were being taught and which were being concealed.

In fact, one question I was thinking about when defining arts education is whether art prepares students for the "real world," or the spaces students learn in are actually their real worlds now. Do we teach students that they must separate their own lived experiences outside their classrooms from what they learn within them? Or can the art room be the place where honest truths about our students' lives are discussed and explored?

Idealistically, I once believed that open dialogue within safe and brave spaces was the tool art educators could use to reveal and not conceal the realities of life around us all. How can people with very different experiences share stories and ideas and be listened to by others who do not agree? This book was going to be a guide to leading discussions. I still believe in dialogue, but I now think the answers to the questions we face as educators are much more complex. Various exertions of cultural and structural power and personal vulnerabilities interplay within our learning spaces and are worked out through the practices of teachers and learners.

My questions about teaching social justice have evolved since a symposium I organized in 2019 at the University of Northern Colorado with teachers interested in art teaching, which went beyond teaching form to conveying social meanings. The teachers listened to presentations of issues and methods by Dr. Lisa Hochtritt and others. The mood of the day changed when Eli Burke, a coeditor of this volume, openly shared his artwork, revealing stories from his life. At the end of the day, participants were asked to tell a story about when they wish they had said something to counter an injustice. The reflective stories brought about a flood of emotions and support for one another. Teachers who came not knowing one another left as friends.

Building upon that experience, this book shares the stories of educators teaching in school, museum, and community settings, engaged in defining art education as a force for voice and change. They look at their own power, privilege, and vulnerabilities as they define practices of good teaching. The stories are from many viewpoints and contain varied descriptions of what we do as educators. In the end, what we give to each other is our own stories. It is hoped that you can find yourself in the writings, and within your own teaching continue the processes of defining what is real, revealing truth, and inviting the voices of all students into spaces for discourse and understanding.

—Connie Stewart

REFERENCES

Coates, T. -N. (2015) *Between the world and me.* Random House.

Morrison, T. (1988). *Beloved.* Penguin.

Acknowledgments

There are many people we would like to acknowledge, including our families, partners, and friends who supported us in our dedication to this project. Special thanks also to the students, colleagues, artists, and educators who generously shared their time in contributing to this anthology. We have learned so much from you in this process.

The idea for this book started in 2019 when Connie Stewart created a symposium for educators and preservice teachers at the University of Northern Colorado on the topic of the role of art in social change. Lisa Hochtritt and Eli Burke participated in the event. The exceptional Sarah J. Biondello, senior acquisitions editor at Teachers College Press, contacted Connie and invited her to submit a book prospectus based on this presentation topic. Connie invited Lisa and Eli, and Eli, who had worked with Toya Northington on an earlier project, invited her to join us. Sarah Biondello supported our project from the start; after her retirement, the dedicated Sarah Jubar became our main contact. Sarah Jubar has been outstanding to work with, and we appreciate all of the efforts of the Teachers College Press staff. A special thank you to Lori Tate and the production staff whose careful eyes and attention to detail brought the work to completion.

We would also like to thank all of the people who submitted an abstract for this book. We received far more submissions than we had space for, and we wish we could have included all of your voices. We appreciate the work you are doing and your interest in strong, innovative educational practice.

Thanks to Dr. James Haywood Rolling Jr., who agreed to write our Foreword. He eloquently captured the spirit of the anthology, and we are honored to have him as a part of this project. And finally, thank you to Eli Burke for his original artwork that inspired the cover and his willingness to share his stories with us. The book is better because of all of you. Thank you.

Cultivating Critical Conversations in Art Education

Introduction

Connie Stewart, Eli Burke, Lisa Hochtritt, and Toya Northington

Art encompasses issues of identity and culture that connect directly to the lived experiences of learners in the art classroom. Our identities as learners and educators can become enmeshed with the political, influencing what we teach and how we learn. How might we respectfully and critically attend to the realities within our classroom spaces while ensuring all students' experiences are validated and heard? The current national discourse often reinforces a polemical climate. The contributors in this book provide examples to help educators teach through critical conversations (Schieble et al., 2020) and cultivate spaces for dialogue.

INSIDE THE ANTHOLOGY

This book introduces and builds upon theoretical frameworks, art education practices, and personal experiences that are based on dialogue and may include civil discussion of opposing viewpoints. It prioritizes questioning, encourages differing perspectives, and examines contexts as embodied teaching practices. We realize that certain viewpoints can be divisive. In these moments it feels especially important to offer educators opportunities to address topics with care and respect while still encouraging learners to expand their thinking and address meanings conveyed through art making in contemporary contexts. As these chapters convey, we believe art can be used as a tool to connect with students and offer a safe space to unpack and discuss differing opinions and lived experiences.

The anthology addresses important topics of lived experience, including racial inequity, gender identity, economic disparity, and immigration. We focus on classroom dialogue with the understanding that by not addressing the experiences of our students, our silence can hurt more than help. However, within dialogue we do acknowledge the need to make space and time for those who are rarely invited to speak. We believe that vulnerability is an important factor in dialogue. As teachers, students, and artists, we are all vulnerable in what we do, when making and sharing are so public. Creating spaces where teacher's and learner's vulnerability is addressed is essential to this topic. Our contributors offer examples through personal stories and the description of teaching practices. To contextualize these stories, we highlight the different ways that power is exercised and negotiated within classroom/community spaces and how art is often used as a tool to disrupt, trouble, or challenge these systems of power, specifically through the artist's personal experience and subjectivities.

We hope this book will be a resource for art educators who want classrooms where every student's story is carefully listened to and each student finds agency to make a difference in their world (Burke, 2019). Educators can sometimes be discouraged from discussing controversial topics in the classroom for fear of repercussions from administrators, institutions, or the school community. However, in our experience, a variety of current social topics can be effectively addressed in the art room. (Quinn et al., 2012). The authors in this anthology address contemporary issues and critical conversations in art education.

We all have our own complex set of life circumstances that inevitably cross over into the controversial. A "controversy" can be defined as any challenge to current homogeneous societal assumptions. We acknowledge that controversy is relative to each individual and learning context. We encouraged authors to share their own definitions of what is controversial and contextualize it through their own experiences. The result is a guide to creating learning environments that are "communities of discourse, spaces of shared and contested meaning" (Gude, 2009, p. 10).

In the spirit of learning from each other, we seek to extend and continue the conversation with art educators about ways they have addressed dialogue and difficult conversations in their teachings. In the spirit of "dialogic looking" (Wilson McKay & Monteverde, 2003, p. 40) the editors highlight various educational practices during a time of cultural change. The reader can compare ideas and practices that can stimulate their own delivery of instruction.

This book addresses how artists, educators, and scholars reflect on the importance of teaching art through dialogue and how they use art and visual culture to bridge learning with culturally relevant pedagogy and curricula. We are aware that practice-based narratives are best when they include the slip-ups and perceived failures, rather than focusing solely on the successes, and we include contributions that examine these moments. This text is a resource for creating learning spaces where interpersonal connections are prioritized, and conflicting opinions, differing experiences, and individual stories are shared and listened to.

CONTEMPORARY ART AND IDEAS

Art responds to its own time, and the social concerns of our time should be directly addressed and openly discussed in art classrooms. Artists today are making work that responds to the world, engages the viewer with questions, and examines social justice issues. Ralph Rugoff (2019), curator of the 2019 Venice Biennale, chose work assuming that "art works do not offer us conclusions as much as deeply engaging points of departure" (p. 37). He quotes artist Jimmy Durham, who says, "I want to see if I can make the object have a conversation with whoever is looking" (p. 41). Rugoff refers to the artist group Slavs and Tatars, who see interaction with current artworks not as unimpassioned, from a distance, but "through a bear hug" (p. 40). A bear hug with art implies comfort but also risk and vulnerability.

Artists, lessons, and ideas are presented that encourage deep engagement even if such teaching triggers strong emotions in participants or discomfort for discussion leaders. Often, art education curriculum is based on teaching skills and formal characteristics of art within a Euro-American tradition (Gude, 2004). For many educators, it may seem comfortable to rely on the same skills, media, and vocabularies that were used in their own education. This seemingly safe choice often reinforces white, Western, and patriarchal power and acts as evidence of bias and systematic oppression (Acuff, 2020). Ignoring the history of white supremacy and colonialism will not save art teaching from its own biases (Kraehe & Herman, 2020). How are educators in different settings addressing the various complicated contexts of art historical images, introducing new artists, and interrupting the assumptions underlying the way they were taught in their own schooling?

The importance of education in basic art skills is not to be discounted. However, artists known for their emphasis on expert technique and beautiful form also show how forms convey complex meaning. An example is how Martin Puryear's expertly crafted and intriguing formal sculptures address slavery, gun violence, and histories that are seldom taught (Rapaport et al., 2019). A discussion of *only* the forms and techniques he uses reinforces modernist priorities and marginalizes the stated purpose of his work. If we can't talk about the art of our time, invite our students to intimately engage with it, and respond to the world through it, then what are we doing as art educators? This book invites teachers/authors/artists who are attempting to put themselves in the "turbulence of transformation" (Kraehe & Herman, 2020, p. 6), challenging the status quo and opening their classrooms to dialogue.

The authors propose models of art education to guide students in times of cultural crisis and change, asking these practical questions:

- How does art education respond to socially sensitive current events?
- How can artists and educators encourage new ideas, creative thoughts, and innovative approaches to learning? How do we allow for different opinions?
- How do we teach students whose beliefs are different from our own?
- How do we create an environment where dialogue is respectful and meaningful, and all are encouraged to participate?
- As we encourage open discussion, what are the nonnegotiable stances and bottom lines? What opinions cannot be allowed, for example, those in support of Nazism, white supremacy, and brutality by those in authority?
- How does a teacher establish those structures for safe and respectful dialogue?

Art educators have been increasingly challenged to both attend to the needs of our students and simultaneously navigate what they can and cannot discuss with their students in the classroom. Administrators may discourage difficult discussions that might counter predominant views in the community. However, students express the need to prepare themselves for agency in the adult world they will soon inherit (Oxfam GB, 2018; Stewart, 2020). Our goal with this book is to share ways that art educators can respond to current political climates, including systems of oppression, to more holistically address the needs of students.

CONTINUING THE CONVERSATION

Contemporary art is a tool to affect change and provide relevance to our students' lived experiences both within and outside the classroom. We argue that art is a nexus of learning as students make and examine visual imagery that responds to political policy, societal structures, and an individual's place within them. We ask the basic question, "What works of art are allowed in the learning space?" Are the models of artistic excellence still predominantly cisgender, male, heterosexual, and White? Do we teach students to emulate artists' forms and techniques but not examine the social concerns they were responding to in the past? One important area of consideration is: Who is left out? This book provides resource materials to use for discussion and introduces artists who challenge assumed artistic norms. Work that is used in the book visits histories that have not been taught, reexamines personal assumptions, and provides students the opportunity to form opinions and find avenues for artistic activism, personal awareness, and societal change.

Conversations in art learning spaces are an essential tool for educators at this time of societal reexamination of norms. This book is intended to equip educators in schools, museums, and community settings to engage in critical conversation and create learning environments that are sensitive to silenced groups, acknowledge the lived experiences of individual students (Rao & Pfeiler-Wunder, 2018), and demonstrate arts' role in the common good. The contributions support art classrooms where invisible privilege and power structures are interrogated, equity is practiced, and stories given attention, space, and respect.

REFERENCES

Acuff, J. B. (2020). Afrofuturism: Reimagining art curricula for Black existence. *Art Education, 73*(3), 13–21.

Burke, E. (2019). Turning the tide: Reframing how we acknowledge and support transgender and gender nonconforming learners in educational spaces. *Art Education, 72*(2),48–50.

Gude, O. (2004). Postmodern principles: In search of a 21st century art education. *Art Education, 57*(1), 6–14. doi: 10.1080/00043125.2004.11653528

Gude, O. (2009). The 2009 Lowenfeld lecture: Art education for democratic life. *Art Education, 62*(6), 6–11. doi: 10.1080/00043125.2009.11519039

Kraehe, A., & Herman, D., Jr. (2020). Racial encounters, ruptures, and reckonings: Art curriculum futurity in the wake of Black Lives Matter. *Art Education, 73*(5), 4–7.

Oxfam GB (2018). Teaching controversial issues: A guide for teachers. https://oxfamilibrary.openrepository.com/bitstream/handle/10546/620473/gd-teaching-controversial-issues-290418-en.pdf?sequence=1&isAllowed=y

Quinn, T., Ploof, J., & Hochtritt, L. (2012). *Art and social justice education: Culture as commons.* Routledge.

Rao, S., & Pfeiler-Wunder, A. (2018). Intersections, identities, and the landscape of preservice education. *Art Education, 71*(1), 32–37.

Rapaport, B. K., Wagner, A., English, D., & Haslett, T. (2019). *Martin Puryear: Liberty/Libertá* [Exhibition Catalog]. Gregory R. Miller & Co.

Rugoff, R. (2019). *May you live in interesting times: Biennale Arte 2019.* La Biennale di Venizia.

Schieble, M., Vetter, A., & Martin, K. M. (2020). *Classroom talk for social change: Critical conversations in English language arts.* Teachers College Press.

Stewart, C. (2020 Apr 17–21). *What do kids want to talk about? Middle school discussions about contemporary art* [Roundtable Session Paper]. AERA Annual Meeting, San Francisco, CA.

Wilson McKay, S., & Monteverde, S. R. (2003). Dialogic looking: Beyond the mediated experience. *Art Education, 56(1),* 40–45.

Part I

CONVERSATIONS IN ART EDUCATIONAL SETTINGS

This section presents educational practices where students engage in deeper conversations in a complex world.

CHAPTER 1

Exploring Debatable Topics With Divergent Thinking Strategies

A Visual Narrative

Rebecca Shipe

I provide in a visual narrative format an instructional strategy for exploring controversial topics in the art classroom that engages multiple perspectives and supports students' abilities to create metaphorical, visual representations of their ideas. This graphic novel–style chapter provides implementation guidance and cites research supporting the strategy's relevance to today's youth and teens.

Exploring Debatable Topics With Divergent Thinking Strategies: A Visual Narrative

In the following graphic novel style (Carpenter and Tavin, 2012; Madrid-Manrique, 2020) visual narrative, I present how a divergent thinking activity can be used to help stimulate imaginative visual responses to debatable current issues.

While using both pictures and words, I highlight how and why art educators can facilitate explorations on controversial topics with secondary-level students in a way that highlights multiple perspectives and supports their ability to create visual metaphors to represent their ideas.

This curricular activity promotes the concept that I refer to as "productive ambiguity."

PLEASE NOTE: I WILL DEFINE PRODUCTIVE AMBIGUITY ON THE NEXT PAGE.

Rebecca Shipe
Rhode Island College

Why should educators develop instructional strategies for addressing controversial topics?

Current discourse highlights how our use of technology and social media can perpetuate the 'filter bubble' dilemma that generates a distorted version of reality based on what computer algorithms think we want to see and believe is true. This also promotes the polarization of our society as individuals restrict their sources of information to media that support their existing point of view (Lee, 2018; Steyer, 2020; Worthington,2001). Scholars emphasize how exercising the ability to critically evaluate both sides of an issue can reveal false dichotomies and promote an awareness of common ground among differing perspectives (Journell, 2019; Noddings & Brooks, 2017; Zimmerman & Robertson, 2017).

Why should art teachers incorporate this into their teaching practice?

Based on my personal experience teaching art in K-12 and higher education, I believe that the process of interpreting as well as creating art and visual culture provides opportunities for students to address and process internal and external conflicts. For example, this might involve analyzing how artists and the media strategically manipulate imagery to convey a particular message on a debatable topic. In addition to empowering students to be more savvy consumers of visual imagery, they can then apply similar techniques to enhance the impact of their own artworks. This specific activity demonstrates how the concept of "productive ambiguity" can be promoted in an art classroom environment.

Defining Productive Ambiguity

My working definition of "productive ambiguity" is the ability to transform tensions that disrupt one's current understandings into opportunities for personal growth. Ambiguity becomes productive when encounters with difference stimulate curiosity, imagination, and consideration of new possibilities and perspectives; as well as occasions to experience self-awareness and empathy for others. Barone and Eisner (2012) used this term while describing how arts-based research generates new understandings when the researcher or audience recognizes and engages with contrasting perspectives.

The following illustration identifies how several specific scholars have influenced my understanding of productive ambiguity.

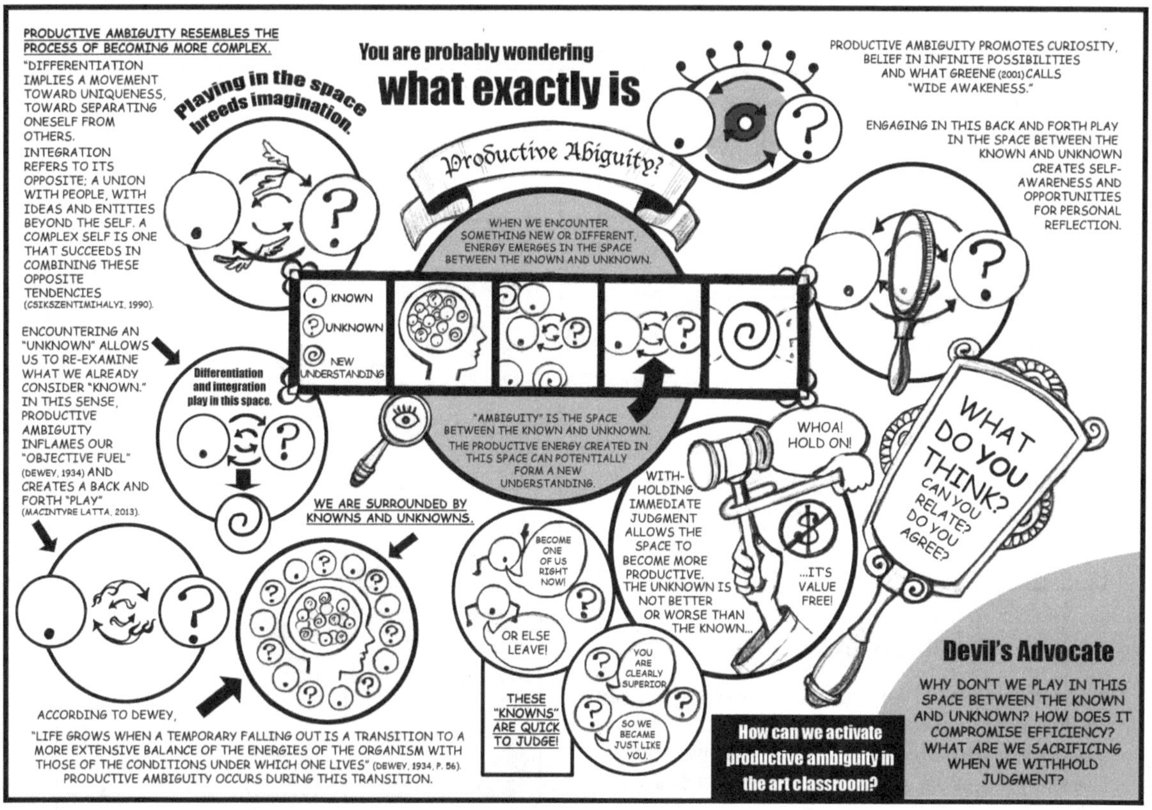

How can art students employ productive ambiguity while addressing controversial topics?

The following instructional tool guides teachers and students through a process of researching opposing viewpoints on a debatable topic and then reflecting on how this new knowledge impacts their existing perspective.
Next, participants use "Divergent Thinking Strategies" (Marshall & Donahue, 2014) to imagine new ways of visually portraying the key terms and concepts that relate to both sides of the issue. After completing this metaphorical brainstorming activity, students are more equipped to create unique, personal, visual responses to the topic that reflect thoughtful consideration of multiple perspectives.

Ideally, this exercise would puncture the participant's 'filter bubble' that protects their sense of stability, but also prohibits their ability to understand and empathize with those who hold different points of view on a debatable topic.

Instructional Tool

I have implemented the framework shown below with pre-service and practicing art teachers to better understand its potential usefulness for secondary-level art students. This instructional tool guides students through the process of reflecting on their existing opinion on a controversial topic, identifying opposing arguments, using divergent thinking strategies to identify visual metaphors that represent these ideas, and ultimately create a piece of visual art that reflects their personal response to the topic.

Using Divergent Thinking Strategies* to Address Controversial Topics in the Art Classroom

Choose a current controversial topic that interests you or one that you foresee being of interest to your future secondary level students.

Examples include:

Medical Marijuana	Gun Control	Animal Testing	Death Penalty
School Uniforms	Illegal Immigration	Abortion	Homework
Euthanasia & Assisted Suicide	Climate Change	Video Games and Violence	Drinking Age- Lower it?

Please identify your current perspective on this topic. Which side of the argument do you usually lean toward? What specific values and life experiences do you think contribute to your perspective? (Please know that it is okay to hold a middle-ground or moderate perspective, or to recognize that your perspective might change.)

Identify specific points made for both sides of the argument. Use the ProCon.org website for helpful examples.

Topic:

PROS	CONS

Pause and Reflect: Has your perspective changed after identifying these Pros and Cons?

Use Divergent Thinking Strategies to Further Expand Your Perspective on this Topic

1. Identify key words/phrases that appear on the "pro" side and key words/phrases that appear on the "con" side. These words/phrases might include people, places, things, concepts, circumstances, values, or belief systems (religious, political, etc.). Identify these key words/phrases below.

PROS	CONS

2. Choose two- three key words/phrases from your Pros and Cons list and complete the metaphorical thinking exercise below. Feel free to include both words and pictures to express your thoughts.

Key word/phrase	Qualities or attributes that describe this key word/phrase	Other beings, places, things, ideas, activities that share these qualities/attributes
PRO:		
CON:		

3. Continue to expand your way of thinking about this topic by completing additional metaphorical thinking exercises. Feel free to include both words and pictures to express your thoughts.

Key word/phrase (PRO):
Recontextualize: Change the context of an idea, object, or image
Extend: Take ideas to logical or absurd conclusions or into fiction and fantasy
Amplify/magnify: Exaggerate a phenomenon; make it larger than life, and call attention to it
Project: Imagine, speculate, or envision what could come next
Abstract: Make visible the simple form (or idea) within a complex one; pare a form (or idea) down to its essentials; pare down information to the underlying concepts or relationships

Key word/phrase (CON):
Recontextualize: Change the context of an idea, object, or image
Extend: Take ideas to logical or absurd conclusions or into fiction and fantasy
Amplify/magnify: Exaggerate a phenomenon; make it larger than life, and call attention to it
Project: Imagine, speculate, or envision what could come next
Abstract: Make visible the simple form (or idea) within a complex one; pare a form (or idea) down to its essentials; pare down information to the underlying concepts or relationships

Create a piece of art that addresses this issue.

The medium/media is open-ended and might take the form of a video, meme, public performance, or any other type of visual culture.

The purpose of the artwork could be:
- a personal response to the issue that is not intended to persuade or support one position over the other
- a personal response to the issue that does intend to support one position over the other
- a less personal commentary that is not intended to persuade or support one position over the other, but rather to highlight common ground
- a less personal commentary that does intend to support one position over the other

* Examples of Divergent Thinking Strategies came from Marshall and Donahue's book *Art-Centered Learning Across the Curriculum: Integrating Contemporary Art in the Secondary School Classroom*.

Implications for Future Use

Participants largely agreed that using the divergent thinking strategies truly challenged them to activate metaphorical thinking skills that they would not have exercised otherwise. I was continually encouraged by the variety of ideas they generated while completing this exercise.

As I consider ways to enhance this activity's learning potential, I recognize that the concept of productive ambiguity could be explicitly addressed in the instructional tool. This would support students' metacognition as they connect learning theories to the intellectual growth that they are experiencing.
How would you adapt this activity for your own teaching practice?
Please share your insights with me at rshipe@ric.edu.

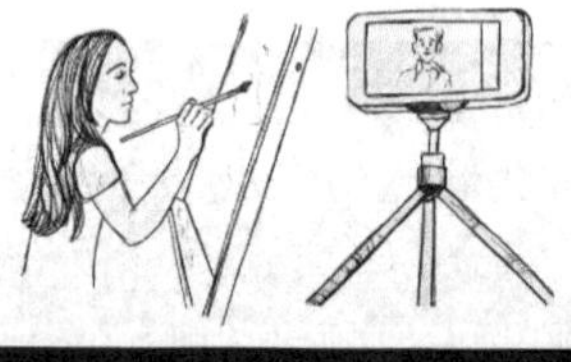

References

Barone, T. & Eisner, E. (2012). *Arts based research.* Los Angeles: SAGE.

Carpenter, II, B. & Tavin, K. (Eds.) (2012). The graphic novel and art education [Special Issue]. *Visual Arts Research, 38(1).*

Csikszentmihalyi, M. (1990). *Flow: The psychology of optimal experience.* New York, NY: Harperperennial.

Dewey, J. (1934). *Art as experience.* New York, NY: Capricorn Books.

Greene, M. (2001). *Variations on a blue guitar.* New York, NY: Teachers College Press.

Journell, W. (Ed.) (2019). *Unpacking fake news: An educator's guide to navigating the media with students.* New York, NY: Teachers College Press.

Lee, J. (2018). *Talking across the divide: How to communicate with people you disagree and maybe change the world.* New York, NY: Penguin Random House.

Macintyre Latta, M. (2013). *Curricular conversations: Play is the (missing) thing.* New York, NY: Routledge.

Madrid-Manrique, M. (2020). Engaging, validating, imagining: A comic-based approach t(non)participation and empowerment. *International Journal of Education Through Art, 16(1),* 43-61.

Marshall, J. & Donahue, D. (2014). *Art-centered learning across the curriculum: Integrating contemporary art in the secondary school classroom.* New York, NY: Teachers College Press.

Noddings, N. & Brooks, L. (2017). *Teaching controversial issues: The case for critical thinking and moral commitment in the classroom.* New York, NY: Teachers College Press.

Steyer, J. (Ed.) (2020). *Which side of history? How technology is reshaping democracy and our lives.* San Francisco, CA: Chronicle Prism.

Zimmerman, J. and Robertson, E. (2017). *The case for contention: Teaching controversial issues in American schools.* Chicago, IL: The University of Chicago Press.

CHAPTER 2

Let's Talk

Engaging in Critical Conversations in the Art Room

Amy Pfeiler-Wunder and Mary Kate Bergh

> To engage in dialogue is one of the simplest ways we can begin as teachers, scholars, and critical thinkers to cross boundaries, the barriers that may or may not be erected by race, gender, class, professional standing, and a host of other differences.
>
> —hooks, 1994 (p.130)

The art room is often buzzing with conversation, a studio environment where topics are discussed, possibilities brainstormed, and ideas exchanged. Often, through engaged dialogue, student voice emerges as learners discuss topics that concern them within and outside the school's walls. Art teachers may overhear snippets of debate and highly charged questions. To illuminate these exchanges, the following is a fictitious amalgamation of how visible and invisible story lines unfold in Ms. Shelley's K–12 art room.

As art class ends, the bustle of clean-up sparks energy and ignites tension. With the news centered on presidential debates, the media and public opinion polls ask: "Does the United States have a race problem?"

My students are not immune to conversations on social media, nor unfolding conversations within their homes. I can hear the students' questions, the hard ones, sometimes questions I want to ignore. They are asking each other, "Who is your family voting for?"

Voices pipe in: "Hey, Ms. Shelley, who you voting for?"

More questions unravel. "I wonder why Ms. Shelley wanted to talk about the flag I drew; it's just the Confederate flag."

Tangled threads of dialogue, I can't process difficult topics, wonderings inside my mind. . . . Should I respond? How would their families respond? What if I say the wrong thing? I am on the verge of attempting a response when a shout comes from the back of the room. "The bus driver is racist and nobody's doing anything about it."

Pause, reflect, consider. How do educators respond to these questions? To controversial images in student artwork? Should they? Is this an opportunity for dialogue? If so, how? When? Where? How might educators and learners engage in critical conversations, creating space for new understandings on challenging topics, especially those that are politicized and polarized? Is this even possible in an educational landscape where concerns are palpable, a landscape filled with challenges, and ongoing changes? Where do teacher and learner voices live in the art room?

VOICES IN THE EDUCATIONAL LANDSCAPE

Teachers and learners find themselves in the midst of shifts in school culture and curriculum due to historical and contemporary forces (Clandinin & Connelly, 2000). Teachers and students are immersed in an educational landscape, navigating school culture and climate, expression of their intersecting identities, and the perceptions or fears held by members of the school community around what has been or will be discussed. How do educators negotiate uncomfortable questions, even uncomfortable and possibly troubling questions, while taking into account the teacher's and students' differing positionalities? Within the interplay of these concerns, educators are faced with district policies and in some cases state laws (Gross, 2022) determining topics acceptable in educational spaces. In turn, educators continue to feel the impact of test mandates (Ravitch, 2016), the pressure of COVID-19's transformation on school life, and teacher shortages—all fueling curriculum disruptions. Is there time to pause and discuss complex topics while meeting curriculum and assessment expectations? How are students positioned amid these cultural, social, and political story lines? Which students bring voice to educational settings? Which students may feel their voices are invisible?

Students come with complex storied lives navigating being a learner, a human in a world where there is always access—access to witnessing environmental impacts, access to political views from a wide spectrum of sources and perspectives, access to wars and conflicts, all among inequities due to race, class, gender, and the intersectionality of identities (Collins & Bilge, 2016). Access to knowledge is *always* available through phones, tablets, and computers, often one-way conversations. Post, push, comment. Step away. Students absorb "news" and information from multiple sources, mingling with family story lines, interpretations, and opinions from various sources. How are these sources layering and mixing with the questions, opinions, and concerns students bring to the art room? If teaching is to be relational, opening a space of vulnerability about one's intersecting identities in relationship to our students' storied lives (Britzman, 1998; Pfeiler-Wunder, 2013), how do educators and learners bring voice to the challenging topics emerging in the art room, especially outside the planned curriculum? We return to a classroom scenario.

It is 2016, the news feels heightened. Tensions feel heightened. As a new teacher, I feel heightened. There is the 2D and 3D arts curriculum focused on skills and techniques, and then there are my students, adolescents navigating a complex world. Students from a predominantly rural and working-class community intermingled with middle-class families; White students encountered students of color; there is diversity in religious and spiritual beliefs; and students with increasing academic, social, and emotional needs. AND I am a White, cisgender teacher from a solid middle-class background. I represent much of the teaching field (Emdin, 2017). I feel heightened . . .

"Hey, Ms. Shelley, who you voting for?" This may seem innocuous, but to me it felt laden with expectations. My student held strong opinions about the candidates, and from the ongoing threads of conversations, quietly discussed at tables; overtly through direct questions, I knew *who they supported. Every conversation, every art piece, every question centered around idolizing their candidate. Students would ask about my political views or stances, looking for a way to engage in the election. "Did you watch the debate last night? Who are you voting for? What is the point of the Women's March?" Should I engage? Could I engage?*

If education is relationally located in the activities between the teacher and the one being educated (Biesta, 2014; Freire, 1994), yet schools increase in diversity from a predominantly White, female, and middle-class field (Emdin, 2016), how do educators create space for learners' voice and therefore agency in the art room?

UNPACKING POSITIONALITY

For voice to enter the art classroom, we suggest educators begin with understanding their own positionality and intersecting identities as a form of "living inquiry" (Irwin, 2013). Living inquiry is an ongoing rhizomatic experience where reflection moves back and forth to praxis, or ways of doing for the sake of becoming. Here, educators are intricately attuned to the intersections between their storied lives as teachers and the storied lives of their students. As art educators and artists, we started with artmaking as a visual reference of our identities. For example, from a book arts class focused on critical social action with Amy, Mary Kate engaged in intrapersonal reflections on her identity, stitching together pieces of an elementary composition book layered with contour self-portraits. Here Mary Kate explored past and present educational experiences in relation to her positionality in a new community (see Figure 2.1).

In tandem with our artmaking, we were critical colleagues for each other navigating the brackish waters of difficult topics. Brackish waters, where salt and freshwater meet, create tension, but also one of the most fertile and vital ecosystems. We worked to create a fertile conversation that also lived in tension through elevating students' voices in our classroom settings.

Being self-reflective entails many layers; one of those layers is knowing that individuals all come from dynamic cultures that shape and shift over time (Chang, 2008). As White educators, we were cognizant enough of our own racial subculture to understand others' cultures (Milner, 2020). "Cultural conflicts" (Milner, 2020, pp. 24–25) are the brackish waters, the challenging topics that emerge between teachers and learners based on race, gender, age, geography, and socioeconomic disconnections (among other factors). White educators often avoid cultural conflicts, not recognizing biases from their own lived experience, which impacts their teaching and views of the learners.

Figure 2.1. ***Stitches: Layers of self in a changing landscape*** **(Mary Kate Bergh).**

BRAVE SPACES FOR DIALOGUE

Traversing discussions on candidate choices, election polarization, racist bus drivers, and the use of the Confederate flag in a student's artwork are just some examples of cultural conflicts within a multilayered context living in/with nuisance—that is, the intersection of the teacher's and learner's stories amid the cultural, social, and political landscape (Rao & Pfeiler-Wunder, 2018). We suggest establishing norms and multimodal practices within the brackish waters of your teaching spaces. This includes co-constructing norms of conversation with your learners. Voice also enters using multimodal forms of expression (drawing, painting, sculpting, dancing, gesturing) with dialogue. Pushing and pulling through discomfort is not always possible as educators or as students depending on enacted identities. There is inherently more risk for many students, especially students of color or other underrepresented/marginalized identities, due to power dynamics and systems of oppression seen and unseen within white-dominated school systems (DiAngelo, 2018). What follows are approaches used in our classrooms, from elementary to high school settings and with preservice learners, to support critical conversations.

VOICE: NORMS AND MULTIMODAL FORMATS

Norms

Mellon et al. (2019) provide examples of creating conversational norms we have found helpful; we have also merged other authors' suggestions into our own practices. Different than rules and "do nots," conversation norms describe how the group will engage in dialogue, while listening to understand. Conversation norms have the potential to create a "culture of care" that honors diverse experiences (Noddings, 1992) and stories of each learner (Pfeiler-Wunder, 2013). Through a culture of caring, potential opens for discussions about difficult topics from multiple vantage points. Although it is difficult to guarantee a *safe* space physically due to the challenges faced within schools (such as gun violence) and emotionally due to the polarization of race relationships in society, educators can foster a *brave* space for learning. Emotionally safe spaces were created so individuals could discuss difficult and sensitive topics, which often translated into groups discussing topics with shared ideologies (Graham, 2021). Brave spaces are intended to go further, opening individuals to vulnerability: spaces of growth where ideas are challenged (Boostroom, 1997).

Suggestions for Creating Norms

- Show empathy: Recognize there are many perspectives due to individuals' diverse experiences
- Curiosity: Be open to ideas and listen to understand others' viewpoints
- Inclusivity: Recognize that all voices matter and seek to understand others' thoughts
- Paraphrase: Restate ideas to check for shared understanding
- Encourage: Encourage individuals who may be quieter to share their ideas and perspectives. How can you provide multimodal opportunities for students to engage?

- Productive Struggle: Be willing to disagree and challenge ideas to learn
- Listen to understand

(These suggestions are condensed from Mellon et al., 2019, p. 20)

Courageous conversations are established to "create conditions for safe exploration and profound learning for all" in conversations about race (Michael, 2015, p. 4). To do so:

- Stay engaged in a space of continuous becoming (Britzman, 1998)
- Speak your truth
- Recognize the truth that comes from your lived experience
    - » *In my experience . . .*
    - » *Help me to understand . . . tell me more.*
- Expect to experience discomfort
- Expect and accept a lack of closure

Multimodal Forms of Expression

When engaging in dialogue, we also suggest implementing strategies for learners to share their perspectives in low-risk ways, where a learner's voice is not limited to speaking, but can be heard through other avenues. Students may be hesitant to share verbally due to feeling anxious about navigating different perceptions of identities in the classroom. Dialogue may certainly emerge through learners' artmaking; there are also approaches to creating voice and dialogue using multimodal approaches: quick writes, chalk talks, temperature lines, visual journaling, and Padlets allow students to use movement, writing, technology, and illustration in conjunction with verbal opportunities, layering and unfolding a range of dialogue.

EMBRACING THE BRACKISH WATERS OF CLASSROOM DIALOGUE

"Hey, Ms. Shelley, who you voting for . . ."

As teachers, we *should* challenge and provide alternative perspectives when the situation allows. When discussing difficult or controversial topics, model the dispositions of voice and agency while checking one's biases. Education is a practice of freedom, as both teacher and students share and confess, *and* empower one another (hooks, 1994). In these conversations, students learn to speak and respond, *and* to listen, together creating an environment where this can occur (hooks, 1994). Norms in a classroom will shift and change as the storied lives of learners and teachers shift and change due to the political, social, and cultural landscape. With our learners, educators make space for dialogue, conversation, and even controversy—embracing vulnerability and discomfort to engage in critical consciousness *together,* listening to understand (Rao & Pfeiler-Wunder, 2018). Conversations can move in many directions, like the brackish waters where opposing forces create tension. This tension also creates the most fertile ecosystem; dialogue emerges and fosters the building of community, understanding multiple perspectives, and seeing differently.

REFERENCES

Biesta, J. J. (2013). *The beautiful risk of education*. Paradigm Publishers.

Boostrom, R. (1997, March 24–28). "Unsafe spaces": Reflections on a specimen of educational jargon [Conference session]. Educational Research Association Annual Meeting, Chicago, IL. https://files.eric.ed.gov/fulltext/ED407686.pdf

Britzman, D. (1998). *Lost subjects, contested objects: Toward a psychoanalytic inquiry of learning.* State University of New York Press.

Chang, H. (2008). *Autoethnography as method*. Routledge.

Clandinin, D. J. & Connelly, F. M. (2000). *Narrative inquiry: Experience and story in qualitative research* (1st ed.). Jossey-Bass.

Collins, P., & Bilge, S. (2016). *Intersectionality*. Polity Press.

DiAngelo, R. (2018). *White fragility: Why it is so hard for white people to talk about racism.* Beacon Press.

Emdin, C. (2017). *For white folks who teach in the hood . . . and the rest of y'all too.* Beacon Press.

Freire, P. (1994). *Pedagogy of the oppressed* (20th anniversary ed.). Continuum.

Graham, L. P. (2021). "Safe spaces" and "brave spaces": The case for creating law school classrooms that are both. *University of Miami Law Review, 76*(1), 84–162.

Gross, T. (2022, February 3). *From slavery to socialism, new legislation restricts what teachers can discuss* [Radio broadcast]. NPR. https://www.npr.org/transcripts/1077878538

hooks, b. (1994). *Teaching to transgress: Education as the practice of freedom*. Routledge.

Irwin, R. L. (2013). Becoming a/r/tography. *Studies in Art Education, 54*(3), 198–215.

Mellon, P., Hixon, R., & Weber, J. (2019.) *With a little help from my friends: Conversation-based instruction for culturally and linguistically diverse (CLD) classrooms*. Teachers College Press.

Michael, A. (2015). *Raising race questions: Whiteness and inquiry in education.* Teachers College Press.

Milner, H. (2020). *Start where you are, but don't stay there: Understanding diversity, opportunity gaps and teaching in today's classroom* (2nd ed.). Harvard College Press.

Noddings, N. (1984). *Caring: A feminine approach to ethics & moral education*. University of California Press.

Noddings, N. (1992). *The challenge to care in the schools: An alternative approach to education.* Teachers College Press.

Pfeiler-Wunder, A. (2013). Social class and the art room curriculum. In F. McArdle & G. Boldt (Eds.), *Young children, pedagogy and the arts: Ways of seeing* (pp. 146–168). Routledge.

Rao, S., & Pfeiler-Wunder, A. (2018). Intersections, identities, and the landscape of preservice education. *Art Education, 71*(1), 32–37. doi: 10.1080/00043125.2018.1389590

Ravitch, D. (2016). *The death and life of the great American school system*. Basic Books.

CHAPTER 3

Children *Can* Talk About Hard Things

Kimberly Lane

Our kids often have to grapple with difficult problems stemming from social media, the news, and conversations with friends and adults. I have been an art educator for more than 20 years, and I have noticed that even our youngest students are aware of and trying to make sense of what is happening in the world around them, including war, gun violence, racial injustice, and climate catastrophe. As an art teacher of elementary-age children, I provide students with opportunities other subject teachers cannot to use a visual language for processing and expressing their responses to difficult topics and life experiences.

BEING BRAVE

I currently teach in an independent school in Minnesota. A crucial aspect of my role as the art teacher is to nurture an atmosphere in which students feel safe to take risks, explore materials, and express themselves, even when the subject is tough and emotional. This approach promotes the development of critical thinking skills, perseverance, self-confidence, and creativity. When children share their work, I encourage their capacity to appreciate new perspectives and to strengthen the bonds within the classroom through open conversation. One powerful way to do this is to discuss examples of work by adult artists about a difficult topic or event and tie it into students' lives, allowing each one to explore content that is meaningful to them.

In Spring 2022, I showed my class a short BBC video (Burgess, 2022) in which street artist Steve "Jenks" Jenkins and pop artist Nathan Wyburn, two contemporary Welsh artists, explain how and why their work expresses solidarity with the people of war-ravaged Ukraine. That day, students in my 4th-grade class entered the art studio and sat on the rug as usual, ready to begin. I opened the discussion by saying, "We are going to watch and discuss a video of two British artists explaining how they are using their work to bring attention to current events in Ukraine. Who has an idea of why artists living as far away as Wales might want to say something in their artwork about Ukraine? I'm wondering what you know about what's happening there?"

Immediately a dozen hands shot up from children eager to share what they knew or thought they knew about the war. Their responses showed a broad range of awareness and accuracy of information around this topic. While guiding the discussion, I affirmed information that was accurate, corrected inaccurate statements, and suggested that the children talk with the adults at home if they had further questions or wanted more information.

After several minutes of discussion, I asked, "Why do you think so many of us are aware of this war in Ukraine? Why might a person care about what's happening across the ocean in Ukraine if it's not happening to them or their family?"

Again, children were bursting to express their point of view.

> "Ukraine is still a part of the world, and nobody wants to have a war."
> "You could have family there."
> "It's just not right."
> "People might have empathy. Like, they'd think, 'If that was happening to my house, I wouldn't want that to be happening to me!'"

It was clear through this conversation that the children had deep empathy for, and could relate to, people experiencing the hardships of war. This response is key to connecting to the children's own lived experiences when it comes time to choose a topic for their own artwork.

In the video (Burgess, 2022), Welsh artist Jenkins explained why he used street art to draw attention to the war in Ukraine. "It's a great way of getting a message across to people," he said. "And you can see something and take it in for a blink of an eye or a millisecond, and it makes you think things and awakens things inside you. It's a powerful tool to use" (Burgess, 2022, 00:30).

In the same video, pop artist Wyburn said,

> I know that I use my artwork to quite often shout about things that I'm passionate about, including showing solidarity for the people of Ukraine. I think quite often words just don't cut it. A piece of artwork is a great way of doing that and a way for the average person to let their voice be heard. (Burgess, 2022, 01:23)

I asked the 4th-graders what they thought the artists meant when they said that art "is a powerful tool to use" (Burgess, 2022, 00:49) and "often words just don't cut it" (Burgess, 2022, 01:33). Here are some of their responses:

> "Sometimes someone might say 'sorry,' but that's not going to fix anything. Like if a tornado came by tomorrow and destroyed someone's house, you can't just say, 'Sorry that happened to you.' You have to actually *do* something."

> "When you do artwork, you put effort into it and it takes a lot of time. That shows that you care."

> "A picture can show something that you might not be able to say with just words."

> "Sometimes with art you can even make something bigger and put in so much detail, and sometimes words just can't match what you can show with that detail."

At this point, I shifted the conversation to connect the idea of art as a powerful means of expression with the children's own experiences. "We are living here in Minnesota, and this war is not coming to us," I said. "We are not going to have to leave our homes the way you described some Ukrainians having to do. But every one of us in this room can tell a story about a moment in our lives when we had to be brave. And by being brave, I mean doing something even though we are scared to do it. If it's not scary to me to jump off a high dive, it doesn't take bravery for *me* to do that, but to someone else, they might really have to dig deep to climb that tall ladder and jump off. Who will share a time in your life when you had to be brave?" Here are some of the students' responses:

> "I feel like the time that stands out most is my first swim meet. There was *a lot* of tension, and I had only swum in practice before."

> "When I started a new school in 3rd grade. I'd been with my best friend since preschool, but then I had to start all over again with no friends."

> "My first time doing a back handspring on the trampoline. I basically spent 20 minutes before just telling myself that I could do it."

> "When I was about to go on a rollercoaster, and I don't like crazy rides."

After the discussion, students wrote brief descriptions of the moment they planned to depict in their painting before sketching ideas for their composition. Over the course of the project, these 4th-graders learned about one another as they shared their stories of bravery.

At the end of the project, students created a new personal connection with the Ukrainian people through their art and their own notion of bravery—a tangible marker in time and history.

The same technique of talking about difficult topics through art works with younger and older students, though it is essential to consider the children's ages and development.

ART AS A SPARK FOR DISCUSSION

This semester, I introduced the students in my kindergarten classes to Ukrainian artist Maria Prymachenko's 1982 painting, "A Dove Has Spread Her Wings and Asks for Peace." Before telling them the painting's title, I asked the children to describe what they saw. They noticed the brightly colored flowers and leaves, the white dove that dominates the painting and the blue patterns painted across its feathers. I asked what kind of bird they thought it might be and got a variety of answers including "a dove." I then told them that sometimes a dove is used to represent the idea of peace. We know that Prymachenko was using this dove to represent peace because she tells us that in the title. She was thinking about peace, and sometimes artists like to make artwork about what is on their mind. I wanted to show them this painting because of the hardships endured by the people of Ukraine, the country Prymachenko was from. I wanted them to know that Ukraine was on my mind. In one class a student raised her hand and told us, "There is a war in Ukraine right now." Yes, I said, there is fighting going on in Ukraine right now. "Today is a day when you get to make art about something that is on your mind," I said, "just as Maria made her painting about what was on hers. Who would like to share what they plan to paint about today?"

It is part of my art teaching practice to discuss current events with learners of every age. In the fall of 2020, I began the school year with my 5th-graders by looking at a wide variety of the mural images that were painted by artists and activists on many of the boarded-up windows after George Floyd's murder in our city, Minneapolis. After discussing these public artworks, I asked the students to consider what topic they would each choose if they were going to make their own public murals aimed at changing the world for the better. Topics ranged from issues of social justice such as support for Black Lives Matter to environmental concerns regarding protecting endangered animals and climate change.

I told the children at the end of the class that sometimes these conversations might make us uncomfortable and that I was nervous before starting this conversation because when I was growing up, racism was not something that we talked about in school. I offered that the only way to end racism starts by conversations like these, and talking about how unfair it is, and that treating people fairly matters. I told them that even though I was nervous about the conversation, I went ahead because Black lives are too important for me to not try or not talk about it.

At the end of the project, I asked the students what they thought about looking at and talking about the George Floyd murals in art class. "It was really interesting and good that we did something that's timely, something that's happening right now," Cyrus Skibell, 11, explained. "It's not just talking about George Floyd, it was connected to art because of the murals, so it made sense that we would talk about that in art." I asked him if he thought that art was a useful way of expressing feelings about these kinds of topics. "Yes! Definitely, because it allows you to be creative and shows how you feel in a way that might not be possible to articulate with words."

In these examples, an adult artist's work was the spark for a broader dialogue that engendered empathy and elicited emotional responses from the children before connecting to their own lived experiences. It's imperative that educators find the time and method to have these talks with students. We cannot always predict where the conversation will go, and sometimes it may go to an uncomfortable place. By facilitating dialogues such as these, we provide our students the opportunity to use the lens of art to reflect critically on events in the world and a visual voice to express their emotions and opinions. These issues, and the processing of them, are too important not to try.

REFERENCE

Burgess, M. (2022, March 8). *How artists are using art to highlight Ukraine war* [Video]. BBC News. https://www.bbc.com/news/av/uk-wales-60665871

CHAPTER 4

Investigating Contemporary Art in the Elementary Classroom

Amy Felder

In my elementary classroom, I use contemporary art to facilitate discussions on a variety of topics from cyberbullying to the refugee crisis to acceptance of the LGBTQIA+ community. My hope is that students see themselves represented in the artists and artwork we discuss. I also want to provide opportunities for students to gain insight into viewpoints that may differ from their own. My goals are to empower students, foster student voice, and ensure that all voices are heard.

In a *What Is My World?* unit, I launched students' investigations of the world with Iranian-born artist Laleh Mehran and her *W3FI* multimedia art installations combining technology, art, and science with her own personal history. My students who are refugees and immigrants like Mehran related to her struggle with cultural identity. After viewing the video *Compilation of the W3FI Exhibitions* (CO-LAB, 2014), we discussed how the installation encourages visitors to think before engaging online. Students learned how Mehran's life experience as a victim of bullying led to her creating anti-cyberbullying art.

In response to the question "What does my world look like?" we examined Shepard Fairey's *We the People* campaign (2017); JR's billboard of a boy peering over the Mexican border (2017); and Christoph Büchel's *Barca Nostra* (2019). Students adopted the perspective of someone or something in the artwork and considered the following questions: "What can this person or thing see, observe or notice? What might this person or thing know, understand, hold true, or believe? What might the person or thing care deeply about? What might the person or thing wonder about or question?" (Ritchhart et al., 2011, p. 178). Students shared their answers with a partner, and a few students shared with the entire class. I elaborated on how Fairey's art celebrates America's diversity and how everyone deserves respect regardless of race, religion, and sexual orientation. I also shared how the artist Büchel wanted to raise awareness of the refugee crisis by displaying a ship that sank with 800 migrants on board (Povoledo, 2019).

For the question "What is my world like?" students crafted their own interpretations of Nani Chacon's *Missing*, a painting of a transparent indigenous woman surrounded by fluttering butterflies. One student said that the disappearing woman shows how when you are not seen or noticed, you feel like you are invisible. I explained that all interpretations are valid, but according to the artist's statement the endangered monarch butterflies are a metaphor for missing indigenous women (Chacon, n.d.).

Students made art in response to the artists we discussed. I interviewed them about what they were making and how it represented their world. One 5th-grader said, "I am creating a tie-dye tree and it's supposed to represent all the new people that come to America from all over the world" (see Figure 4.1).

Figure 4.1. Isabella Swainston, *The Willow Whisperer* (2020)

Her appreciation of newcomers coming to the United States is evidenced through her use of different colors. Through investigating contemporary art, students not only gain insight into viewpoints that may differ from their own but also on how their own art may provide viewers with insight into a different viewpoint.

REFERENCES

Chacon, N. (n.d.). *Original artwork by Nani Chacon: Artist statement about the piece*. Sing Our Rivers Red: Raising Awareness for Murdered & Missing Indigenous Women. https://singourriversred.wordpress.com/original-artwork-by-nani-chacon/

CO-LAB (Producer). (2014). *Compilation of the W3FI exhibitions* [Video]. http://thew3fi.com/

Povoledo, E. (2019, May 6). Wreck of migrant ship that killed hundreds will be displayed at Venice Biennale. *The New York Times*. https://www.nytimes.com/2019/05/06/arts/design/migrant-boat-venice-biennale-christian-buchel.html

Ritchhart, R., Church, M., & Morrison, K. (2011). *Making thinking visible: How to promote engagement, understanding, and independence for all learners*. Jossey-Bass.

CHAPTER 5

Challenging Content and Critical Conversations in the Classroom

Kryssi Staikidis

This chapter introduces the multiple strategies of looking at contemporary artists and artworks, discussing historical and contemporary readings, and offering an artmaking lesson, to examine social issues and inspire critical conversations. Undergraduate and graduate preservice art education students incorporate contemporary art in a postcard-sized visual image to examine complex social issues. Simultaneously, students also read historical and contemporary theoretical writings to inspire dialogue about human rights, issues concerning race, LGBTQIA+ communities, issues of gender and sexualities, Indigenous rights, and multicultural histories that are central to these conversations. Finally, students challenge themselves to courageously face their own assumptions and biases in preparation for the eventual design of middle-level lessons, which they will teach to 5th–8th grade students in the second half of the course. The chapter will focus on some specific curricular and pedagogical approaches I take to scaffold wonderful, difficult, challenging topics and conversations. I want university students to view their own learning and teaching as transformed and to enter the teaching profession prioritizing justice and equity as primary goals of their PK–12 visual arts curriculum and pedagogy.

SCAFFOLDING OF DISCUSSION TOPICS

When I begin the course, I choose certain topics that might feel more accessible, such as sexism and feminism, since many students are intimately familiar with these topics, whereas issues of heteronormativity, White privilege, and antiracism come later in the curriculum. I teach at a research university in the Midwest, a rural farming area, and the majority of art and design education students are first-generation college students from rural or suburban areas and are of White Euro-American descent. I find that a thoughtful approach to the introduction of challenging content and its implications of accountability with a focus on topic sequencing has helped us to hold critical conversations.

Even with my careful scaffolding of discussion topics, I still have students questioning me about my inclusion of social justice issues in a middle-level curriculum class. Nevertheless, I am absolutely committed to a justice equity–based curriculum; it is through holding such critical conversations in a higher education art-learning space that students can choose to go beyond "tolerance," moving instead toward critique and the ethics of self-examination. It is clear from years of feedback from graduates that this course changed their lifelong perspectives and helped them teach in ways that fostered a sense of belonging for students in their own classrooms.

Introducing Critical Perspectives Through Contemporary Art

I start the semester-long middle-level methods curriculum introducing students to the work of contemporary artists whose work reflects their critical perspectives. This approach introduces students to potentially controversial ideas. Scaffolding dialogues away from the self at first lessens students' defensiveness when they later witness their own participation in and complicity in dominant cultural assumptions and ideologies. This in turn enables them to question their histories and positions, and the power dynamics these imply.

Quinn (2006) observed that working for social justice within art education "requires attention to the complex contexts of peoples' lives, and then, engaged responses aimed at change" (p. 291). Therefore, providing an inclusive art education curriculum becomes necessary for "analysis and action" (p. 290), in which teachers and students are encouraged to "link the arts to social justice or plan arts curricula around conceptions of citizenship in a democracy" (p. 291).

Embedding Dialogue in Multileveled Ways

In the many years I have taught future art educators at the university level, I have found that not only holding dialogues, but teaching students how to *build* dialogues, is an essential pedagogical strategy. Dialogue needs to be embedded in multileveled ways throughout the curriculum. If dialogic possibilities are modeled when viewing art, when responding to readings, when consulting with peers in pairs, in small-group conversations, and in the whole-class group, opportunities are created for disclosure when talking about difficult issues. Norms need to be set for how conversations should be held; for example, care must be exercised not to put any student on the spot by asking a student of a particular sexual orientation, or a student of color, to speak for and represent an entire community. It is essential to lay ground rules agreed upon and chosen by students before starting. For example, we may agree to disagree, but we will focus on respecting difference, exercising utmost care not to attack the individual as we engage with points of view that differ from our own. Such modeling of dialogue at all levels enables future teachers to incorporate similar strategies in open-ended lesson design and course curricula with their own students.

As we view work, I use the sequencing of dialogic questions: Topic, Association, Visualization, Transition (Burton, 2009; Burton et al., 2000; Smith, 1994) to help guide the students to think more fully about translating their ideas and choices into the artmaking process. When I ask students to share their social issues and the like-minded contemporary artists they have chosen to study independently, we create a forum for initial dialogues. In our first classroom studio art assignment, I ask students to incorporate contemporary art in a postcard-sized visual image to examine complex social issues relevant to them. I ask students in the class to think about the following questions related to their selected topic and a social justice perspective:

- **Topic Question:** What issue (local/global/social) are you personally concerned about that affects the individual and the collective?
- **Association Question:** How have you experienced this in your own life? Or how have you witnessed such experiences in the lives of others? What are your deepest concerns about these experiences? How might you advocate for change at local or global levels?
- **Visualization Question:** If you were to visually represent any one of your ideas, what image(s) might you begin with? Who has a different idea? How else might you create an image to express this idea and action? What will determine the visual choices you make to communicate your point of view or perspective about your key issue/idea/concept?
- **Transition Question:** Where would you place your image on the cardboard used for the final postcard-sized artwork? What colors might you use? How might you integrate the text? What would you want to emphasize most through scale and composition?

After students participate in the roundtable discussion in class, each sharing their social issue and chosen contemporary artists' ideas, they brainstorm visual strategies for their own images and compositions guided by the sequenced dialogic questions that ask them to connect making with their lived experiences and to articulate their perspective or point of view about a social issue that affects them. They make the work both in class and at home. Such initial dialogue about their own lives brings out concern and empathy from their peers, thus setting the stage for mutual understanding. This does not mean that students are asked to agree with each other's views. Rather, they are asked to listen actively, which fosters open communication in their beginning conversations. Working together on the same assignment with its multiple solutions models a collaborative viewing and making of art and visual culture. Pre-artistic process questions add to the creation of a dialogic forum for sharing and critical reflection.

INTRODUCING ARTMAKING AS A POINT OF ENTRY

Over the years, students have brought up LGBTQIA+ concerns; environmental conservation content; antiracist, antisexist, and human rights content; animal abuse; child abuse; sexual abuse; migration injustices; border crossings; and marginalization in schools, to name just a few. In these initial dialogues, students are representing themselves and their positions through visual statements and explaining why their concerns matter. Such conversations generate empathy. Students are able to recognize the impact that chosen issues have on classmates' lives. Students' images in the form of postcard-sized visual statements intermingled with text reflect their deepest concerns.

This first assignment is an entry point for teaching difficult topics, but the content emerges from the students and therefore takes on meaning for the collective. In expressing personal views about difficult topics (Hsieh, 2016; Keifer-Boyd, 2010; Kraehe, 2015; Kraehe et al., 2018; Lampela, 2005; Lilienthal et al., 2018; McIntosh, 1990), art and visual culture are used to bridge learning with lived experience. Difficult topics made personal enable heartfelt dialogues that disarm through narrative (Barakett & Sacca, 2002; Wellman & Bey, 2015). Some examples of student work from this lesson are included below (see Figures 5.1 and 5.2).

Examples of Class Lesson Postcard Studio Exploration Outcomes

Artist Statement: "In my piece I explore the idea of how we disregard others. My theme is ownership based on materialism. I begin with a background that is washed out, symbolic of the mining of our natural resources leading to an unfertile environment that is destroyed. I have come to the conclusion that capitalism is one of the major evils of our modern world."

Artist Statement: "I chose to depict police terrorism using graphite, ink, pen, watercolor, and charcoal. I feel we take on a subliminal numbing trauma through seeing news and footage of Black Americans being murdered regularly. The background includes a long, winding list of names of Black Americans murdered through police brutality. It is up to White people to recognize and use their privilege to act against their privilege in order to create safe ground for people of color."

SOME CONCLUDING REMARKS

Controversial topics enable questioning and examining each other's opinions, which is a messy process and never neatly packaged. The challenging ideas in students' readings, viewing, and research, as well as in their studio explorations and writings, provide dynamic conversational spaces for ideas about the roles students themselves play in the institutional constructs of issues of privilege, racism, sexism, heteronormativity, and cultural stereotyping. I have attempted to

Figure 5.1. Juan Pablo Ramirez Quiroz, *How Did Humans Decide They Owned the Earth?* (mixed media collage, Spring 2021)

Figure 5.2. Isabella Monet Gomez-Welsh, *Police Brutality* (mixed media drawing, Spring 2021)

share how I address opportunities for students to critically examine, in many cases for the first time, their own positioned assumptions. This book asks how art educators might center the voices of students, democratize the classroom so all are equally represented, and create a space where everyone has the choice to both speak and be silent. This chapter attempts to contribute to the larger conversation of art educators who are engaged in democratizing our classrooms. It is my hope that we might do better as we raise a next generation of art educators whose humanism is centered in their every teaching act and whose priorities are to create spaces of access and equity for all students.

REFERENCES

Barakett, J., & Sacca, E. (2002). Narratives empowering teachers and students: Educational and cultural practice. In Y. Gaudelius & P. Speirs (Eds.), *Contemporary issues in art education* (pp. 39–49). Prentice-Hall.

Burton, J. M. (2009). Creative intelligence, creative practice: Lowenfeld redux. *Studies in Art Education, 50*(40), 323–337.

Burton, J. M., Horowitz, R., & Abeles, H. (2000). The configuration of meaning: Learner centered art education revisited. *Studies in Art Education, 41*(4), 330–345.

Hsieh, K. (2016). Preservice art teachers' attitudes toward addressing LGBTQ issues in their future classrooms. *Studies in Art Education, 57*(2), 120–138.

Keifer-Boyd, K. (2010). Visual culture and gender constructions. *The International Journal of Arts Education, 8,* 1–24.

Kraehe, A. M. (2015). Sounds of silence: Race and emergent counter-narratives of art teacher identity. *Studies in Art Education, 56*(3), 199–213.

Kraehe, A. M., Gaztambide-Fernández, R., & Carpenter, B. S. (2018). *The Palgrave handbook of race and the arts in education.* Springer International Publishing.

Lampela, L. (2005). Writing effective lesson plans while utilizing the work of lesbian and gay artists. *Art Education, 58*(2), 33–39.

Lilienthal, L. K., Matyo-Cepero, J. A., Messinger, L., & Mims, M. J. (2018). Creating an inviting classroom for all students: Inviting teachers to learn about LGBTQ diversity. *Delta Kappa Gamma Bulletin, 85*(1), 13–19.

McIntosh, P. (1990). Unpacking the knapsack of white privilege. *Independent School, Working Papers.*

Quinn, T. (2006). Out of cite, out of mind: Social justice and art education. *Journal of Social Theory in Art Education, 26*, 282–301.

Smith, N. (1994). *Experience and art: Teaching children to paint* (2nd ed.). Teachers College Press.

Wellman, S., & Bey, S. (2015). Refugee children and art teacher training: Promoting language, self-advocacy, and cultural preservation. *Art Education, 68*(6), 36–44.

CHAPTER 6

"Yes, and . . ."

Extending Conversations in Art Classrooms

Nikki Sandschaper

I have witnessed a coming-of-age drama happening in art classrooms across the world. A well-intended teacher looks out at their classroom of young artists. Students have been asked to think about an artwork, and it's time to share their ideas. "Anyone? Anyone?" the teacher begs from the front of the room. The longer the pause goes on, the more the pressure piles on. Students swing from feeling nervous about having the "right" answer to simply thinking about other distractions. The teacher starts to wonder whether they chose an interesting enough artwork, and everyone is feeling a little self-conscious. Then it happens. One brave soul offers an interpretation, breaking up the silence. It's not a serious answer. It might be silly, maybe mischievous. Whatever it is, it's clear that the rest of the class is watching. Postures are more upright, and the spotlight is on the teacher.

I have led discussions about contemporary art in classrooms in different countries with students from various cultures and privileges. The conversations in my classroom range from playful and joyful to deep and serious. I love the way one artwork can inspire a broad range of interpretations. When I was a teacher in Denver, Colorado, in Title I schools, I learned that authentic questioning with students can be unpredictable. I thrived on the rambunctious dance of inquiry that students with loud reputations and fearless opinions can bring to a classroom. I enjoyed the playful push and pull where participants take turns leading and following as they metaphorically whirl around the classroom. My most rebellious students have been my best teachers, and I found myself baiting students for wacky answers when I wanted to get the ball rolling.

When I shifted my career into international teaching in Seoul, South Korea, I wondered how the skills I had learned at public schools would transfer to an exclusive private school where I expected quiet compliance. Creating a safe space where students are free to be vulnerable sets the stage for authentic aesthetic experiences. One simple approach that has influenced both conversations and creations that happen in my classroom is the technique used in theatrical improvisation of "Yes, and . . ." This high-impact move encourages the flow of conversations and thought processes in a validating and encouraging way, no matter the level or background.

This magical moment created by saying "Yes, and . . ." carries the possibility of showing students that there are infinite "right" answers and what matters most is that they find their own answers, whatever they may be. Making "Yes, and . . ." a cultural norm in your classroom shows students that their truth is their own and not for you to define. Whatever direction the conversation takes, validate, engage, and encourage with sincere curiosity. Your students will notice and become more inquisitive and courageous. Their answers won't always be silly, but when even the most ludicrous answers are acceptable and engaged with, students are empowered to be risky with their deeper interpretations.

CHAPTER 7

Challenging Implicit Bias

Using Contemporary Art to Understand the Power of Personal Autonomy

Kristin A. Ponden

Conversations around identity are a key touchstone for my 5th-grade visual arts class. Developmentally, each student is in the process of figuring out who they are and where they fit in the world, so this is a critical time to help them reflect on the power that comes from having personal autonomy and the negative consequences that can result from unexamined bias. Implicit bias occurs when our brains unconsciously place people and things into categories, which often results in negative stereotyping. Using contemporary art as a basis for classroom discussion is one way I help my students identify their own bias and work to overcome it.

We consider the following three essential questions as a framework for this process:

1. How do our life experiences and identities influence the way we look at art?
2. How can we control the way others view us (or can we)?
3. Why is it important to consider representation when looking at art?

To begin, I have students look at photographs from Joel Parés' *Judging America* (2014) series. Parés presents two photos of his subjects side by side: one based on stereotypes of the cultural or ethnic group the subject belongs to and the other revealing the subject's actual identity. Showing only the former, I ask students to make assumptions about the subjects based only on the available visual information. They must back up their opinions using visual clues; for example, in one photo a man is wearing soiled clothes, gardening gloves, and holding a rake. Many of my students perceive the man as being Latinx, which influences their view of him with some interpreting him as a laborer rather than someone gardening for pleasure because of their association with migrant farm worker stereotypes. In Parés' photo series, race, ethnicity, and socioeconomic status are unavoidable topics. When the man working in the garden is revealed to be the CEO of a Fortune 500 company in a second photograph, some of the students are confronted with their own implicit bias, or the assumptions we make unconsciously. This leads into a discussion about how we perceive others and how we ourselves might be perceived based only on our outward physical appearances. Most importantly, students consider how to acknowledge and challenge their own biases and address stereotypes and prejudice when they encounter it.

We next look at the art of William H. Johnson, working as part of the Harlem Renaissance, a time when African Americans celebrated their culture publicly and were able to define themselves apart from how they had been stereotyped and oppressed by White society. I show Johnson's painting *Street Life, Harlem* (1939–1940) to my students and ask them to describe the couple depicted, who are dressed up for a night out and embody the style and vivacity of the period. After a brief discussion of the Harlem Renaissance, we listen to a recording of Langston Hughes reading his poem "One-Way Ticket" (1949). Hughes refers to: "[people] Who are scared of me/ And me of them" (pp. 60–61). We discuss what Hughes meant by that statement and students reflect on the pressures of being perceived a certain way. We also talk about the desire to escape, the way many Southern African Americans did when they journeyed North during the Great Migration. The freedom of individuals to authentically express themselves through art, dance, music, poetry, and fashion contributed to the cultural revitalization in Harlem in the 1920s.

Following this historical context, I show students the work of contemporary African American artists Kehinde Wiley and Amy Sherald. We watch Wiley (TIME, 2018) speak about the honor of painting President Barack Obama and the significance of being a Black artist selected by the first Black President of the United States to paint his official portrait. We listen to Sherald (CBS Sunday Morning, 2019) discuss the intimacy of her portraits and how her characteristic gray skin tones represent the inner lives of her Black subjects. We discuss the lack of portraits of Black individuals in museum collections, most notably in the Grand Manner style that much of Wiley's work emulates, and I explain that Wiley involves his subjects in choosing how they would like to be portrayed. I again ask students to use visual clues to interpret the subjects in Sherald and Wiley's portraits; their answers now reflect a broader understanding of identity and personal authenticity after having been confronted with their own implicit biases earlier. They consider their own experiences as viewers in museums and begin to question who decides what is displayed and why. Without their prior knowledge of how non-White identities and experiences have been shaped by harmful stereotypes, students will not have a complete understanding of the significance of Black artists painting portraits of individuals who have been historically excluded from collections of fine art.

Giving students the space to question institutional practices that have long been accepted allows them to move forward with the goal of supporting equity and personal autonomy within the art world and beyond. Contemporary art provides an opportunity to illuminate critical issues such as stereotyping and implicit bias. Empowering my students to recognize their ability to effect positive change in their own lives and in the broader community is the most important lesson I try to impart to them in the art room.

REFERENCES

CBS Sunday Morning. (2019, October 18). *Amy Sherald on painting "everyday people"* [Video]. YouTube. https://youtu.be/kuF3NxF-ACc

Hughes, L. (1949). *One-way ticket.* Alfred A. Knopf.

Johnson, W. H. (1939–1940). *Street life, Harlem* [Oil on plywood]. Smithsonian American Art Museum, Washington, DC, United States. https://americanart.si.edu/artwork/street-life-harlem-11857

Parés, J. (2014). *Judging America* [Photograph series]. http://www.joelpares.com/judging-america-1

TIME. (2018, April 19). *Kehinde Wiley on President Obama's official portrait: "This is the real thing"* [Video]. YouTube. https://youtu.be/44TTnTO443k

CHAPTER 8

Approaching a Liberatory Future of Museum Education

Reflections on Practice and Pedagogy

Ariana Robles, Amara Higuera, Gladys Preciado, and Alice Bebbington

We are four educators who have collectively worked in the education departments of six arts and culture museums across the United States over the last 7 years. We believe it is essential that museum education curriculum be executed with an anti-oppressive and liberatory lens. Psychologist Jamila Codrington (2014) points out that if the curriculum does not serve the student's needs and goals within the classroom, "we run the risk of promoting education reform strategies that continue to serve the needs of the dominant group and perpetuate the status quo" (p. 1017). The status quo in Western history leans toward the celebration of colonialism, whiteness, and capitalism—a legacy museums tend to reflect. J'net AyAyQwaYakSheelth, now Director of Indigenous Relations and Community Engagement at the National Film Board of Canada, reported that the lack of education about Indigenous histories "leaves a vacuum of details, experiences, and social injustices that are not taught in the Western education system, which is a systemic form of erasure" (AyAyQwaYakSheelth & Ng, 2018, para. 10).

We will share our firsthand experiences in museum arts education settings that point to the need for liberatory spaces, critical thinking, and antiracist work cultures, and offer practical suggestions as to how these values can be extended to all learning spaces. This chapter is a resource for anyone interested in liberatory pedagogy who works in an education space, whether as a teacher, administrator, or teaching artist. By practicing reflection and action, creating a healthy work environment, centering student voices and knowledge, acknowledging their sources of knowledge, and understanding them as whole individuals who exist outside of the classroom, we can begin to create liberatory learning spaces.

A PATH TOWARD LIBERATORY PEDAGOGY

So, what is liberatory pedagogy? Paulo Freire (2000) suggests the goal of liberatory pedagogy is for teacher and student to achieve *conscientiza¢ão*, an active effort to learn to perceive social, political, and economic contradictions and to take action against the oppressive elements of reality. In our practice, we aim to achieve conscientiza¢ão through *praxis*, a conscious practice of reflection and action to affect change.

Some reflective questions to begin praxis in your teaching practice are:

- Who is the population you are supporting?
- What are their immediate and long-term needs and how are you supporting them?
- How are you reflecting on your progress and your success with the community, and making space to incorporate changing needs?
- Are your collaboration and feedback in the classroom in support of the larger goal of liberation?
- How do you sustain this work, both financially and physically?
- How are you making time for rest to avoid burnout?

Being in a practice of praxis means taking action from theoretical starting points, reflecting, and acting upon continued reflection.

In addition to prioritizing individual reflection and action, the organization must be a safe place for the education worker alongside the student. Unfortunately, our current educational and capitalist system is structured in a way that overworks individuals and makes praxis a challenge. Workers must be paid livable wages; this is one starting point to build liberatory pedagogy. The investment in educators' practices will support the kind of work needed to build antioppressive teaching. Unions are examples of how workers can be protected and supported to help build liberatory learning spaces. If you are in an administrative position and want to support this change within your own institution, begin with reflective questions, then start changing the answers to those questions with action. In our own work, we established praxis at one institution we worked for by advocating for paid time to read theory, and collectively built a liberatory pedagogy with our team of educators. We worked to create a student-centered community by engaging in critical conversations and advocating for change, receiving training on trauma-informed teaching, working with students with disabilities, and applying liberatory teaching, and multilingual classroom techniques.

LESSONS FROM OUR OWN CLASSROOMS

What does an authentically student-centered learning space look, feel, and sound like? The first thing we noticed before this work was implemented was that our students had little space to openly participate in class discussions. We hold power as educators, and our goal was to distribute it back to students. We learned from the practices of other educators, like Keonna Hendrick, Alyssa Machida, Flavia Zuñiga-West, and Alisha Mernick, who all write and offer resources to support an antiracist and antioppressive classroom. We began every class by cocreating community agreements that defined and regulated how we interacted with each other as a classroom community. Our community agreements were simple and challenged classroom norms. During virtual learning, we attempted to meet students' diverse needs by allowing them to turn off cameras and participate using chat and reaction functions. While we were not able to gather hard data on classroom engagement, anecdotally we noticed that after the introduction of our community agreements, students opened up almost immediately in positive ways that voiced their needs.

Intentional language is also key to building an anti-oppressive classroom. Changing how we think about language and how we utilize it alters our worldview (hooks, 1994). Language creates concepts that become our reality. hooks helped us theorize how the English language is linked to domination. She explains that "standard English . . . is the language of conquest and domination; in the United States, it is the mask which hides the loss of . . . diverse native communities" (hooks, 1994, p. 168). In our work, we try to subvert this domination by examining the meaning of some words and concepts to create new perspectives than we are used to. Think about the keywords and terms you often use in your classroom: Do these create an expansive understanding of the world? Do they limit you and your students to a Western-canonical way of thinking?

In our classrooms, we made it a point to allow students to share their lived experiences that connected to the material. When teaching with historical objects that featured staple crops, we would ask students, "What is your favorite way of eating these foods?" Broad questions during guided conversation center students' personal preferences and opinions, like music, food preferences, or movies that frame their worldview. This is another crucial aspect of agency where we seek to empower the whole student and their sources of knowledge versus one aspect of their experience like their cultural background or how many facts they can recall on a subject.

When teaching objects from the museum collection, we centered students' experience by showing them that object history could be in their own kitchen! A classroom favorite was a *metate*, a flat grinding stone used specifically to grind corn. Many students shared that they had metates or similar objects in their homes. We made space for them in conversation to see themselves in the material that created out-of-the-classroom, intergenerational conversations between students and their elders. Crooke (2007) suggests, "It is people who bring value and consequence to objects and collections; as a result, if a museum cannot forge associations with people, it will have no meaning" (p. 131). We argue that education and learning, likewise, have no value if they do not reflect the people who are learning and who can apply this knowledge in their life.

CONCLUDING THOUGHTS

Returning to the work of Dr. Codrington (2014), we agree that "culturally responsive teaching can move from a focus on the racial academic achievement gap and improvement of 'minority' graduation rates and labor market success, to outcomes that reflect a real advocacy for anti-racism and social justice" (pp. 1022–1023). Conscientizaçăo is a process that takes years of trust and mutual collaboration on the side of the teacher, and that of the student. We would like to reiterate that our reflections are not a step-by-step guide on how to establish a liberatory pedagogy, nor would we claim that we have perfected or even fully developed this pedagogy within our own practices. We also did not develop this practice alone; we built it in community with one another and learning from the labor, scholarship, and cultural resilience of Black and Indigenous activists, leaders, scholars, and cultural workers, working towards an actively antiracist future.

We wanted to share how we attempted to work toward one version of liberatory pedagogy within the structures of museums and the school systems we partnered with. This is in the hopes of sharing concepts, resources, and support systems that are needed to begin establishing antioppressive environments for our students. With better tools, they can shape the world and the function of old systems into something new and liberated.

REFERENCES

AyAyQwaYakSheelth, J., & Ng, W. (2018, June 28). *Decolonize and Indigenize: A reflective dialogue*. Viewfinder. https://medium.com/viewfinder-reflecting-on-museum-education/decolonize-and-indigenize-a-reflective-dialogue-3de78fa76442

Codrington, J. (2014). Sharpening the lens of culturally responsive science teaching: A call for liberatory education for oppressed student groups. *Cultural Studies of Science Education*, *9*(4), 1015–1024. https://doi.org/10.1007/s11422-013-9543-2

Crooke, E. M. (2007). *Community spaces: Ideas, issues and challenges*. Routledge.

Freire, P. (2000). *Pedagogy of the oppressed* (30th anniversary ed.). Bloomsbury.

hooks, b. (1994) *Teaching to transgress*. Routledge.

CHAPTER 9

Addressing Facilitator Power in Youth Museum Programs

Simona Zappas

I am a skeptic of any program that describes itself as "youth-led." Adult facilitators in "youth-led" programming do hold power and can acknowledge the implicit power structure in the program. Holding power isn't a negative thing, but willfully not acknowledging power structures can subvert equity goals and cause harm. Striving for equity requires an understanding of the systems of power that affect it.

It is a fallacy to call a program youth-led if it has an adult facilitator. I don't say this to be (entirely) glib, but rather to recognize the power and impact facilitators have. My cynicism may seem surprising given that I oversee Youth Programming at the Walker Art Center in Minneapolis, Minnesota, which has a format similar to other "youth-led" programs. The Walker Art Center Teen Arts Council (WACTAC), made up of a dozen 10th- through 12th-graders who have applied to the program, meets weekly at the museum. We leverage the Walker's collection to build the students' critical thinking abilities, visual literacies, and collaboration-based leadership skills through leveraging our collection, staff, spaces, and ample snack budget. The teens learn the behind-the-scenes functionalities of the museum, plan events for their peers, and explore a group research project of their choosing. The teens make a majority of the content decisions, but I would never call it *youth-led*. Let me explain why.

In WACTAC, my interactions with teens may be informal and laid-back, but I'm still the one in charge. I'm older, I control the money, I hold institutional knowledge, and I plan the program. In designating a program as youth-led, there is a danger of underplaying the positionality of the facilitator and so (un) intentionally avoiding acknowledgment of the program's power structure. Accepting and openly communicating the power we hold as adult facilitators or administrators allows us to guide the program ethically.

This acknowledgment should be done at the start of a program or project by having the facilitator describe their responsibilities; when establishing group norms, the facilitator would explain their role in enforcing those norms. This sets the expectations for what the youth are responsible for while demonstrating to the youth the facilitator's commitment as a contributor to the group's goals.

I found success building distinct opportunities for teens to take the lead by identifying and communicating clear parameters, including roles, goals, capacity, and time limits, in every project we do. In my program design, I intentionally scaffold learning to ensure that the beginning of the year frontloads the youth with information and time to practice skills that they will use when doing projects in the latter half of the program, where they can take a stronger lead. For example, in WACTAC, the year culminates in the teens determining a question or critique they have of the museum, figuring out how to research it, and sharing what they've learned. When introducing a project, I explain the parameters and the purpose. I give the participants past examples and a budget with sample costs, and describe projects that would be out of scope and explain why. I build in reflective activities to discuss what they've learned so far. I arrange the curriculum around key activities and learning goals that support the open-ended project that balance student choices with the needs of the program. I can designate areas where I could be responsive to their interests. This allows me to provide them opportunities to take ownership over projects that are driven by their interests.

As art educators and administrators, our work holds gravity because of the potential impact we can have on the youth we serve. In my reflections on my practice, I think about how not acknowledging my power can create a space where power is implicit and youth are expected to passively accept it. When I recognize my power and model a transparent use of it, it can open up opportunities to meaningfully engage in dialogue on how to share power or how to expand the autonomy within our programs. It is my hope that I can provide youth with a safe space to practice interrogating power dynamics, leading to discussions on how they would shift other systems of power. Critical reflections on our power are necessary for programs that call themselves youth-led. Our work is important and should be celebrated for its dynamic challenges, skill sets, and efficacy.

CHAPTER 10

Rethinking Feelings in Antiracist Art Pedagogy

Injeong Yoon-Ramirez

How can art educator-scholars understand and question *feelings* as a key dimension of a critical learning process? As a partial answer to this question, I reflect on my experience of teaching an art education course focusing on diversity and equity. To better understand emotion and its relation to antiracist art pedagogy, I first share how my perspective on emotion has shifted over the past couple of years and the importance of reflecting on emotions to bolster antiracist art pedagogy.

I am a university professor working primarily with undergraduate and graduate students in the fields of art and art education. In 2016, as a doctoral student, I taught an upper-division art education course on diversity at a medium-sized university in the Southwest. More than half of the 15 undergraduate students self-identified as White. I found that engaging students on topics related to racism was challenging. When I brought up the term *White privilege*, for example, there was awkward silence in the classroom; later, several White students wrote in their reflections that they did not feel comfortable to speak up about racial issues, and often felt blamed. Two students in particular wrote that the idea of White privilege did not make sense to them and discussing its concept in class made them uncomfortable and frustrated. These emotional responses from White students—including shutdown, guilt, withdrawal, and anger—were no surprise to me. At that time, I just considered the students' feelings as obstacles to learning about structural racism and as signs of my teaching failure.

Over the years, I started thinking more about this experience, the emotions that I sensed, and how those feelings affect antiracist work. I wondered what emotions were dominant in my classroom at the time and how they affected the classroom dynamics and my teaching practice. Specifically, I was curious why I perceived some of my students' responses as a sign of my failure.

With this question in mind, in this chapter I reflect on feelings and their relationship with antiracist art pedagogy. As some critical race feminists argue (Berry, 2010; hooks, 1994), emotions are not subsidiary effects of learning, but key dimensions of intellectual and aesthetic engagement, especially in critical learning. By unpacking the sociocultural dimension of emotions, I argue that feelings can be a pedagogical site for transformation. That is, the pedagogical practice of antiracism can be amplified when art educators recognize, question, and reorient habitual patterns of feelings.

UNDERSTANDING EMOTIONS VIA A CULTURAL LENS

When I first taught about racism, I regarded emotions as things contained and expressed by individuals. For instance, if one student wrote that they felt frustrated by the conversation about White privilege, I considered that feeling as something that individual student possessed, due to their background, experience, or knowledge. However, I noticed some similarities among students' emotional responses, especially from White students during the class conversations. A few White students mentioned that they felt blamed, or they didn't feel comfortable to speak up when the class discussed white privilege and structural racism. On another occasion, several students almost habitually recentered their good intentions by saying "I treat everyone equally" or "I am trying to do good," even when no one accused them of racism. I was curious where this defensiveness stemmed from.

A few years later, I reanalyzed my students' responses from the course taught in 2016 through a cultural theory of emotions (see Ahmed, 2015; Gibbs, 2001; Pedwell & Whitehead, 2012; Sedgwick, 2003). This time, I examined how certain ways of responding to racial dialogues, whether they entailed explicit emotional responses or implicit avoidance of engagement, were habitually normalized and circulated in my classroom (Yoon, 2019). I employed a critical lens of emotions because they allowed me to see how seemingly individualized feelings are imbricated with sociocultural relations and power. In other words, emotions are a significant circuit through which power relations and social norms are imagined and contested (Pedwell, 2012). From this perspective, what one feels, or feelings that are evoked in learning, are more than a mere reaction contained within or expressed by an individual. Instead, emotions are a site where social norms and power are collectively sensed and maintained. Thus, it is crucial to examine how certain feelings are centered, circulated, and maintained, and more importantly, whose feelings, at what expense, are constantly recentered in the classroom.

The other important learning I gleaned through this research is that feelings are set off not in an isolated individual body, but rather in moments of encounter with others and objects. In her theorization of the politics of emotions, Ahmed (2000, 2015) pays attention to the social encounter and the interanimation of emotional energies that are triggered within certain dynamics. Emotions and feelings are not produced within an individual, but "come from without and move inward" (Ahmed, 2015, p. 9). Ahmed (2015) explains,

> Emotions create the very effect of the surfaces and boundaries that allow us to distinguish an inside and an outside in the first place. So emotions are not simply something "I" or "we" have. Rather, it is through emotions, or how we respond to objects and others, that surfaces or boundaries are made; the "I" and the "we" are shaped by, and even take the shape of, contact with others. (p. 10)

When I started recognizing the cultural and political aspects of emotions, I was able to better understand how some feelings, such as defensiveness and discomfort, are more frequently shared in my classroom and how I routinely perceive them in either a negative or positive way. In my predominantly White classroom, White students' feelings around racial dialogues are often distributed more dominantly. It was not because they are numerically dominant in my classroom. Rather, it seemed like emotional habits of responding to racial dialogues were already established in line with values of whiteness. Feelings, as Ahmed (2015) points out, work to register a judgment of a thing, the judgment becomes the quality of a thing, and the quality becomes socially shared. In this light, I could recognize how my students were already socialized to participate in conversations about racism by sensing, inhabiting, and expressing socially shared feelings.

This reflective analysis offered me an important lesson that emotions are not just cues of positive or negative learning outcomes, but a circuit where norms and values are constructed and maintained. Where whiteness operates as a normative power, it becomes almost instinctive to feel and share emotions of discomfort, denial, and defensiveness toward the topic of racism. I presumed discomfort may be a result of racial dialogues; however, whose emotions was I mainly considering? When I collected written responses about the readings and class discussions from the students, I was pleasantly surprised by the different responses toward our class discussion on racism, which was heated to some extent. Many Black, Indigenous, and People of Color (BIPOC) students in my class responded that the discussion was not emotionally charging. Instead, several BIPOC students noted that they felt their experiences were validated. Reading these students' responses allowed me to see that even I, as a female teacher of color, was not centering emotions that BIPOC students might bring into the class discussion at the beginning. This reflection challenged my perspectives on emotions in antiracist pedagogy and enabled me to see how norms around emotions powerfully shaped the perception of my teaching practice.

REFLECTIONS ON NICENESS

To understand emotions as a site where normalized power is distributed, a key part of antiracist art pedagogy, is to recognize habitual feelings that maintain the status quo. According to Matias (2016), White feelings of guilt, shame, anger, defensiveness, and discomfort are often conjured up in racial dialogues and perpetuate racial inequities. Similarly, it is important to pay attention to how "niceness" as a value is prevalent in antiracist dialogues. As I briefly mentioned above, some of my White students underlined their good intentions to be nice to everyone during the conversations about racism. At first, I didn't consider this type of response harmful. I just had to point out how structural racism is sustained not just by malicious intentions, but through ordinary practices of doing one's job, for instance.

However, critical whiteness scholars argue that creating a culture of niceness is one of techniques in which whiteness maintains its power (Haviland, 2008; McIntyre, 1997). In the context of teacher education, Picower (2009) and Matias (2016) both argue that White preservice teachers overly rely on "niceness." "Niceness" is a main pedagogical stance; they believe if they are open-minded and nice to everyone, their young students, regardless of their background, will flourish in school. Matias (2016) argues that declarations of caring and empathy for all students often become a shallow and empty signifier, especially when teachers do not examine their positionality in relation to the oppressive system in schooling. Critical whiteness scholars point out that being nice to students, in and of itself, is not the problem. How it operates to disguise the actual issue of inequity that shapes students' lives as well as how it recenters White agency is problematic.

Based on these critical whiteness studies, I started recognizing how niceness was habitually brought up in difficult conversations. The emphasis on niceness quickly shifted the attention from issues of racism affecting BIPOC communities. Several White students overemphasized their good intentions to treat everyone equally as a response to the class discussion on structural racism. It seemed these students considered antiracist education as teaching niceness, instead of examining and challenging the roots and effects of racism. Niceness and white saviorhood together can mislead teachers into thinking their role is to be a good helper or loving fixer, while unknowingly perpetuating racial and sociocultural hierarchies (Picower, 2009).

I also witnessed how often "doing good" is mentioned in racial conversations. Ahmed (2008) says that "good feeling"/happiness becomes a technology of reconciliation "which in allowing us to leave bad feeling behind, enable us to embrace a common good" (p. 9). In a classroom where whiteness is predominant, a common good tends to be oriented toward the colorblind and celebratory, in Ahmed's (2008) words, "a happy smiling multiculturalism" (p. 9). When this orientation is set, the thing that gets in the way—for instance, a conversation on structural racism that evokes any feeling of discomfort or guilt—turns into a disruptive, unhappy thing. In the normative narrative of whiteness, any disturbing feelings are easily shifted and replaced by a good feeling (Ahmed, 2008). This is especially problematic in antiracist pedagogy, as niceness becomes a strategy to perform antiracism without deeply engaging in the issue and challenging the status quo; ultimately, it recenters whiteness and secures the racial hierarchy.

CONCLUDING THOUGHTS

Through my reflection, I learned a couple of things. Emotions are entwined with the power structure. Through emotions, dominant norms and values are circulated and maintained in our pedagogical practice. A prevalent emotional response based on niceness or good feelings, for example, operates to maintain whiteness by decentering the oppressive racial reality. Thus, it is important to reflect on what, and how, values are shared through emotions in the classroom, as well as whose emotions are dominantly circulated. This way, educators can also revisit the sense of teaching failure and how it is formed through dominant values around emotions involved in teaching. For me, I had to let go of my own desire or expectation of feeling good after teaching, especially when I invited students to be open, vulnerable, and even courageous to take part in antiracist work.

I believe the arts have a unique strength in the reflective work on emotions. This is because the arts allow us to pause, to notice things, people, and sensations in unfamiliar and meaningful ways. Perhaps art educators can guide a critical reflection on emotions for antiracism by creating works about how emotions travel or how their emotions often are aligned with dominant values. Students can explore their own emotions, confronting what makes them uncomfortable, by talking about artworks. By collectively cultivating the reflective capacity to examine norms and values around emotions, art educators can enhance existing antiracist endeavors in our field.

REFERENCES

Ahmed, S. (2000). *Strange encounters: Embodied others in post-coloniality*. Routledge.

Ahmed, S. (2008). The politics of good feeling. *Australian Critical Race and Whiteness Studies Association Journal, 4*(1), 1–18.

Ahmed, S. (2015). *The cultural politics of emotion* (2nd ed.). Routledge.

Berry, T. R. (2010). Engaged pedagogy and critical race feminism. *Educational Foundations, 24*(3–4), 19–26.

Gibbs, A. (2001). Contagious feelings: Pauline Hanson and the epidemiology of affect. *Australian Humanities Review*. https://australianhumanitiesreview.org/2001/12/01/contagious-feelings-pauline-hanson-and-the-epidemiology-of-affect/ *24*(December).

Haviland, V. S. (2008). "Things get glossed over": Rearticulating the silencing power of whiteness in education. *Journal of Teacher Education, 59*(1), 40–54.

hooks, b. (1994). *Teaching to transgress: Education as the practice of freedom*. Routledge.

Matias, C. E. (2016). *Feeling White: Whiteness, emotionality, and education*. Brill.

McIntyre, A. (1997). *Making meaning of whiteness: Exploring racial identity with White teachers*. State University of New York Press.

Pedwell, C. (2012). Economies of empathy: Obama, neoliberalism, and social justice. *Environment and Planning D: Society and Space, 30*(2), 280–297.

Pedwell, C., & Whitehead, A. (2012). Affecting feminism: Questions of feeling in feminist theory. *Feminist Theory, 13*(2), 115–129.

Picower, B. (2009). The unexamined whiteness of teaching: How White teachers maintain and enact dominant racial ideologies. *Race Ethnicity and Education 12*(2), 197–215.

Sedgwick, E. K. (2003). *Touching feeling: Affect, pedagogy, performativity*. Duke University Press.

Yoon, I. (2019, September 19–21). *Exploring emotions and (dis)comfort in teaching and learning art for social transformation* [Conference presentation]. Art Education Research Institute symposium. New York, NY.

CHAPTER 11

Shifting the Conversation

Scaffolding Sociocultural Dialogue in the Elementary Art Classroom

Beth Link

How do art teachers navigate conversations about cultures they are not part of? As a White woman, and a former elementary art teacher myself, I was curious to see how race factored into the curriculum work of other White elementary art educators. To explore these questions, I conducted an ethnographic case study, spending nearly a year with two White elementary art teachers to observe how they navigated sensitive cultural conversations. I then used the data to lead critical reflections and collaboratively reflect on decentering whiteness. In this chapter I introduce one of the teachers, provide a snapshot of her practice, and detail reflections from our work. I also offer a framework for scaffolding intentional sociocultural dialogue drawn from this research.

SNAPSHOT OF SOCIOCULTURAL DIALOGUE

Sharon is a White female art teacher with over a decade of experience. She grew up in a "little bitty town" where her "world was all white." Her perspective expanded as she attended college and moved to larger cities with more racial diversity. She now works to intentionally learn more about race and power in the wake of our nation's racial reckoning, which brought racial tensions into sharper focus for her. Her work to educate herself is coupled with an effort to help students gain "a little piece of understanding that broadens their lens to see a bigger world beyond their white home" (Link, 2022, p. 245).

Recently, Sharon has made substantial shifts to teach more multicultural art projects, including during her "art of the day" series where she begins each class with a brief discussion of an artwork by a contemporary artist of color. She projects an image and asks, "What do you notice?" before sharing information to provide context. During one of my observations, she discussed *Past Times* (1997) by Kerry James Marshall (see Figure 11.1).

The dialogue began with student observations such as "I see a guy playing golf" and "I see blue birds." Sharon then asked, "What do you think the mood of this painting is?" A student answered, "Happy and joyful," and she probed, "What makes you think that?" He replied, "Everyone's getting along well." After more observations a student noted that "The color of their skin is chocolate," prompting laughter. Sharon urged them to "be respectful" and moved on to contextualize the work. She shared Marshall's name, nationality, and birthday, and told them, "When he started making art he noticed a lot of the art about Black people was negative, it was not positive, did not show them living everyday life like we do. . . . Here's them out here at the lake and it just shows them in everyday life."

REFLECTIONS AND SHIFTS

When we met to reflect on her teaching, I shared sections of my notes and asked Sharon if she thought her identity as a middle-class White woman shaped how she discussed this piece. When looking at the lesson through this perspective, she was taken aback because she had not considered how the inclusion of an artist of color could be anything but positive when she had good intentions. Through our dialogue I led Sharon to examine how her well-intentioned efforts performed inclusivity without meaningfully disrupting white supremacy.

Her discussion facilitation focused on aesthetics, innocuous facts (like the artist's birthday), and shallow observations. When her student labeled the painting's mood as "happy and joyful," Sharon did not draw students' attention to the dissonance between

Figure 11.1. Kerry James Marshall, *Past Times* (1997). © Kerry James Marshall. Courtesy of the artist and Jack Shainman Gallery, New York

the cheery setting and the figures' stoic gaze; she simply moved past it. I wondered how the conversation could have deepened if she had elicited other interpretations about the figures' expressions.

Other teachable moments were missed. When another student named the color of the subjects' skin as "chocolate," Sharon shut the dialogue down in vague terms, preserving civility rather than fostering "discourse across difference" (Mayo, 2004, p. 35). It was unclear what was disrespectful: The naming of Blackness? Likening it to chocolate? Laughter? This moment could have been a chance to discuss Marshall's intentional choice to paint his figures with undiluted black pigment, but she ended the conversation rather than furthering discussions of race.

Although this lesson included an artist of color, it continued to be framed by whiteness. Sharon's insistence that "everyday life" is filled with activities like golf, croquet, and water-skiing presented a skewed perception of what average Americans have access to. Additionally, her language describing Marshall's motivation as a desire to show *them* living everyday life like *we* do (italics added) presumes White subjects as the collective and normative "we" and labels Black subjects as "them," preserving racial divisions in practice and in speech.

On the surface Sharon attempted to be inclusive, but upon a closer look the enactment of this "inclusive" curriculum caused harm. It failed to substantively address the culture of white supremacy that has kept Black artists excluded from the canon and prevented people of color from building political power and generational wealth. Kraehe and Acuff (2021) argue that art teachers who fail to grapple with how white supremacy informs their teaching may inadvertently "alienate" (p. 107) and "inflict trauma" (p. 124) on students of color. After we reflected on these points together, Sharon was so moved that she decided to share her experience at a conference. She told the audience about our reflective work and pin-pointed the Marshall conversation as something that "really, really, really hit me," noting, "You have to be careful when you are talking—and it's hard, even when you don't intentionally do it . . . [to] make sure you don't make it sound like it's them versus us." Her experience also prompted her to advocate for district-wide professional development to help practicing art teachers discuss strategies to help them "see color" in their classroom dialogue.

SCAFFOLDING SOCIOCULTURAL DIALOGUE

The practice of including artists of color only on a surface level of observation and aesthetic appreciation is commonplace. Meaningful inclusions require careful research and dialogic scaffolding to disrupt whiteness as the cultural center (King, 2004). Art teachers should devote the same attention to scaffolding dialogue as they spend scaffolding artistic tools and techniques. Scaffolding sociocultural dialogue should be intentional and flexible, and account for depth, disruption, and connection.

Intentional and Flexible Scaffolding

Intentional scaffolding of sociocultural dialogue through art uses art as a provocation for talking about challenging issues. Facilitation is inquiry-based, asking students questions that move beyond observation to make connections that are relevant to society and students' lives. These dialogues require careful research and planning held loosely to seize teachable moments and follow students' conversational detours. Just as skilled jazz musicians master their craft so they may improvise in the moment, teachers need to do the research and internal reflection necessary to guide their students through sensitive dialogues about identity.

Scaffolding for Depth, Disruption, and Connection

Scaffolding for sociocultural dialogue involves a willingness to instigate deep conversations that may produce productive discomfort.

- Depth: Carefully planning questions and strategically sharing context about an artist's life and work can suggest conversational pathways to lead students to make connections to identity and the world around them.
- Disruption: Art can be curated to disrupt stereotypes by highlighting counternarratives and divergent perspectives. Rather than attempting to include every culture, art teachers can prompt students to examine larger themes by highlighting disruptive knowledge, which calls truth and knowledge production into question (Kumashiro, 2000). By asking why artists or students have different perspectives, teachers can disrupt "common knowledge" often accepted as truth.
- Connection: Relating across difference involves disrupting the common practice of one-way looking in which non-White cultures are objects of the anthropological gaze rather than relational subjects (Sabzalian, 2019). Scaffolding for connections asks students to look at art in order to reflect back on themselves. This might look like a lesson exploring a theme (i.e., Journey, Home, Citizenship) from multiple perspectives and then asking students to express their ideas on this topic. The goal in this approach is not to learn more about "others" perceived as different, but to consider why they have been constructed as "other" in the first place.

SHARON'S CONTINUING JOURNEY

Sharon's journey to change how she facilitates dialogue provides a road map for the future of sociocultural dialogue in art education. From her story we see the importance of scaffolding intentional and flexible dialogues that include disruptive knowledge and forge connections across difference. Sharon's teaching is now driven by thematic explorations across cultures, and she strives to go deeper with discussions of race by planning for critical dialogue so students can better understand one another. Her willingness to change course, share how her biases impact her teaching, and advocate for meaningful professional development can inspire other art teachers ready to do the work to shift the conversation in their own classrooms.

REFERENCES

King, J. E. (2004). Culture centered knowledge: Black studies, curriculum transformation and social action. In J. Banks & C. McGee Banks (Eds.), *Handbook of research on multicultural education* (pp. 349–380). Jossey-Bass.

Kraehe, A. M., & Acuff, J. B. (2021). *Race and art education.* Davis Publications, Inc.

Kumashiro, K. K. (2000). Toward a theory of anti-oppressive education. *Review of Educational Research, 70*(1), 25–53.

Link, B. (2022). *Examining whiteness in elementary art education.* [Unpublished doctoral dissertation]. University of Texas at Austin.

Mayo, C. (2004). The tolerance that dare not speak its name. *Counterpoints, 240,* 33–47.

Sabzalian, L. (2019). *Indigenous children's survivance in public schools.* Routledge.

CHAPTER 12

Artistic Responses to Race

Naomi Lifschitz-Grant, Robb Epps, and Taylor Styles

This essay is a visual response to a graduate class discussing Culturally Responsive Pedagogy.

THE FAMILY STORIES TOLD WERE OF A HETEROSEXUAL WHITE COUPLE MARRIED... THIS MODEL EXCLUDES SO SINGLE-PARENT HOUSEHOLDS, GAY PARENTS, INTERRACIAL FAMILIES, FOSTER FAMILIES, AND MANY MORE.
I THINK OF MY DAD GROWING UP WITH 7 SISTERS AND ONLY ONE BATHROOM.
MY FAMILY DOESN'T HAVE MANY CONVERSATIONS WHEN TALKING ABOUT FAMILY STORIES. THE ELDERS IGNORE THE TOPIC, AND WE, AS THE YOUNG, TEND NOT TO ASK QUESTIONS.
MY FOLKS WERE DIVORCED, AND I GREW UP WITH A SINGLE MOM ... MY CORE VALUES INCLUDE LAUGHING THROUGH THE TEARS AND CHERISHING OUR ROOTS.
CHRISTIANITY PLAYS A HUGE ROLE. I WOULD SAY THAT BIBLE VERSES WERE REFERENCED LIKE "HONOR THY FATHER AND THY MOTHER... BETTER IS THE POOR THAT WALKETH IN HIS INTEGRITY, THAN HE THAT IS PERVERSE IN HIS LIPS, AND IS A FOOL, ETC."

MY FAMILY DIDN'T HAVE MUCH MATERIALISTICALLY, BUT THEY HAD GOD, LOVE, PEACE, JOY, AND EACH OTHER. WE FACED EVERY BATTLE TOGETHER.
WE WERE TOLD TO NOT COME INSIDE THE HOUSE BECAUSE THE ADULT HAD WORKED A SIXTEEN-HOUR SHIFT AND NEEDED REST... A PICTURE OF EXHAUSTION THAT CAN DEPRIVE ONE'S HEALTH.
BOTH MY PARENTS COME FROM BEING PART OF MILITARY FAMILIES AND WE ALWAYS USED OUR MANNER, "MRS./MR. OR YES MA'AM/NO MA'AM OR YES SIR/NO SIR.
I CAN REMEMBER STORIES ABOUT PICKING COTTON FROM MY GREAT-GRANDMOTHER. MY GRANDMOTHER WOULD OFTEN TALK ABOUT HOW THEY WERE VERY POOR, AND HOW THE OLDER SIBLINGS WERE EXPECTED TO HELP THE FAMILY ONCE THEY GOT SETTLED... TIME IN THE BLACK COMMUNITY IS ALL WE HAVE. IT'S LIKE WE HURRY UP TO WAIT. WE ARE NOT CONCERNED ENOUGH TO TEACH OUR CHILDREN ABOUT WHO WE ARE. WE DON'T PASS DOWN TRADITIONS. TIME ALLOWS US TO FORGET ABOUT OUR PAST, BUT IT DOES VERY LITTLE FOR OUR FUTURE BECAUSE WE WASTE SO MUCH OF IT.
HOW DOES THINKING ABOUT YOUR BACKGROUND INFLUENCE YOUR TEACHING?
SELF-REFLECTION HELPS US REALIZE OUR BIASES AND OUR EXPECTATIONS. FOR EXAMPLE...
IF MY CULTURE/LIFESTYLE EMPHASIZES TIMELINESS, IT WILL LIKELY SEEM DISRESPECTFUL IF A STUDENT CONTINUALLY COMES TO CLASS 5 MINUTES LATE. WHAT I NEED TO CONSIDER, IS MAYBE THIS STUDENT IS COMING FROM A CULTURE/FAMILY THAT 5 MINUTES LATE IS RIGHT ON TIME! I AM NOT SAYING THE EDUCATOR NEEDS TO CHANGE THEIR EXPECTATIONS FOR THIS STUDENT BUT SHOULD BE AWARE OF THEIR EXPECTATIONS AND CLEARLY COMMUNICATE.
I NEED TO REALIZE WHERE THEY ARE COMING FROM, HOW THEY HAVE BEEN TAUGHT IN THEIR OWN HOMES, AND WHAT CORE VALUES THEY ARE CARRYING FROM THEIR PARENTS.
MY STUDENTS ARE EXPERIENCING REAL ISSUES, AND I SHOULD NOT IGNORE THEM BUT HELP. I ASK QUESTIONS, LET THEM TALK, AND GIVE ASSIGNMENTS THAT HELP THEM SPEAK WITHOUT SAYING WORDS.
I TRY TO REMEMBER THAT "FAMILY" COMES IN MANY DIFFERENT PACKAGES, AND WE NEED TO INCLUDE ALL OF OUR STUDENTS AND THE FAMILY PACKAGE THAT COMES WITH THEM. I TRY NOT TO SAY "MOM" OR "DAD", I SAY "FAMILY OR "GROWN-UP" OR "ADULT" UNLESS THE CHILD REFERS TO A CERTAIN PERSON A CERTAIN WAY... BEING A GROWN-UP ISN'T ALWAYS EASY, AND IF A KID COMES LATE, IT REALLY ISN'T THEIR FAULT. SOME OF THE ADULTS AT MY SCHOOL DON'T ALWAYS REMEMBER THAT. I TRY NOT TO BE THAT ADULT AND MAKE SURE THOSE STUDENTS GET A HAPPY START TO THEIR DAY TOO.

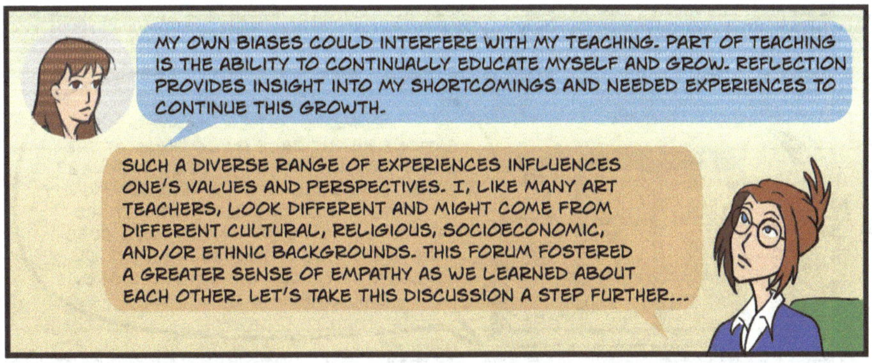

Discussion Board: Race in School

Instructions: *The National Network of State Teachers of the Year (NNSTOY) has produced several short videos that are intended to "promote a deeper, more authentic discussion about issues of racial equity in schools" (https://www.nnstoy.org/equity-education-courageous-conversations-race/).*

How did race impact your own experience as a student in P-16 schools?

STUDENTS DESCRIBE SPECIFIC DETAILS AND ASK QUESTIONS THROUGH CONSTRUCTING EXPLANATIONS; STUDENTS MAKE CONNECTIONS BETWEEN AN OBJECT AND THE CONTEXT IN WHICH IT WAS CREATED. THINKING ROUTINES ARE FACILITATED WITHIN A GROUP DYNAMIC, ALLOWING STUDENTS TO HEAR AND LEARN FROM ONE ANOTHER. (TISHMAN, MACGILLIVRAY, AND PALMER, 2006). A "ROUTINE IS A PROCESS, PROCEDURE OR A PATTERN OF ACTION USED CONTINUALLY" ("BACKGROUND ON PZ'S VISIBLE THINKING, 2019A, PARA. 1).

INSTRUCTIONS: IN THE CHAT WRITE YOUR RESPONSE. (STUDENTS RESPOND TO ONE POINT BEFORE MOVING ON TO THE NEXT):

I see...	I think...	I wonder...
• family • two men • camo • a chain • gang members 'reppin' their set. • two men who look to be rappers. • hand signals	• they are tight, possibly family • two guys having fun • it's a music videos because they look to be on location (set) • In a skate park • they smoke weed, carry guns	• what do the hand signs represent? • what the tattoo on his neck represents? • if they are rappers or famous and just have a street persona? • what is their location is and the importance of the location?

SOME OF YOU MENTIONED THAT YOU THINK THAT THESE YOUNG MEN MIGHT BE IN A GANG. WHAT MAKES YOU SAY THAT? DO YOU THINK THAT IT IS BASED ON A STEREOTYPE OF HOW ONE PERCEIVES YOUNG MEN OF COLOR THAT ARE DRESSED IN A CERTAIN WAY?
ACCORDING TO THE SMITHSONIAN, NATIONAL PORTRAIT GALLERY, (2019) "MICHAEL VASQUEZ'S DYNAMIC LARGE-SCALE PORTRAITS EXPLORE IDENTITY AND ACCEPTANCE THROUGH THE EXPERIENCES OF YOUNG MEN COMING OF AGE WITHIN UNDER-SERVED COMMUNITIES". THE TWO YOUNG MEN IN THE PORTRAIT MAKE THE HAND SIGN FOR THEIR UNDERGROUND HIP-HOP CONGLOMERATE.
DOES THIS INFORMATION CHANGE THE WAY YOU THINK ABOUT THIS PAINTING?
NO, NOT REALLY. THEY ARE IN A GANG OR A CONGLOMERATE. IT'S HIP-HOP, SO THERE'S GUNS AND SMOKING IN HIP-HOP. I CAN SEE THAT THEY ARE RAPPERS.
IT IS IMPORTANT FOR US TO BE AWARE OF THE TERM "GANGS" IN REFERENCING YOUNG MEN OF COLOR ARE CULTURALLY LOADED AND CAN BE PERCEIVED NEGATIVELY. WE NEED TO RETHINK OUR LANGUAGE AND HOW WE SPEAK, ESPECIALLY ABOUT THESE SUBJECT MATTERS BECAUSE THEY CAN CAUSE HARM TO OUR STUDENTS, AND DO NOT WANT THEM TO FEEL SOLATED OR SHUT DOWN.
WHEN WE GO TO A MAJOR MUSEUM, WE ARE NOT USED TO SEEING PAINTINGS OF YOUNG MEN OF COLOR, AT LEAST, UNTIL RECENTLY.
THE THINKING ROUTINES ENCOURAGED US TO CAREFULLY EXAMINE WORKS. YOU ASKED THOUGHTFUL QUESTIONS; DESCRIBED SPECIFIC DETAILS; AND MADE CONNECTIONS BETWEEN THE ARTWORK, THE CONTEXT IN WHICH IT WAS CREATED, AND HOW THESE IMAGES ARE RELEVANT TO OUR LIVES AND EXPERIENCES. THROUGH HEARING CLASSMATES' VIEWPOINTS, ONE CAN EXPAND ON THEIR UNDERSTANDING OF ARTWORKS.
AS CULTURALLY RELEVANT ART TEACHERS WE NEED TO UNDERSTAND OUR STUDENTS' BACKGROUNDS AND EXPERIENCES AND HOW THEY IMPACT THEIR WORLDVIEWS (LEE, 2012). THROUGH THIS CRITICAL DIALOGUE AND OBSERVATIONS OF CONTEMPORARY ARTISTS AND PERSONAL REFLECTIONS, COLLECTIVELY WE EXPLORED RACIAL JUSTICE AND SOME HISTORICAL RACIAL ISSUES.
DURING SUCH DIALOGUES, ONE CAN ADDRESS PREJUDICE, BIASED, AND OPPRESSIVE VIEWS. EDUCATORS THAT ACTIVELY PLAN FOR LEARNING OPPORTUNITIES ADDRESSING REAL-WORLD TOPICS, SUCH AS RACE CAN HELP STUDENTS TO DEVELOP SKILLS TO COMMUNICATE WITH EMPATHY AND PROFESSIONALISM. SIMULTANEOUSLY, ACCORDING TO TATUM (2020), TO AVOID THE SILENT OMISSION AND DISTORTION OF HISTORICAL, SOCIETAL, AND CULTURAL EVENTS, EDUCATORS CAN PROVIDE STUDENTS WITH EXAMPLES OF ARTWORK FROM DIVERSE BACKGROUNDS, ETHNICITIES, RACES, ETC. THAT CAN FOSTER ANTI-RACIST VIEWS.

REFERENCES:

HAMMOND, Z. (2015). CULTURALLY RESPONSIVE TEACHING AND THE BRAIN: PROMOTING AUTHENTIC ENGAGEMENT AND RIGOR AMONG CULTURALLY AND LINGUISTICALLY DIVERSE STUDENTS. CORWIN.

HARVARD GRADUATE SCHOOL OF EDUCATION, PROJECT ZERO. (2019). SEE, THINK, WONDER. HTTPS://PZ.HAR
VARD.EDU/SITES/DEFAULT/FILES/SEE%20THINK%20WON
DER_2.PDF

LEE, N. (2012). CULTURALLY RESPONSIVE TEACHING FOR 21ST-CENTURY ART EDUCATION: EXAMINING RACE IN A STUDIO EXPERIENCE. ART EDUCATION, 65(5), 48–53.

MARSHALL J., & DONAHUE, D. M. (2014). ART-CENTERED LEARNING ACROSS THE CURRICULUM. INTEGRATING CONTEM
PORARY ART IN THE SECONDARY SCHOOL CLASSROOM. TEACHERS COLLEGE PRESS.

SMITHSONIAN INSTITUTE, NATIONAL PORTRAIT GALLERY. (2019). MICHAEL VASQUEZ. HTTPS://PORTRAITCOMPETITION.SI.EDU/EX
HIBITION/2019-OUTWIN-BOOCHEVER-PORTRAIT-COMPETI
TION/CSPG-SOUTHWAY-ZOO-TROPICAL-BOYZ?LANG=ENG

SMITHSONIAN INSTITUTE, NATIONAL PORTRAIT GALLERY. (2020). ELEMENTS OF PORTRAYAL: DEFINITIONS. HTTPS://N
PG.SI.EDU/SITES/DEFAULT/FILES/ELEMENTS_OF_PORTRAY
AL_DEFINITIONS.PDF

TATUM, B. D. (2010). DEFINING RACISM. IN M. ADAMS, W. J. BLUMENFELD, H. W. HACKMAN, M. L. PETERS, & X. ZUNIGA (EDS.), READING FOR DIVERSITY AND SOCIAL JUSTICE (2ND ED., PP. 66–78). ROUTLEDGE.

ACKNOWLEDGEMENTS:

THANK YOU TO THE FALL 2021 APPLIED ART EDUCATION PEDAGOGY: SECONDARY STUDENTS (AMMA, KELLY, ALLISON, BRE, CATHERINE, JEMEIKKA, CONCETTA, TAYLOR, AND KAIT) WHO CONTRIBUTED HONESTLY TO OUR CLASS'S DISCUSSION BOARDS.
YOUR THOUGHTS AND IDEAS OPENED OUR MINDS AND HEARTS.

CHAPTER 13

Using Group Reflection and Dialogue as Tools for Antiracist Teaching

Amanda Tobin Ripley, Hannah Heller, and Michelle Antonisse

Dialogue is one of the most effective pedagogical tools in art museum teaching (Burnham & Kai-Kee, 2011; Hooper-Greenhill, 1999; Hubard, 2015). Many museum educators work to hone their dialogic skills, in preservice programs or through ongoing professional development. These efforts usually coalesce around facilitating "good" dialogue, and less frequently examine how educators' positionalities, such as race, gender, and class, and dominant worldviews, including whiteness, shape and constrict the dialogues we craft—to the detriment of our teaching. We share examples of reflexive dialogue as an invitation to gallery educators to join in the pursuit of critical, equity-focused, liberatory visitor engagement.

EXAMINING WHITENESS IN OUR MUSEUM TEACHING

Dr. Hannah Heller focused her doctoral research at Columbia University's Teachers College on understanding the role of whiteness on gallery teaching practices in museums (Heller, 2021). She virtually convened a small group of White museum educators from 2019 to 2021 to conduct a practitioner inquiry group for White educators to identify and name where whiteness shows up in our teaching. One finding was a frequent glossing-over of race talk (Haviland, 2008), especially when discussing Blackness. To model how White practitioners might move through anxiety and fear toward accountability and equity, what follows in this chapter are excerpts (lightly edited for clarity) of our group dialogue, highlighting moments of anti-Blackness in our teaching and our attempts to understand this phenomenon.

Dialogue #1 (asynchronous Google Groups conversation, January 16 & 30, 2020)

Amanda: The moment I was kicking myself about afterwards was when we were discussing a portrait by E2 in which they photoshopped a painting of Washington crossing the Delaware to replace the figures with women of various races; the figure of Washington is replaced by a Black woman. We discussed the gender and racial dynamics overall [in a tour with 4th-graders], but then when we got to the placement of that figure and the ways the artists were showing us how important she is, I totally dropped the ball and said that Washington had been replaced by a woman, without saying by a Black woman. I think it just comes from the discomfort I feel as a White person naming race in front of people of color and is such a strong reminder about how I need to practice naming race and how ingrained that impulse is in me.

Hannah: Right, this idea of explicitly stating someone's race (going to go out on a limb and say in general White people are more reluctant to name Blackness specifically, than say Asian or another race or designation). I saw this again and again in collecting my pilot data, observing that and the various euphemisms we use instead. Even the term "people of color" when we mean Black is silencing. But then I also have this feeling like sometimes I'm saying "Black" a lot [when discussing work centering Blackness]? And from my mouth, with a group of predominantly Black students, I do wonder how it comes off.

Dialogue #2 (focus group conducted via Zoom, January 28, 2021):

Amanda: Well, to your point about timing, I think given what I've been noticing with the public this year with the Wendy Red Star show, White people are very different in this space and have been much more able to name that [Red Star is] Native American or ask what her race is in a way that I didn't see with *Still I Rise* [which focused on portraits of Black women]. No one would say, "They're Black," in the way that they say, "This is a Native American woman," as they're explaining things to their kids. And I think that there is anti-Blackness at work in that.

Hannah: Yeah . . . There's something about saying—okay, I don't know if any of you are *30 Rock* fans, but Elisa, one of Jack's girlfriends, is Puerto Rican and they're like, "You can't say that!" [Laughter] "But, I'm Puerto Rican!" There's something that feels similar about naming Blackness, it almost feels like we're saying something racist because of the negativity that's become associated with it.

Michelle: I agree. There's also this feeling that naming Blackness is othering as well. Or maybe because there is the specificity in the ways that other groups are talked about, like, being Puerto Rican, from a really specific place. And then just saying someone's Black—I still have discomfort, sometimes, around making that identity call for someone else between African American and Black or Cuban American. It feels important, and it's something I've learned over the summer [of 2020], the importance of maybe naming Blackness and specifically, anti-Blackness, over naming racism [more broadly]. And thinking a little bit about the ways that that discomfort is born of a larger culture of anti-Blackness that's just so deeply systemic.

NEXT STEPS

As these excerpts demonstrate, White museum educators' socialized discomfort with naming race, specifically Blackness, exemplifies anti-Blackness and a culture of whiteness (Okun, 2001) that prioritizes the comfort of the White educator over the learning and potential identification Black students might be able to feel (Acuff et al., 2012; Charland, 2010; Wilson, 2017). El-Amin and Cohen (2017) stress how explicit race talk helps students of all races develop critical racial literacy; White museum educators' reluctance to do so has direct consequences on all our visitors. Without naming dynamics of racial (mis)representation, museum experiences reinforce, rather than challenge, visitors' inculcation into the hidden curriculum of racial hierarchies (McLaren, 2002). If we want to truly enact radical pedagogies, we—museum educators in general, and White educators in particular—need to understand where and how anti-Blackness and other hegemonic attitudes live in our teaching, interrogate the roots of these tendencies, and work to build new habits. The findings of this study raise questions around the nature of training and professional development for (White) museum educators. Training should aid educators in developing competencies facilitating anti-racist conversations, and reflect on how art museums uphold or can help dismantle systems of oppressions.

REFERENCES

Acuff, J. B., Hirak, B., & Nangah, M. (2012). Dismantling a master narrative: Using culturally responsive pedagogy to teach the history of art education. *Art Education, 65*(5), 6–10.

Burnham, R., & Kai-Kee, E. (2011). *Teaching in the art museum: Interpretation as experience*. The J. Paul Getty Museum.

Charland, W. (2010). African American youth and the artist's identity: Cultural models and aspirational foreclosure. *Studies in Art Education, 51*(2), 115–133.

El-Amin, A., & Cohen, C. (2017). Just representations: Using critical pedagogy in art museums to foster student belonging. *Art Education: The Journal of the National Art Education Association, 71*(1), 8–11. https://doi.org/10.1080/00043125.2018.1389579

Haviland, V. S. (2008). "Things Get Glossed Over:" Rearticulating the Silencing Power of Whiteness in Education. *Journal of Teacher Education, 59*(1), 40–54.

Heller, H. D. (2021). *Naming and dismantling Whiteness in art museum education: Developing an anti-racist approach* [Doctoral dissertation, Teachers College, Columbia University, New York]. Columbia Academic Commons. https://academiccommons.columbia.edu/doi/10.7916/d8-1ea0-d793

Hooper-Greenhill, E. (1999). Museum learners as active postmodernists: Contextualizing constructivism.

In E. Hooper-Greenhill (Ed.), *The educational role of the museum* (2nd ed.) (pp. 67–72). Routledge.

Hubard, O. (2015). *Art museum education: Facilitating gallery experiences.* Palgrave Macmillan.

McLaren, P. (2002). Critical pedagogy: A look at the major concepts. In A. Darder, M. Baltodano, & R. D. Torres (Eds.), *The critical pedagogy reader* (pp. 61–96). Routledge /Falmer Press.

Okun, T. (2001). White supremacy culture. In T. Okun & K. Jones (Eds.), *Dismantling racism: A workbook for social change groups.* Dismantling Racism Works. https://www.dismantlingracism.org/uploads/4/3/5/7/43579015/okun_-_white_sup_culture.pdf

Wilson, G. J. (2017). Fictive kinship in the aspirations, agency, and (im)possible selves of the Black American art teacher. *The Journal of Social Theory in Art Education, 37,* 49–60.

CHAPTER 14

Shaming Queerness in Art Spaces

Would You Change That If You Could?

Libya Doman

"Who are your go-to diverse artists?" This is the question I am most asked as a veteran K–12 art educator, former adjunct professor, and cultural responsiveness facilitator who engages with teachers throughout the United States. I encourage educators to make conscious choices to learn about and share work by queer artists. I also direct educators to concepts and resources emphasizing how—more than what—one teaches. The intention behind "the diverse artist question," as I call it, is to find pathways toward being a more inclusive art educator by engaging in topics perceived to be challenging in art spaces geared to youth. Following the murder of George Floyd and in view of legislation like Florida's so-called "Don't Say Gay" law, there has been, in my observation, a seismic shift in desire to include BIPOC and queer artists as meaningful artmakers in our curriculums. There is still a lot of work to do.

MANY ART DOUBTS IN THE AGE OF "DON'T SAY GAY"

I often hear of teachers expressing concerns about a possible backlash to openly naming queer artists or indicating that gender exists beyond the binary in the art room. Common questions include: Will students misrepresent the art teacher's statements to their families? (Anonymous 2, personal communication, February 3, 2022). Will parents or caregivers accuse the instructor of impropriety? Will educators who prioritize inclusivity open their school districts up "to legal risk" (Fields, 2022, p. 11)?

Keeping art teachers "plagued by a host of doubts" (Gude, 2002, p. 73) perpetuates the widespread discrimination against LGBTQIA+ communities. White, male, heteronormative artists and artworks have prominent place in art curriculum, while "queer aspects of lives are ignored, erased, camouflaged or denied" (Wolfgang & Rhoades, 2017, p. 76). Art educators would do well to ask, "Would you change that if you could?" What would you change to foster agency instead of dictating solutions (R. Compton, personal communication, December 1, 2021)?

We exist in an era of state-sanctioned, current, and pending mandates (Movement Advancement Project, 2022) that explicitly tell teachers to not mention sexual orientation and gender identity in manners that are deemed age- or developmentally inappropriate (Florida Senate, 2022). Many states are prohibiting gender-diverse curriculum choices, banning students from entering restrooms or joining sports teams, and reducing medical access to gender-affirming care.

The vagueness of "age and developmental" appropriateness as a standard has allowed Gustav Klimt's *The Kiss* (1907–1908), a painting of a man and woman kissing, to be shared with little incident in elementary settings around the world for decades. Yet vague notions of inappropriateness would likely cause an educator pause when considering Marcos Chin's illustration featuring two men engaged in a kiss. The artist stated,

> As a gay man, I remember what it was like growing up in a closeted space; at that time, the media supported the shame that I felt about my queerness and my body by describing gay characters on TV or in film in a negative way by calling us sissies, faggots, carriers of disease, less-than and the other. (LBB, 2017, para. 5)

No one should feel excluded from visual narratives. Through the eyes of a middle-schooler choosing to don nail polish despite narrow gender expression norms, there is positive representation in Amy Sherald's painting *Try on Dreams Until I Find the One*

That Fits Me. They All Fit Me (David, 2017). Similarly, there is power in being conscious of visually representing family diversity within a primary school unit because children with two mothers are a reality. Representation is a subtle means of welcoming everyday acts of showing up as our true selves.

CHECKING OUR BIAS IN ART

In art spaces, are we perpetuating the shame of queerness that Marcos Chin laments? Does the assumption of heterosexual superiority guide which artists are shared? Do we name heteronormativity when it shows up in our art rooms? Are we able to audit our image selection inclinations (The Phillips Collection, n.d.)? I regularly juxtapose commonly accepted and frequently censored artworks addressing similar subject matters as a strategy to visualize bias in society and within schools. I use juxtaposition as a teaching strategy to interact with my own biases when I present Klimt's and Chin's kissing images side by side.

It is vital to unpack our own explicit and unconscious bias that may leave us hesitant and unsure. We must commit to learning about and from marginalized community members to bolster our capacity to facilitate informed discussions without causing harm. We may need to read state bills to know the specifics of mandates as we prepare ourselves to articulate the value of our inclusive curriculum decisions to students, guardians, administrators, colleagues, school boards, politicians and legislators, and voters.

Noticing and Naming Ourselves

In February 2022, a parent contacted the principal of one of my schools to share concerns about the use of "sexual orientation" in my class. The parent questioned why this would be mentioned not just in school but particularly in an art class. The school principal was familiar with the unit I was teaching and had observed me teaching it in a previous semester. He understood its purpose. Well beyond learning the formal and technical skills of producing art, my students were encouraged to defy stereotypes assigned to them to reveal their self-affirming identities. Students selected which identities to explore from a list of nearly 25 categories. During the observation, the principal talked to the student artists and took notes.

Student A: "This person is dressed up as a sports person and is surrounded by sports but he has a tear coming out of his eye because he is not sports but sports is everywhere."

Student B: "Up here is all the things that everyone assumes girls like. Here is me playing soccer with some of the girl things but not all. I am a combination of both."

Neither of the middle-schoolers quoted identified as queer, which demonstrates the benefit of all students—cis and queer—having the freedom to recognize the dynamic range and intersections of their identities in relationship to others and to social constructs. A high school art educator shared, "I don't tell a student that an artist is gay. But it is implied that art is not just for straight White males. I was teaching a lesson on graffiti while in grad school. A student stated that all the artists you shared were men. She changed the way I write my lessons; all my lessons" (C. Raubacher, personal communication, February 2022). As artist Mickalene Thomas stated, "I'm queer . . . but it's not necessary to always read my work as, 'Oh, Mickalene is a queer woman" (Aperture, 2016, para. 6). An artist's sexual orientation and gender identity do not always need to be named.

Art Educators as Decision-Makers

LGBTQIA+ gender-affirming spaces within schools are well documented to significantly reduce student stress, depression, self-harm, and suicide risk, which are especially pronounced for transgender and nonbinary youth (American Psychological Association, 2021; Kociw et al., 2021; The Trevor Project, 2020). Consider what is at stake if art educators do not see themselves as decision-makers cultivating spaces of belonging for all students. In 2019, nearly 70% of LGBTQIA+ students surveyed reported that they were regularly called derogatory names and were threatened in school (Kociw et al., 2021). "Less than one-fifth of LGBTQ students (13.7%) reported that school staff intervened most of the time or always when overhearing homophobic remarks at school" (p. xix). A high percentage of LGBTQIA+ students experience increased rates of school absences, depression, self-harm and suicide attempts compared to their heterosexual peers. In art classes, the same national study indicated that only 14.2% of LGBTQIA+ students felt that positive representations of LGBTQ-related history, people, or events were shared (p. 6).

We can normalize speaking up when derogatory remarks are made. What if art spaces reliably served as buffers to the name-calling, bullying, and assaults gender-nonconforming students are most likely to experience in our schools' restrooms, locker rooms, and PE classes (Kociw et al., 2021)? I have pushed my students' thinking about the complexity of gender, stating, "I am a woman. But I am not the model of a woman. There are many ways to show up as a woman." When I have heard students use words like "faggot," "sissy," or "gay" as derogatory terms, I choose to connect to the students' understandings by asking some grounding questions: What do you think "sissy" means? What does a boy act like? Do you think that is a kind word? Would you change that if you could?

Art educators must be willing to "experience discomfort" (Singleton, 2005, p. 70) by confronting some topics while scared and uncertain. As the author Ibram X. Kendi (2019) has written, being against bias is not enough. This work requires practice through action. Mistakes will be made by all of us. As a Black, cisgender woman, I have misgendered a student. Misgendering is a mistake that needs to be apologized for and corrected by practicing the use of the pronouns that currently align with our ever-evolving understandings of gender.

Art educators are decision-makers in our students' lives. Committing to our ongoing growth by pursuing gender-affirming professional development in the forms of workshops, learning communities, book studies, and conferences is highly encouraged. Resources with links are shared below to help us explore relevant terminology, mandates, artists, and standards. Note that the documents are not exhaustive; there is so much more that needs to be done.

As art educators, we can disrupt practices of centering White, cisgendered, heterosexism in our field because the stakes are especially high for queer students and colleagues who may feel invalidated and unseen. We must actively uplift the parts of our identities that are too often ignored or erased in our art spaces.

REFERENCES

American Psychological Association. (2021, October). *Students exploring gender identity.* https://www.apa.org/ed/schools/primer/gender-identity.pdf

Aperture. (2016). *Muse: Mickalene Thomas Photographs and* tête-à-tête. https://aperture.org/wp-content/uploads/2016/09/MUSE_EducationResource.pdf

David, C. (2017). Amy Sherald: Painter of the beautiful ordinary. *Crwn Magazine.* https://www.crwnmag.com/blog/2017/3/amy-sherald-painter-of-the-beautiful-ordinary

Fields, K. (2022, May 23). Teachers, deputized to fight the culture wars, are often reluctant to serve. *Hechinger Report.* https://hechingerreport.org/teachers-deputized-to-fight-the-culture-wars-are-often-reluctant-to-serve/

Florida Senate (2022). Parental Rights in Education Act, HB 1557. https://www.flsenate.gov/Session/Bill/2022/1557/BillText/er/PDF

Gude, O. (2002). There's something queer about this classroom. In L. Lampela & E. Check (Eds.), *From our voices: Art educators and artists speak out about lesbian, gay, bisexual, and transgendered issues* (pp. 73–86). Kendall Hunt.

Kendi, I. X. (2019). *How to be an antiracist.* One World.

Kociw, J. G., Clark, C. M., Truong, N. L., & Zongrone, A. D. (2021, April). *The 2019 school climate report: The experiences of lesbian, gay, bisexual, transgender, and queer youth in our nation's schools.* GLSEN. https://www.glsen.org/sites/default/files/2021-04/NSCS19-FullReport-032421-Web_0.pdf

LBB. (2017, August 31). *In conversation with: Marcos Chin, illustrator.* https://www.lbbonline.com/news/in-conversation-with-marcos-chin-illustrator

Movement Advancement Project. (2022). *LGBTQ curricular laws* [Map]. https://www.lgbtmap.org/equality-maps/curricular_laws

Phillips Collection. (n.d). *Checking in on our biases: Using artworks to confront biases.* https://www.phillipscollection.org/media/10813

Singleton, G. (2015). *Courageous conversations about race:A field guide for achieving equity in schools.* Corwin.

Trevor Project. (2020, December). *The Trevor Project research brief: LGBTQ & gender-affirming spaces.* https://www.thetrevorproject.org/wp-content/uploads/2021/07/LGBTQ-Affirming-Spaces_-December-2020.pdf

Wolfgang, C., & Rhoades, M. (2017). First fagnostics: Queering art education. *Journal of Social Theory in Art Education, 37,* 72–79

CHAPTER 15

Rethinking Disability in Art Classrooms

Kelly M. Gross

A few years ago, a graduate student asked: "How has your research changed since your dissertation?" I admitted to the student that today I would develop my research methods from a disability studies perspective to emphasize the voice and artmaking of disabled students. That perspective has impacted not only my research, but also my approaches to teaching about disability and preparing art educators to support inclusive settings.

I am currently a college professor of art education; I started my professional career as a special education teacher working with elementary students labeled with emotional and behavioral disorders. My background and training in education, influenced by No Child Left Behind (2001), instilled a deficit-based model focused on high expectations and remediating deficits in learning. I measured successful instruction through academic gains. However, I struggled with this approach to education, as I found it to be in contrast to what I valued in my own educational experiences.

When I started teaching, artmaking became a means of exploring my own experiences and making sense of what I was seeing in the classroom. For example, one of my pieces at that time depicted the students' faces, their enthusiasm, and the barbed wire that surrounded our school. I thought they were bright, intelligent boys who had been hidden away, and through my artwork I wanted to center the students and examine the situations that restricted them.

It was not until I read Freire's (1972) *Pedagogy of the Oppressed* that I started to encounter those who imagined a different way of approaching education, especially for disabled students. Freire argues that the traditional banking approach where teachers deposit knowledge into students' minds minimizes their creative power and treats those who deviate from the norms by changing the students rather than the situation that opposes them. Later, economist and philosopher Amartya Sen's theories on capabilities and the importance of the opportunities and potential available to persons as a means of achieving social justice moved me to reframe my thinking about educational situations and the availability of resources and opportunities for different learners (Walker & Unterhalter, 2007).

These ideas about equity and opportunity influenced my thinking and teaching. As I started to teach preservice courses for art teachers, I began to introduce comics and graphic novels as a means of critically examining disability experiences and representation (Gross, 2018). In dialogue with students, students in the class would analyze how depictions reinforced or challenged typical tropes of disability (Biklen & Bogdan, 1977). Our class would consider:

1. What aspects of society, schooling, or environment are causing this person to be disabled?
2. What does the intersection of race, language, culture, gender, and/or sexual orientation with disability look like in these comics and graphic novels?
3. How can visual media be used to express disability experience?

Art education curricula are often developed with a goal of the refinement of technical fine motor skills and dexterous hands (Penketh, 2017). Rather than teaching art educators how to accommodate students to meet the normative designed lessons, I suggested that "there is no neutral body from which our bodies deviate" (Morales, 2016, p. 9). To develop enabling curriculum, my teaching approaches no longer focus on the individual impairment as the cause of disabled students' lack of successful inclusion, but rather on the design of curricula to be accessible for all students (Titchkosky, 2011). I ask students to consider, "How can you design a lesson for which there is no right answer?" and "How can we allow students to demonstrate ability through a choice of modality or material?" These approaches affirm autonomy for disabled persons and universality for all students through open-ended lessons with opportunities for choice-making, self-expression, and problem-solving.

I recognize that some of my previous research and teaching was framed through a deficit-based approach and that my evolution of perspective and research practice that focuses on a capacity- and asset-based model has not happened overnight, nor is it complete. Through sharing my own experience, I hope others can recognize the need to improve, engage in dialogue, and be open to different ways of enacting teaching and research.

REFERENCES

Biklen, D., & Bogdan, R. (1977). Media portrayals of disabled people: A study in stereotypes. *Interracial Books for Children Bulletin, 8*(6–7), 4–9.

Freire, P. (1972). *Pedagogy of the oppressed.* Herder and Herder.

Gross, K. (2018). Representation, re-presentation, and representin' through graphic novels. *Synnyt/Origins: Finnish Studies in Art Education, 2*(2018), 25–40.

Morales, A. (2016). *Kindling: Writings on the body.* Palabrera Press.

Penketh, C. (2017). "Children see before they speak": An exploration of ableism in art education. *Disability & Society, 32*(1), 110–127. doi:10.1080/09687599.2016.1270819

Titchkosky, T. (2011). *The question of access: Disability, space and meaning.* University of Toronto Press.

Walker, M., & Unterhalter, E. (2007). The capability approach: Its potential for work in education. In M. Walker & E. Unterhalter (Eds.), *Amartya Sen's capability approach and social justice in education* (pp. 1–18). Palgrave Macmillan. https://doi.org/10.1057/9780230604810_1

Part II

STRUCTURING THE LEARNING ENVIRONMENT FOR OPEN DISCUSSION

This section describes learning climates where vulnerability and opinions are honored.

Chapter 16: Creating Spaces to Support Difficult Dialogues

Lisa Hochtritt

Suggestions for structuring classroom spaces to address complicated issues

Chapter 17: Centering Culture Through Critical Conversations

Katie Coogan and Margaret Walker

Sharing personal culture and reframing socially acquired perspectives through artmaking

Chapter 18: Conversations over Wi-Fi: Reorienting Student-Centered Art Discussions Online

Ashley Mask

Online learning environments that cocreated paths of inquiry in art discussions

Chapter 19: Building Community by Using Opening and Closing Circles

Valeska Maria Populoh

Cofacilitated opening and closing circles to build connections and trust

Chapter 20: Gallery Art Hive as Dialogic Space

Natasha S. Reid

Using an Art Hive in a contemporary gallery for encounters between the public and artists

Chapter 21: Artists as Activists: Engaging Middle School Artists in Creating Art That Matters

Julie Toole

Making art that makes a difference with middle school artists

Chapter 22: Finding the Hidden Questions

Alice C. Pennisi

Structure, openness, and thoughtful questions for engaged discussion in the classroom

Chapter 23: Talking about Art: When Questions Are the Answer

Erica Richard

Facilitating conversations with museum docents

Chapter 24: Critical Conversations in Conservative Communities

Kelly Beach and Dianna Montano, with Connie Stewart

Inclusive teaching in politically charged environments

Chapter 25: Facilitating Dialogue about Loss and Grief in the Gallery

Harrison Orr and Carissa DiCindio

Addressing stories of loss and grief in museum settings

Chapter 26: How Superficial Themes in the Art Classroom Can Erase the Narrative of Marginalized Students and Communities

Ketal Patel

Narrative inquiry with preservice teachers to center the humanity of their future students

Chapter 27: Problematizing Conversations: Creating Art to Engage in Difficult Discussions

William Estrada

Creating brave spaces to engage in difficult conversations through public art workshops

Chapter 28: Two Colleagues Talk About Care: Responding to the Emotional State of Our Students

Chris Cain and John Humphrey, with Connie Stewart

The use of artmaking and trained counselors to provide care to K–12 students

CHAPTER 16

Creating Spaces to Support Difficult Dialogues

Lisa Hochtritt

How can educators create a space to support difficult dialogues that invariably occur while teaching? Most art educators have dealt with conflict and controversy in their work in some way or another. Challenging conversations and complicated issues are all around us. We encounter them in our daily lives, current events, school curricula, and popular culture. Artists are essential in the work of making sense of the world; they can address challenging topics through creative encounters, and this can help to spur on conversations to engage with difficult imagery and issues. What follows in this chapter is a description of a workshop I attended that focused on equity, diversity, and inclusion and employed suggestions from educators and organizers who work to make all voices heard.

COMMUNITY AGREEMENTS

In a racial equity workshop I attended at the college where I teach, facilitator Jesse Villalobos, from the organization Race Forward (www.raceforward.org) in New York City, started by asking graduate faculty participants to think of a question, concern, or hope that we brought to the meeting. We shared our thoughts in small groups and then after a few minutes we reported out. In addition to making sure that participants felt comfortable in the space, an important part of setting the tone of the workshop was the joint establishment of community agreements. Because we were going to be talking about potentially sensitive and personal topics, he wanted to make sure that we were aware of how to navigate the possibly uncomfortable moments that might occur. These were the rules of engagement for the workshop:

1. Share the air
2. Anticipate conflict and discomfort
3. ~~"Safe space"~~ *"Brave space"*
4. Impact vs. intent
5. One mic!

We discussed these agreement points collectively, interpreting in our own words what we thought it meant for our current conversation. This was a useful exercise, as it established the expectations for the kind of space we were creating together for the workshop.

Teachers are familiar with setting rules of engagement in their classrooms so all students can learn and be successful. Norms and community agreements are similar in that they encourage a respectful and compassionate classroom that is open to all opinions. In my college classes, we start with a review of a set of community commitments similar to those stated in this chapter, and work in pairs to augment and rewrite them based on our group's particular set of needs during the semester. These agreements are part of a living document that, in order to remain relevant, has to be revisited frequently during the school year and collaboratively reviewed, revised, and refined when needed.

The organization Amplifier provides some examples of other norms that can be used in education settings. They suggest:

- Speak from the "I" or address the topic, not the person
- Speak from a place of love and respect. Start your comment with phrases like "Thank you for sharing!" or "Tell me more about_____."
- Give everyone the opportunity to speak
- Ask yourself if sharing your thoughts will contribute to the conversation in a positive way
- Assume everyone in the space has good intentions
- Give everyone time to think about a response before raising your hand

- DICTIONARY: Raise your hand and say, "dictionary," if you don't know what a word means or would like clarification
- Confidentiality: What is said here, stays here. What is learned here, leaves here. (Amplifier, n.d.-a, p. 3)

This list of suggestions can be used in all learning spaces with variations based on your particular context. I also found this list immediately transferable to situations with colleagues and in workplace conversations. Some of the points are applicable in interpersonal communications and our daily lives.

PERSONAL STORY SHARING

Because of my work in social justice and art education, I have been interested in how groups of people engage in artmaking to amplify voices that are underrepresented. A few years ago, I was invited to the University of Northern Colorado to speak as part of a symposium asking, "How can the art classroom be a space to discuss controversial issues?" The participants were undergraduate and graduate students in art education, arts administrators, artists, and art teachers. The day consisted of presentations, activities, workshops, and opportunities for story sharing and honest exchanges. We started with a community-building spectrum activity where we physically placed ourselves on a continuum in response to questions about how much support we had in our schools to engage in difficult topics. The continuum activity helped us to gain a visual understanding about where we were all entering the conversation.

Throughout the day we heard from current art teachers in rural, urban, and suburban areas talk about situations they have dealt with in their classrooms, including white supremacy, racial injustice, and inadequate funding. They also discussed self-censorship of topics and artists they used, or could not use, in teaching because of certain community viewpoints. We talked about how, what, and who can bring up difficult topics in the art classroom and our roles and responsibilities in doing so. "As educators, we are not expected to have all the answers. Rather, developing effective approaches to discussing controversial issues enables teachers to challenge their own views and explore ideas in greater depth with young people" (Oxfam GB, 2018, p. 2).

This work is critical not only in supporting the learners in our classroom, but also in finding ways to share our own vulnerabilities effectively and safely while addressing difficult topics.

THE IMPORTANCE OF DIALOGUE

Why would a teacher want to invite youth-initiated dialogue and difficult conversations into their classroom? In my own experience I have found that adults often ignore the knowledge and worldviews young people possess. It is important for us to remember that they have lived a life before meeting us; adults owe it to them to listen to what they want to share. Cinquemani and Kraehe (2020), in writing about working and learning alongside young children, suggest that it is not up to educators to "give" voice to young people, but rather, "their voices already exist, and seeking ways to authentically and respectfully bring them into the conversations we are having" (p. 6) is vitally important.

Conversations with young people while I was a high school art teacher showed their concern about topics of relationships, race, body image, social standing, and controversial current events. They wanted to talk about and make artwork about global issues and topics that affected their lives. I found that contemporary art was an excellent way to introduce issues of personal relevance. In addition to looking at and talking about art, Oxfam GB (2018) suggests that young people need to articulate their own values and that exploring "controversial issues can help develop thinking skills" (p. 5). Students of any age know things are happening in the world, and discussing uncomfortable topics and exploring art in a supportive space can help them in unpacking and making sense of these events.

Since controversy is everywhere and is encountered at every age, cultivating a classroom climate and space for open dialogue is important for people to feel comfortable in sharing their thoughts; a *brave space* is one that encourages honesty and courage. Amplifier encourages the creation of a brave space for dialogue and shares ideas with educators about how to facilitate conversations. They suggest,

> To create a brave space for all students to share and learn, you can co-create a list of norms with your students that will maintain a space of respect and provide opportunities to hold each other accountable. A "brave

space" is an environment where students accept and celebrate difference, assume the best intentions of each other, and accept responsibility of affecting the emotional well-being of another person. (Amplifier, n.d-b, Q + A, para. 6)

In their guide to creating a brave space, they offer these ideas: Assume the best intentions; time is valuable; affirmation; wait time; draw expertise from your students; check your privilege; and hold everyone accountable (Amplifier, (n.d-a, pp. 1–2). Because teachers spend a lot of time with young people, they have the responsibility to support the learners as they explore these topics in both a safe *and* brave space.

Kraehe and Evans (2019) discuss the importance of language and of acknowledging our implicit biases when we work with participants in settings such as museums and classrooms. Implicit biases are unconscious beliefs we have about a certain group. When talking about art, for example, some of these biases can come out in the dialogue. It can be challenging for some when they are trying to reconcile new information with their belief systems and personal experiences. Kraehe and Evans (2019) found in their work that when topics are uncomfortable, "in the rush to smooth over our unease, we become more susceptible to making snap judgments . . . [and these] snap judgments are problematic as they reinforce our implicit biases" (Kraehe & Evans, 2019, para. 36). They share seven strategies they have developed for inclusive dialogue that can be useful in all settings. Two of these are that as a community of learners it is important to "be curious about each other and seek understanding" (para. 30) and "be willing to experience discomfort" (para. 33). Our ability to be compassionate and respectful of everyone's opinion can set the tone for open conversations and a space of understanding.

CONSIDERATIONS FOR MOVING FORWARD

As we strive to create a space for honest dialogue, these are a few things to keep in mind on this journey:

- *Know your audience.* Lists and resources are useful to support teachers in this important work, but it is also essential to know your school, community, and the young people you are working with before engaging in any type of activity that you think may be challenging to the participants. What will work in one place of learning may not work in another.
- *Find a supportive educational community.* This work takes sustained energy, and we need a community of friends to inspire and support us. Find an interested educational partner to discuss ideas and share stories about how things are going and brainstorm together about ways to approach uncomfortable situations drawing upon current research and resources. Reflecting on our own implicit biases and discussing these with a set of trusted colleagues can help us to better navigate this important work.
- *Collaboratively set and revisit community agreements.* Try collectively setting community norms for how participants will interact in the space and to create an inclusive space for all voices. Young people know what kind of learning environment they want to learn in, and their voices are critical in establishing these norms and keeping them going throughout the year. Trying out strategies appropriate to your situation is an important first step in creating environments to support difficult conversations. And being attentive to, and encouraging of, inclusive dialogue is essential. If participants do not feel safe and heard, thoughtful exchange of ideas cannot take place.

These community commitments can be created and utilized in every space and with every age. Creating a space that is guided by respect and compassion is everyone's responsibility. The arts are essential in these conversations and can open up new ways of thinking about topics relevant to young people and their daily lives.

REFERENCES

Amplifier. (n.d-a). Creating a brave space for dialogue. https://www.rooseveltufsd.org/site/handlers/filedownload.ashx?moduleinstanceid=3566&dataid=4472&FileName=Creating_A_Brave_Space.pdf

Amplifier. (n.d-b). Education Amplifier. https://amplifier.org/education/

Cinquemani, S., & Kraehe, A. (2020). Thinking alongside children: Explorations of artistic practice and research in early childhood. *Art Education, 73*(6), 4–7.

Kraehe, A., & Evans, L. (2019). *"That depends on how you define it": Reflections on inclusivity language as a flashpoint in museum staff and docent development*. Viewfinder. https://medium.com/viewfinder-reflecting-on-museum-education/that-depends-on-how-you-define-it-reflections-on-inclusivity-language-as-a-flashpoint-in-museum-a7be0326e2f2

Oxfam GB (2018). *Teaching controversial issues: A guide for teachers.* https://oxfamilibrary.openrepository.com/bitstream/handle/10546/620473/gd-teaching-controversial-issues-2904 18-en.pdf?sequence=1&isAllowed=y

Race Forward. (n.d.). https://www.raceforward.org

CHAPTER 17

Centering Culture Through Critical Conversations

Katie Coogan and Margaret Walker

I (Katie Coogan) wasn't expecting the group hug. We had just finished sharing final projects in our first art ed course together, artwork responding to the Big Idea *shifting perspectives*, when my preservice undergrads embraced me and one another. "Is this awkward?" I wondered. But it wasn't; it felt completely natural. We had shared a lot about ourselves throughout the course. This hug validated my decision to purposefully model culturally responsive pedagogy through readings, assignments, and discussions to build connections.

Focusing on culturally relevant and responsive teaching methodologies, like identifying the unique cultures and customs of individual students to guide teaching and learning (Hammond, 2015; Ladson-Billings, 1994) and avoiding cultural appropriation in the art room (which can lead to the trivialization of cultures taken out of context [Ballengee-Morris & Taylor, 2005]) led to deep discussions on systemic racism, bias, and the need to create inclusive classrooms. These conversations and corresponding art projects prepared students to openly examine their unique identities. What's more, they learned about one another.

WHY ARE THESE CONVERSATIONS IMPORTANT IN THE ART ROOM?

When teachers fail to reflect on their students' culturally diverse backgrounds, they neglect to acknowledge the assets that these individuals bring to the table (Delpit, 1995). Educators can play a major role in teaching about diversity and antiracism, and because culture and identity are a natural part of the visual art curriculum, the art room creates a natural environment for students to "come to understand cultural diversity, social inclusion, and antiracist behaviors" (Lee, 2012, p. 48) if the teacher is well-versed in culturally responsive teaching. Art education has been shown to teach tolerance, help students embrace sexual and racial diversity, and challenge cultural assumptions (Agid & Rand, 2007; Knight, 2006; Prettyman & Elisa, 2006; Roeck, 2009). Modeling critical conversations provides a foundation for educators to engage students in similar dialogues that confront and celebrate our culturally driven differences.

Laying the Foundation for the Conversation

To establish a framework for the semester-long conversation, we focus on Zaretta Hammond's (2015) Ready for Rigor Framework for Culturally Responsive Teaching. The first part, *Awareness*, includes seven steps, and our process concentrates on two of these: Learning to "know and own your cultural lens," and recognizing the "socio-political context around race and language" (p. 17).

To begin, we discuss the relationship between *implicit bias* and *structural racialization*. Each of us harbors culturally driven implicit bias that, if unchecked, may negatively impact how we respond to our students' needs. Structural racialization, the "social, economic, & political structures that are harmful to people of color & to our society as a whole" (p. 29), and implicit bias play off one another. Understanding the dynamic that structural racialization plays in the development of one's own implicit bias can help us first acknowledge, and then reframe, the internal triggers.

Second, we ensure that the preservice art education students we work with understand the negative effects of cultural appropriation in the art room. Lessons that inadequately relay information about cultural artifacts or have students mimic them in their artmaking "do not respect the complexities of cultures, cultural products, and individual artists" while also disregarding the "meaning of materials . . . and diversity within cultural groups" (Buffington & Bryant, 2019, p. 20). When students re-create cultural artifacts using materials that disregard their intended meaning and significance, they may acquire "superficial knowledge and misunderstandings of cultures" (Buffington & Bryant, 2019, p. 22). Engaging in conversations around cultural appropriation ensures that preservice art educators maintain a high level of culturally responsive teaching in their future classrooms that does not unintentionally dismiss the cultures of students who enter their classrooms or the artists and artworks they introduce.

Finally, we introduce Hammond's (2015) three levels of culture: surface, shallow, and deep. *Surface culture* is what most people think of first when discussing culture in the classroom: holidays, traditions, dress, and food. *Shallow culture* includes learned social norms around eye contact, physical touch, and respect. *Deep culture* is where our ethical compass and ideas around good and evil come from. Culture impacts how students learn and how they respond to authority figures; therefore, understanding the three levels of culture helps preservice teachers look beyond the outward-facing cultures of their students and into their deeper selves so they can effectively respond to and support students' varying needs in the classroom.

Getting to Work

Through the *Unique Culture Assignment*, students reflect on their own culture to understand their positionality and to recognize the assets of other cultures. The learning outcomes of this project are directly aligned to the Social Justice Standards (Learning for Justice, 2022) involving *identity* and *diversity*. The standards ask students to recognize how "multiple identities interact and create unique and complex individuals" (Identity, para. 4), to "express comfort with people who are both similar to and different from them," (Diversity, para. 5), and to "accurately and respectfully describe how people (including themselves) are both similar to and different from each other and others in their identity groups" (Diversity, para. 5), among others (Learning for Justice, 2022).

Students create a mixed media artwork that represents the three different levels of their culture (surface, shallow, deep) and reflect on their artistic choices. One student reflected that understanding these levels from a personal viewpoint helped them "see the importance of the aspects of culture that some people hide" (personal communication, December 2019). What's more, it made them aware of how they are influenced by hidden cultural bias. Another student was able to highlight several aspects of his unique culture, including his "strong Islamic roots, pie-in-the-sky American values, and deep African mystery and ambitions" that make up his faceted self (personal communication, December 2019). This assignment challenged students to learn about how culture influences many aspects of their identity and to value the unique perspectives of each of their peers.

Shifting Perspectives Assignment

After the *Unique Culture Assignmen*t sets the foundation, students move on to a larger artistic project that focuses directly on their *Shifting Perspectives*. While focusing on the essential question "How does my unique and layered perspective impact meaning and decision-making in my artwork?", students draft three ideas, share and receive feedback from one another, then begin their final project. At the project's end, students participate in a final critique and write an artist's statement. This particular semester, the students explored mental illness, sexuality, migration, and racism through this project. Projects investigated, for example, the unique perspective of a Muslim student grappling with hearing the former U.S. president declaring his parents' homeland a "shithole"; the feelings of a student from a socially conservative household upon coming out as bisexual; the struggles of living with mental illness; and what it feels like to be transgender. This student created a surreal self-portrait with their chest removed (see Figure 17.1).

These are but a few of the unique and layered perspectives we shared and learned from.

Student Reflections

When asked how working on the *Unique Culture* and *Shifting Perspectives* projects impacted their learning, students said this work showed them how to create safe spaces for their students to reflect on their personal identities. One student commented:

> Foundations was one of the first classes where I intentionally investigated and described my own unique culture. I had taken classes before that superficially . . . talked about how everyone's experiences of the world are different and how that both informs and is informed by our identities. In these projects, though, we put that into context. . . . It helped me further the process of understanding myself, which in turn allowed me to understand others. Hearing other people's views and experiences was another form of that context that I

Figure 17.1. Morgan Fitrell, *Shifting Perspectives Project*

> needed to best understand the ways my dominant culture as a white person has affected my identity. The project also further established the class as a safe place. (personal communication, March 12, 2022)

Another student (now alumnus) remarked that the "biggest benefit was seeing how accepted my culture was and how many similarities me and the others shared" and that he continues to "use the practices we learned" during that Foundations class in his own classroom (personal communication, March 14, 2022).

CONCLUDING THOUGHTS

While these art pieces and the dialogue we shared around them touched on difficult topics like race, sexuality, religion, and politics, laying a foundation of a safe place that honored the unique perspectives of each individual allowed students to share freely despite differing views and opinions. These critical conversations, fueled by self-reflection and sharing personal art pieces based on unique cultures and shifting perspectives, allowed us to recognize and honor the assets each individual brought to the classroom and to reframe our socially acquired perspectives. It also set us up for an epic group hug.

REFERENCES

Agid, S., & Rand, E. (2007). Teaching beyond "tolerance." *Radical Teacher, 80*, 2–5.

Ballengee-Morris, C., & Taylor, P. (2005). You can hide but you can't run: Interdisciplinary and culturally sensitive approaches to mask making. *Art Education, 58*(5), 12–17.

Buffington, M., & Bryant, A. (2019). Changing practice: Culturally sustaining pedagogy in art education. *Art Education, 72*(2), 20–25.

Delpit, L. D. (1995). *Other people's children: Cultural conflict in the classroom*. New Press.

Hammond, Z. L. (2015). *Culturally responsive teaching and the brain*. Corwin Press.

Knight, W. B. (2006). Using contemporary art to challenge cultural values, beliefs, and assumptions. *Art Education, 59*(4), 39–45.

Ladson-Billings, G. (1994). *The dreamkeepers*. Jossey-Bass Publishing Co.

Lee, N. (2012). Culturally responsive teaching for 21st-century art education: Examining race in a studio art experience. *Art Education, 65*(5), 48–53.

Learning for Justice. (2022). *Social justice standards*. https://www.learningforjustice.org/frameworks/social-justice-standards

Prettyman, S. S., & Gargarella, E. B. (2006). Community, collaboration, and creativity: The potential of art education to create change. *Mid-Western Educational Researcher, 19*(4), 12–19.

Roeck, K. T. (2009). Embracing diversity. *Journal of LGBT Youth, 6*(1), 1–6.

CHAPTER 18

Conversations Over Wi-Fi

Reorienting Student-Centered Art Discussions Online

Ashley Mask

Art museum education scholars have in recent decades acknowledged the power of group discussion, reorienting museum educators from lecturers talking at students to interlocutors conversing with students (Burnham & Kai-Kee, 2011; Hubard, 2015; Mayer, 2005). Hubard (2015) stated that interpretive dialogue in art museums requires "a flexible, web-like, or rhizomatic sequence of actions" that "allow for avenues of inquiry to emerge organically" (p. 36). By doing so, art discussions can manifest bell hooks's (2010) vision that "we break with the notion that our experience of gaining knowledge is private, individualistic, and competitive" and that we might instead "engage mutually in a learning partnership" (p. 43).

The repositioning of educators as adaptable, responsive dialogue partners with students brings to mind Sara Ahmed's (2010) concept of *orientations*, or how our bodies are oriented toward the world, because "to be oriented in a certain way is how certain things come to be significant" (p. 235). In this chapter, I will reflect on my own reorientation as a museum educator, based on experiences teaching an online after-school art program for middle schoolers. In doing so, I hope to provoke a reconsideration of the interactions among educators, students, and artworks by exploring how online spaces might encourage student agency, teacher risk-taking, and cocreated paths of inquiry in dialogue-based teaching and learning in ways that are unlikely, or even impossible, in physical spaces. As Ahmed (2010) states:

> Spaces too are oriented in the sense that certain bodies are "in place" in this or that place . . . To say spaces are oriented around certain bodies is to show how some bodies will be more "in place" than others. (p. 235)

BACKGROUND ORIENTATION

In early 2020, I was hired by the Metropolitan Museum of Art in New York City to co-lead (with another museum educator) a partnership with a Brooklyn middle school, where the student population was 70% Black, 25% Latinx, 3% White, and 2% other. The school reported that 90% of students were economically disadvantaged. Because the school had no art teacher on staff, the partnership was viewed as an important opportunity for students who showed an affinity for art and would commit to 10 weekly after-school sessions and three museum visits during school hours.

As with previous partnerships, my coteacher and I designed a curriculum based on conversations with the school's administrators and museum staff as well as our own prior experiences with middle school students. The question "How do artists express identity?" guided our curriculum development. The goals were to have students experiment with a variety of art materials and processes; explore artworks that encouraged discussions around identity, race, gender, class, disability, and/or social (in)justice; and express their unique perspectives through art-looking and artmaking.

The COVID-19 Pandemic Forces a Reorientation

In March 2020, we learned that the museum was closing and postponing all off-site programs. It wasn't until a year later that we were finally able to begin working with the middle school through a completely virtual partnership program. Rather than meeting in person at the museum to look at artworks and at school to make art together, we would meet online each week. Each student, school administrator, and museum educator would log in separately from their own home.

Conversations Over Wi-Fi

Our first session began slowly, as students trickled in and we worked through tech issues. We then took time to look through the art supplies that had been delivered to the students, and together we created community expectations for the program ("We respect each other," "We will get out of our comfort zones," "Participation is key!"; the school counselor added, "Cameras should stay on"). I asked students to locate one object in their home that represented a part of their identity and introduce themselves and their object to the group. We then looked at several self-portraits from the Met's collection and discussed how differently artists choose to depict themselves. We finished the session with students choosing how to depict themselves artistically on the cover of their new sketchbooks.

As the weeks went on, we learned a lot about our group, because the virtual nature of the program created new avenues for getting to know one another. In essence, we were invited into one another's homes every week. This kind of exposure—of seeing one another in our personal spaces, in relationship with our families—led to casual interactions that would never have taken place in the museum, encouraging a special kind of vulnerability between us. The time my toddler barged through my office door, Mateo responded, "He's my little brother's age!" and brought his little brother over to say "Hi." On another day, Natalie chimed in to say that it was her birthday. This led to repeated "Happy Birthday!" comments and smiling emojis in the chat box. Students would occasionally turn their cameras off, saying "I've gotta go talk to my mom for a minute," returning moments later to jump back into the art discussion. When I had technical difficulties, a student would unmute and suggest a solution. During the third session, we were joined by a new student, Rosa, who had just moved to New York. Rosa was still learning English, and when the translator didn't show up, another student, Emmanuel, jumped in, saying "I can help her, Ms. Mask." Using the chat, Emmanuel then typed in Spanish everything I said for the rest of the session, and for all of the following sessions.

REORIENTING ART DISCUSSIONS AND STUDENT AGENCY

Had we been in the museum, we would obviously have benefited from being in front of an original work of art, as well as from being in the unique space of the museum itself. However, museums are also notoriously elitist, with unspoken social norms that insist on silence and stillness. By not being in the museum, and instead accessing these experiences through our computers, art discussions looked quite different. Compare the following:

When teaching at the museum, I would typically facilitate an art discussion by having students sit on the floor as a group. I would then stand in front of students, between them and the artwork. The students in the back of the group might not be able to see the details in the artwork. I would ask, "What's going on in this picture?" and expect that students would raise their hands to be called on, one by one. We might hear Emmanuel whispering translations to Rosa in the background. I would paraphrase and synthesize the students' ideas, while incorporating contextual information about the art, until we reached a satisfying (to me) conclusion to the discussion.

In our virtual classroom, we were all oriented toward the artwork from the same perspective, seeing the artwork image displayed on our computer screens. When I asked, "What's going on in this picture?", students responded by typing into the chat box, as well as by unmuting and sharing their observations one by one. This allowed simultaneous responses to emerge, and we heard from students who might not speak up otherwise. Emmanuel's translations for Rosa were also intermixed in the chat, making his labor—and Rosa's experience—visible, taking up space along with everyone's observations. If a student commented that the artwork reminded them of another artist's work, I could easily pull up images of the other artist's work for comparison.

With inevitable technological complications, there were moments of the teacher not-knowing, and accepting direct instruction from students—after all, they had a year of extensive remote learning experiences. One might argue that the virtual space was "oriented in the sense that certain bodies"—middle school bodies, in this case—were "more 'in place' than" mine (Ahmed, 2010, p. 235). And while our art discussions were more chaotic—more organic and less likely to end in a neat conclusion—they were also more student-centered. It was as if we had truly explored the artwork side by side, making our way together as dialogue partners. Students were empowered in ways they may never have been in the museum, and conversely, as an educator, I took risks and gave over the space in ways I wouldn't have in the museum. Finally, while our bodies were situated toward our computers, we were each in our homes, where, assuming we felt safe and supported there, we could be ourselves, sitting more comfortably than on the hard museum floor and moving around when we needed to.

Coming back to the concept of orientations, Ahmed (2010) said, "While bodies do things, things might also 'do bodies'" (p. 245). Our bodies were "done" differently by computers and our online learning environment. Rather than adapting to the museum space, and all of its associated expectations, we were empowered in the virtual space to engage with artworks and each other in new ways. Ahmed (2010) described orientations as "the direction we take that puts some things and not others in our reach" (p. 245). Put this way, online learning places artworks and group dialogue within a different kind of reach. In looking forward, I wonder how this reorientation will change my teaching and learning back in the museum, and in the virtual learning spaces that are here to stay. As Ahmed (2010) said, "If orientations are an effect of what we tend toward, then they point to the future, to what is not yet present" (p. 247). I am hopeful about what is not yet present, and what new directions might become possible, as we all re-orient ourselves in a post-pandemic world.

REFERENCES

Ahmed, S. (2010). Orientations matter. In D. Coole & S. Frost (Eds.), *New materialisms: Ontology, agency, and politics* (pp. 234–257). Duke University Press.

Burnham, R., & Kai-Kee, E. (2011). *Teaching in the art museum: Interpretation as experience*. J. Paul Getty Museum.

hooks, b. (2010). *Teaching critical thinking: Practical wisdom.* Routledge.

Hubard, O. (2015). *Art museum education: Facilitating gallery experiences*. Palgrave Macmillan.

Mayer, M. M. (2005). Bridging the theory-practice divide in contemporary art museum education. *Art Education, 58*(2), 13–17.

CHAPTER 19

Building Community by Using Opening and Closing Circles

Valeska Maria Populoh

Community and trust-building among students, and between the students and the teacher, in a learning space is critical in order to hold space for the challenging and difficult conversations we are called to engage in. Conversations and experiences that require us to take risks and be vulnerable also require that we have the opportunity to practice ways of being with each other that are accessible and low-stakes. The practice of student-led opening and closing circles has been a powerful tool to cocreate a supportive learning environment in my classroom. During opening and closing circles, all class participants are invited to sit in a circle facing each other. The practice, which extends beyond the physical orientation of class members to each other, is rooted in traditions that aim to facilitate conversation and connection among participants.

Opening and closing circles are a deeply rooted practice of bringing people together in a nonhierarchical way in societies around the world. I have learned this practice in relationship with community organizers and cultural workers and want to acknowledge the debt I owe to my many teachers in helping me develop this part of my pedagogy, specifically Ọmọlará Williams McCallister, Sheila Gaskins, Rebecca Yenawine, Robin Marquis, Mama Kibibi Ajanku, and Mama Rashida Forman-Bey. The practice of opening and closing circles intentionally builds time into each class for our learning community to come together and build interpersonal relationships over time.

COURSE FORMAT

Our studio classes at the Maryland Institute College of Art (MICA) meet once a week for 6 hours, with a one-hour break. Before each class, my teaching assistant and I form a circle of chairs in the classroom, pushing tables toward the perimeter of the room, leaving some chairs along those tables as optional seating for students. I welcome students as they enter on the first day of class. Most students choose to sit in the circle, though there are usually a handful of students who opt to sit at a table, facing the circle.

On the first day, I facilitate the circle. I welcome everyone, introduce myself, and invite my teaching assistant to introduce themself. Then students respond in writing to a short survey, in which they share their name, pronouns, major, and other reflections, such as what they are most excited to explore in the class. Once everyone has completed the survey, students are invited to find the other person in the room who has the same number printed on their survey. They have 10 minutes to connect and then introduce their partner to the rest of the class. This circle signals that everyone is welcome and invited to speak and participate.

After this round of introductions, we review the syllabus (a shared digital document); during this review I invite students to add their names to the syllabus if they would like to facilitate a circle in an upcoming class session. They are welcome to cofacilitate with another peer. No one is required to facilitate. I ask students to keep the opening and closing to around 10 minutes (though we sometimes go over that time). The teaching assistant facilitates the second class session, so that students have an opportunity to experience two approaches before stepping into the role themselves. Usually, about two-thirds of the students choose to facilitate, with some students facilitating two to three times. During weeks when no one signs up, or when the volunteer is absent, people are invited to step up for the day. On most occasions, students volunteer with an impromptu activity. If no one volunteers, I read the room to see what might be beneficial for the class that day. In the next section I share examples of the kinds of activities students and I have facilitated.

CONTENT AND CULTURE

The people who make up each class and the culture that forms among students over time shape the opening and closing activities. The activities can be categorized as follows:

- Mindfulness and Grounding: short, guided breathing exercises or visualizations, as well as gentle stretching
- Reflective Questions: questions related to subject matter we are exploring in class, or related to issues students are navigating more collectively, such as the stress of finals or a political event they want to talk about. Often, these are very simple questions that make it easy for everyone to participate, such as "What song are you listening to on repeat right now?" or "What is your favorite movie?"
- Interactive Games and Play: playful activities or games, such as inviting each other to describe a dish they would bring to an imaginary potluck, or playing games like Telephone or Red Light, Green Light (the facilitator explains these and we provide accommodations for students based on their needs and abilities)

STUDENT VOICES

I interviewed six students who facilitated circles. These students ranged from first-year students to a graduate student in her 60s, and encompassed a variety of other lived experiences, including being first-generation college students, identifying as LGBTQIA, and encompassing ethnic and racial identities including Latinx, East Asian, Black, White and South Asian. Two students were from Baltimore, and the others from other regions of the United States. Some had experienced these circles in my other classes, both online during the remote learning of the pandemic, and in person; others had experiences of circles from community settings in their lives, while some had no prior experience with circles. I asked students to reflect on the circles, what they found challenging about the format, and how, if at all, the circles supported their learning. Students also reflected on other impacts of this weekly practice. In reviewing their comments, I noticed five themes: acknowledging students' humanity; supporting student-led facilitation; developing empathy; building connection; and practicing risk-taking and vulnerability.

1. Acknowledging students' humanity: Several students reflected on the value of having a ritual or familiar way to start the class that acknowledges their lives beyond the classroom, that they are more than just students, and have time to "arrive," check in with themselves and each other before getting started with the work of the day. "You reminded us that we're human. We don't always get that. We're just expected to go, go, go." (Bobby Blazek)
2. Supporting student-led facilitation: The circles allow students to engage each other in conversation and build comfort and confidence with stepping into leadership. As Kris Tapia reflected, "It gives students . . . more opportunity to take more control of their learning . . . to make their own relationships with their classmates . . . rather than relying on the professor. . . . When students are given that opportunity to lead themselves, facilitate themselves, that translates to other things. If students want to have a conversation about something else, they aren't waiting for someone else's permission to have it, they can just do it."
3. Developing empathy: Being asked to facilitate activities also encourages students to think about each other's experience. As Kris Tapia reflected, "It allows students to think about their role in the family of the class . . . and to think outside of yourself." The circles help students take into consideration the needs and abilities of their peers. Kris added, "If the teacher always does the activity, then you don't really have to think about the experience of your peers. But when you have to think about what kind of opening activity you are going to do, you have to think about whether people in the class will feel comfortable doing that activity, or whether they will even feel able to participate."
4. Building connection: Several students reflected on the value of these activities in

building connections among the students and with me, their teacher. "Laughter is the best connector . . . so as soon as we're laughing at ourselves and with each other, you're building connections a lot faster" (Alia Payne). "Doing it every week made it part of the routine . . . and you're building connections in the class so then you become more comfortable and more vulnerable and more willing to participate" (Achmad O'Brien).

5. Practicing risk-taking and vulnerability: The circles allow students to learn about each other in ways that go beyond their art making or academic lives. "We shared vulnerabilities in that circle . . . we shared how we were feeling and that made . . . us . . . real people to each other" (Mama Rashida Forman-Bey). The circles allow students to explore emotions and practice behaviors in smaller, less high-stakes ways. "You have to get used to getting silly. . . . People don't want to embarrass themselves or seem immature, but sometimes that's the fun of it. That's how you make friends and get close to other people" (Kris Tapia).

CONTEXT, CONSENT, AND CHOICE

The opening and closing activities are supported by a set of shared agreements that the class comes to collectively. These are built on a preliminary set of common agreements that I bring into class and students amend. One agreement is that everyone always has the right to pass—meaning that no one is ever forced to participate. No one *has* to sit in the circle, but everyone is welcome. No one *has* to facilitate an opening and closing activity, but everyone is welcome. No one *has* to respond to the question asked or activity offered. You can always pass. This is critical. In my experience, it is rare that a student chooses not to participate. But choice is paramount, because being required to participate can get in the way of building a space of trust and safety that these circles are supposed to cultivate.

"I'm glad you didn't force us. You gave me the time to familiarize myself with the other students and with you. Being able to have that choice, to have my own space, because I need that space, I felt very respected and I felt like I had the autonomy" (Bobby Blazek). Another student reflected, "I just don't feel comfortable with all of the attention centered on me, so that is why I never facilitated, but I always felt like there was space for me to step into it when I felt ready" (Achmad O'Brien).

CONCLUDING THOUGHTS

Over the years, my students have taught me to place greater amounts of trust in them to carry this part of the class. Students feel that trust, which is strengthened when I also participate in the activities they initiate. Students are understandably also more in tune with the vibe among the student body than I could ever be, and so are able to read the room in a way that I cannot, and thus have a better sense of whether a fun activity, a restorative stretch, or a more serious reflective question is appropriate. Ultimately, the opening and closing circles have created a critical space for me as a teacher to learn about my students' lives, needs, and perspectives; to practice being vulnerable; and to build connection with them.

CHAPTER 20

Gallery Art Hive as Dialogic Space

Natasha S. Reid

As the Executive Director (2017–2021) of the Visual Arts Centre (VAC) in Tiohtiá:ke (Montreal), I was very interested in finding ways to transform our gallery into a more inclusive and active dialogic space that would encourage new meanings to flow between and amongst diverse participants (Bohm, 2013), supporting our diversity, equity, and inclusion work. In this effort, we established a monthly Art Hive in the art gallery in 2019. Art Hives offer a welcoming free-access arts-based community space that encourages both self-directed and group-based creative learning. Grounded in choice-based experiences and nonevaluative creative engagement, these community art studios recognize all participants as artists (Lewis et al., 2021; Timm-Bottos & Chainey, 2015). Gathered around a table adorned with a wide variety of materials, as well as refreshments, participants are encouraged to engage in dialogic exchange. The type of dialogue promoted in these spaces aligns with Paulo Freire's (2002) conception of dialogue as "an act of creation" (p. 89) between people, where they learn *with* each other in a nonhierarchical exchange grounded in respect, love, and humility. In my role at the VAC, during the McClure Gallery Art Hives (MGAH), I witnessed such dialogic encounters between artists and the public, among members of the public, and between the public and the gallery.

PUBLIC/ARTIST DIALOGUES

At the beginning of each MGAH, the exhibiting artist or a VAC artist-teacher offered an open-ended mini-workshop focused on a medium, technique, or theme in the exhibition. Inviting members of the public to engage with the workshop if they desired, the artist was situated as an active facilitator. During these 1-hour workshops, these facilitators typically offered a short demonstration, providing a potential starting point for the public to engage in artmaking activities. In this relaxed atmosphere, the public and artists discussed their artwork, the exhibition, the art world, and their lived experiences. Rather than simply passively viewing the artist's artwork or listening to an artist talk, participants engaged in an active dialogic exchange with the artists, centered on hands-on artistic explorations.

DIALOGUES AMONG MEMBERS OF THE PUBLIC

It is typical for visitors to contemporary galleries to experience artworks in silence or, when they attend with others, to keep their hushed conversations within their visitor group. Within Art Hives, participants are encouraged to engage in meaningful and lively exchanges with others. Sitting around a table filled with art materials and refreshments, traditional barriers between visitors in our gallery were removed. They engaged in spontaneous and dynamic conversations about the art materials, art on the wall, the artist, and their daily lives. As is common in Art Hives, folks are often naturally engaged in skill-sharing, helping each other in their artistic explorations, enabling participants to take turns being the teacher and the student (Timm-Bottos & Chainey, 2015). For example, I saw one participant teaching another participant a knitting technique and a daughter encouraging and assisting her mother in her artmaking journey. Frequently, participants in the MGAH expressed how meaningful such social exchanges in this space were to them.

PUBLIC/GALLERY DIALOGUES

Within this space, the gallery shifted from the traditional white cube to a dynamic and even messy creative space. I witnessed some individuals' confusion and even frustration with the space being different from what they had grown to expect from galleries.

Others were amused at the changes. Some people were drawn to enter the gallery after seeing the ludic activity in the space through the street-view window. All such reactions led to dialogues between the public and the gallery about what a gallery is, who it is for, and how it is used, as well as the need to shift these conceptions through activities such as Art Hives. These dialogues between visitors and the gallery staff often started on the peripheries of the Art Hive table and eventually led to visitors becoming participants in the Art Hive, making art alongside gallery staff, flattening the traditional hierarchy in galleries that can stifle dialogic encounters.

CONCLUDING THOUGHTS

The McClure Gallery Art Hive shifted the traditional roles of the artist, the public, and the gallery, emphasizing dialogue as an act of creation *with* others. The gallery became a nonhierarchical playground for dialogic exchange, contributing to our diversity, equity, and inclusion efforts. Establishing arts-based spaces grounded in dialogic exchange and an ethic of care in institutions traditionally viewed as exclusionary or hierarchical can contribute to efforts to transform these locations into dynamic relational sites for learning with others.

REFERENCES

Bohm, D. (2013). *On dialogue*. Routledge.

Freire, P. (2002). *Pedagogy of the oppressed*. Continuum.

Lewis, L., McLeod, H., & Li, X. (2021). Art Hive: A relational framework for social change. In H. Mreiwed, M. R. Carter, & C. Mitchell (Eds.), *Art as an agent for social change* (pp. 35–43). Brill.

Timm-Bottos, J., & Chainey, R. (2015). *Art Hives how-to-guide*. Concordia University. https://arthives.org/sites/arthives.org/files/art_hives_how-to-guide_1.pdf

CHAPTER 21

Artists as Activists

Engaging Middle School Artists in Creating Art That Matters

Julie Toole

Art has the power to question the status quo and move people to social change. This educational work cannot thrive without first creating a space for healing, connecting, and advocating. I have found in my 25 years as an art educator that brave environments are built through identity work and community-building. An important part of my teaching practice is to introduce artists who document societal inequities and challenge social norms.

In this chapter I will discuss an elective class I created for 6th–8th-graders, Artists as Activists, as a space for my students to explore all aspects of their identity and use their art to bring focus to social justice issues that are important to them. The students learn about contemporary artists who tackle today's most critical questions and inequities, and then create murals, cartoons, prints, posters, and installations to inform viewers, stimulate conversation, and (hopefully) affect change.

To engage in art activist work as an educator and a White woman, I first held up a mirror to understand my identity, privileges, biases, and blind spots. Sonia Nieto (2003) explains:

> Teachers bring their entire biographies with them: their experiences, identities, values, beliefs, attitudes, hang-ups, biases, wishes, dreams and hopes. It is useless for them to deny this: the most they can do is acknowledge how these may either get in the way of, or enhance, their work with students. (p. 24)

It is a lifelong journey for me to understand systems of oppression so they can be interrupted and dismantled. I learn by listening deeply to others with identities and perspectives different from my own. My participation in a Seeking Educational Equity and Diversity (SEED) Project (National SEED Project, n.d.) was life-changing. This diverse cohort met in person monthly for a year and was led by two trained facilitators. The work included personal reflection and testimony, listening to others' voices, and learning experientially and collectively, in the context of each participant's intersecting identities. I experienced a safe and brave space to unpack my identity, have courageous conversations, and be comfortable being uncomfortable. Through this work, I began acknowledging systems of power, oppression, and privilege to move beyond my white guilt and shame—which I learned is a tool of avoidance—into action. I became a trained SEED facilitator and gave back by co-leading SEED groups for my community, for parents and staff. In addition to SEED, I have been a member of my school Equity Action Team (EqAT). Because of these experiences, I have made a commitment to use my voice and positions of power and privilege to break down systems of oppression, create seats at the table, and give up my own if needed, for those voices who are constantly silenced and diminished.

I created my middle school art elective course, Artists as Activists, as one way to put commitments into action. The students and I explored questions such as: What issues do you care deeply about? How does your identity inform your art? What stories and voices are heard, and which ones are silenced? What are injustices that you see around you? And most importantly, what can you do about it? Since the class was a multiage group with 6th- through 8th-graders, I began with community-building and setting group norms. The students shared their ideas, describing how they want to feel in this class, what they need from me and their peers, and how they will show up for this class and for one another. Agreeing, co-constructing, debating, and posting group norms is the foundation that we come back to each time we meet. Norms have included: Active listening, speaking from "I," respecting others' narratives, leading with questions, assuming positive intent, taking risks, and what is said here stays here.

The art of collaborative artmaking can be transformational for a group in building a community of respect and joy. I curate experiences for my students such as TASK parties, an interactive artmaking experience created by performance artist Oliver Herring (Grimes, 2014); drawing games, including Exquisite Corpse; and collaborative murals. Initial artmaking experiences are not about the product, but about creating connections and community that are needed for socially meaningful work. Building on these connections, we begin exploring our own identities, myself included. This definition from Learning for Justice grounds us: "Our identity consists of the various characteristics we use to categorize and define ourselves and the various characteristics that are constructed by those around us" (Learning for Justice, n.d., para. 4).

It is important for the students to understand that our identity is both visible and invisible, it is often projected onto us by others, and it can be both stable and fluid. Identity wheels, digital collages, Jamboards, and photography are some of the ways that student artists share elements of their identities. Students consider questions such as: Which part of your identity would you like to know more about? What part of your identity do you think about most often? Which part of your identity is invisible? Which part of your identity do most people get wrong? These are useful to deepen the conversations and get beyond physical characteristics and basic hobbies. Sharing these identity characteristics leads us into an awareness of our intersecting identities and builds empathy for our unique qualities.

Naming, understanding, and having open conversations about white supremacy culture includes decolonizing the usual art history canon that I teach. "White supremacy culture is the idea (ideology) that white people, and the ideas, thoughts, beliefs, and actions of white people are superior to [BIPOC] and their ideas, thoughts, beliefs, and actions" (Okun, n.d., para. 3). The traditional canon is predominantly men of European descent, without including women, openly LGBTQ+ artists, and artists of color. The canon overlooks historical Indigenous, African, Asian, and folk artists. We look to contemporary artists who are embracing their identity and using their art as a form of activism, beginning with the work of Titus Kaphar (2017), using his TED talk, "Can Art Amend History?" Other artists we have discussed include Tatyana Fazlalizadeh, Roberto Lugo, Adrian Brandon, Wendy Red Star, Daniel Arzola, Alexandra Bell, Bisa Butler, Tonika Lewis Johnson, Jane Kim, Ekow Nimako, and Shamsia Hassani. The list is evolving, curated each trimester to meet the needs and interests of my students and of our world. We examine works of art through the lens of "What does your eye see?" and "What does your mind see?", looking deeply at the art and interpreting the artist's intent. After sharing our own thoughts, we read the artist's statements to understand the intent and message from the artist's point of view. The rest of the class is spent in studio time. Students reflect on their identity characteristics and areas of social justice that they feel most passionate about as they begin to create their art.

Because I run a Teaching for Artistic Behavior) (https://teachingforartisticbehavior.org) studio, student voice and choice are at the core of my teaching. Topics that students in the class have addressed in their artwork include LGBTQ+ identities, mental health, social media impact, microaggressions, war, gun control, animal rights, racism, sexism, gender gaps, sports equality, immigration, global warming, and ableism.

After they choose their general topic, I encourage the students to research data and statistics related to their topic. As a class, we discuss contemporary artists' frequent use of data as jumping off points for their art. Student artists in my classroom have full access to all media, including drawing, painting, collage, clay, sculpture, printmaking, fiber arts, and mixed media. They post weekly updates with photos on Padlet, our virtual class bulletin board, and we host critiques as they progress through their artmaking process. Student artists can choose to work alone or to collaborate, and all final works are completed with an artist statement.

The final step is sharing. This has included school installations, public art shows, gallery walks, and websites. Sharing their art in a public way and engaging with the viewers gives the student artists the opportunity to see the power of their art to make a difference. The art they create is personal, powerful, and meaningful. I am moved by their voices and I hope they deeply embrace that their art matters. We are on this journey together and I can only show up and do the work, every day. I have hope that my fellow artists will do the same as they bravely go out into the world.

REFERENCES

Grimes, W. (2104, September 7). Making art on the spot and on the fly. *The New York Times*. https://www.nytimes

.com/2014/09/08/arts/design/oliver-herring-at-a-task-party-at-madison-square-park.html?smid=url-share

Kaphar, T. (2017, April). *Can art amend history?* [Video]. TED Conferences. https://www.ted.com/talks/titus_kaphar_can_art_amend_history?language=en

Learning for Justice. (n.d.). Social justice standards: Unpacking identity. https://www.learningforjustice.org/professional-development/social-justice-standards-unpacking-identity

National SEED Project. (n.d.). *What is SEED?* https://nationalseedproject.org/about-us/about-seed

Nieto, S. (2003). *What keeps teachers going?* Teachers College Press.

Okun, T. (n.d.). *System of white supremacy and white privilege.* Racial Equity Tools. https://www.racialequitytools.org/resources/Fundamentals/Core-Concepts/System-of-White-Supremacy-and-White-Privilege

CHAPTER 22

Finding the Hidden Questions

Alice C. Pennisi

How do war, technology, and art influence one another?
How do Dix, Beckmann, and Kollwitz each represent different ways war impacts people?
Why and how were modern art and artists misrepresented and used as propaganda by the Nazis?

These were discussion questions asked by students in *AED315: Arts in Living*, a contextual art history course I teach at a public college in upstate New York. The course is designed chronologically and is essentially a history course taught through artworks. Together, the students and I examine how artworks have shaped the Western world's visions of war, empathy, and heroism. Our guide is a quotation attributed to James Baldwin that "the purpose of art is to lay bare the questions that have been hidden by answers" (as cited in Rankine, 2014, p. 115). The theme threads through the semester, prompting our questioning of how art and artists influence society and how society impacts both.

Analyzing and discussing artworks are essential to art education. It helps us to better understand art's importance to the world and to see art as a meaning-making endeavor steeped in ideas. It also is essential to the artmaking process, as artists of all ages find inspiration from the creations of others. Our class builds understandings by asking questions together and analyzing specific historical events as they are represented through numerous artworks and genres.

Our "textbook" consists of films pertaining to the time periods of the course's seven modules (late 1800s to the Civil Rights Movement), two for each module: one created in the period, and one recent film about that period. All are chosen for historical content and cultural significance. We analyze the films, along with readings, websites, visual art, documentary photographs, poetry, and music, all centered on issues of their time, and I weave the teaching of history through these resources.

The course is shaped by "structured uncertainty," allowing for inquiry. I structure conversations by providing a central theme for each module, and model forming critical thinking questions that encourage purposeful conversations. Throughout the course students also consider, "What does this work value?" The question can allow for focused and divergent answers, providing structure and openness to interpretations. The uncertainty is not knowing the shape of class discussions. We rely on questions, comments, and quotes students bring to every class. They come with short written responses to syllabus questions and their own well-crafted discussion questions and comments connected to class themes and resources (yes/no questions are not allowed, as they do not engender discussion). Students assigned to semester-long facilitation groups rotate initiating class discussions, starting with a Do Now question and Quote-of-the-Day. As I teach the historical context intertwined with artworks, we incorporate students' learning gained from homework assignments using their questions and comments.

The students' questions highlighted at the beginning of the chapter helped shape discussion during our World War I/Weimar Republic section. They helped our class understand how German Expressionist artists Dix, Beckman, and Kollwitz represented in different ways the bodily, psychological, and emotional impact of World War I and how its brutal technologies reshaped the world. Later, we discussed how these artists were persecuted for their political artworks, which were used as negative propaganda in the Hitler regime's demonization of what it called " Degenerate Art."

Not all questions can be asked in discussion. All of the questions are submitted at the end of class and assessed as part of students' participation grade, which includes the quality of their questions and their class interactions. I return submitted questions with comments and encouragement. For thoughtful questions not asked in class, I often write "Please read this aloud in our next class" or use them for class activities. Sometimes I ask students to analyze their group members' questions and then the students choose two to present for class discussion. Over time students understand which questions work best because they are most useful in generating meaningful discussion. Excellent student questions often become syllabus questions in later semesters.

As the syllabus states, participation grading focuses on how each student, verbally and in writing, "helps positively shape discussions by making us think." Students are rewarded by class members for thoughtful, imaginative contributions. We highly value those hidden questions that have been hidden by their answers (Baldwin quoted in Rankine, 2014) and challenge what we have been told to believe. Students become eager to write them, ask them, discuss them, and submit them. Often artworks themselves challenge unexamined answers and ask hidden questions. For example, after analyzing the novel *All Quiet on the Western Front* (Remarque, 1928) alongside its film adaptation (Milestone, 1930) and comparing opposing narratives in two World War I poems, John McCrae's "In Flanders Fields" and Wilfred Owen's "Dulce et Decorum Est" (Hollander, 1999), students determined what questions these works ask in terms of war truisms. Such activities help students become adept at asking in-depth questions and noticing which ones enable thought-provoking discussions. Rewarding such questions through assessment and feedback incentivizes and engages students. The dynamic tension between my structure and students' participation helps support their meaning-making and learning.

The structure is designed so that students know what to focus on while reading or watching resources assigned as homework, though they also can follow their curiosities and concerns. This helps them prepare to participate in class with less anxiety. Shy students read aloud their prepared questions or know theirs will be read. There is enough structure for students to feel supported in expressing themselves openly, while we take the time to develop an ease discussing war, poverty, fascism, racism, intolerance, violence, and more war, through the discussion of art and its contextual events and issues.

How *are* art, technology, and war interconnected? How *were* art and artists misrepresented and used as propaganda fodder by the Nazis? And, more recently, how can art represent what frightens some people into submission and silence and spurs others to protest? These are the kinds of questions we grapple with to connect art with society. Student-generated, inquiry-based/critical thinking questions can help students to connect information from the past to the present. The practice of finding hidden questions takes time and preparation, but including this routine as part of the course can strengthen student participation and uncover meaningful connections in history through art.

REFERENCES

Hollander, J. (Ed.) (1999). *War poems*. Alfred A. Knopf.

Milestone, L. (Director). (1930). *All quiet on the western front.* [Film]. Universal Pictures.

Rankine, C. (2014). *Citizen: An American lyric*. Graywolf Press.

Remarque, E. M. (1928). *All quiet on the western front*. Ballantine Books.

CHAPTER 23

Talking About Art

When Questions Are the Answer

Erica Richard

Educators at the Denver Art Museum (DAM) are reimagining how to implement student-centered dialogue in our student programming. We have learned that to create space for student voice, we must allow space for facilitators' growth in training as well. In this chapter, I address the following questions: How do you work with docents in a museum who are not current teachers or educated in contemporary art? What are their fears in facilitating student visits to the museum through dialogue? How do you address their hesitancies?

The DAM, like many museums, relies on an unpaid volunteer corps of docents to facilitate its school programs. The volunteers have varied backgrounds, from homemaker to social worker. As part of a new tour experience called "Supported Investigation for Grades 6–12," docents conduct an inquiry-based conversation utilizing supplementary resources that help students investigate the sociopolitical context surrounding a work of art. To create liberating art viewing experiences, DAM educators have embarked on a journey to help volunteer facilitators embrace productive ambiguity and recalibrate expectations to support more than a single correct answer.

The new program is rooted in developing students' analytical and reasoning skills while embracing student choice to foster personal connections. A training manual for facilitators and docents was developed for each object, including discussion questions, readings, and video resources representing multiple perspectives. We intentionally engage in complex conversations illuminating topics such as colonization, racism, mixed-race identities, globalization, appropriation, and oppression.

Our facilitator and docent training has evolved to mirror our approach with students. Acknowledgment of the cognitive struggles and individual voices of our facilitators is essential. It was important in each training to ground facilitators by reviewing what teachers were saying about their students' experiences at the museum. Teachers who visited the museum said, "My students felt heard when they were asked for their opinion and feedback" and "My students felt heard when they felt like their perspective mattered." We discussed how these comments could guide our conversations in the galleries. Through the training workshop, facilitators concluded that the activities are about letting students talk and not prioritizing their own knowledge. Docents recognized students and chaperones as equal participants in the conversations.

When facilitators were asked to share what felt most challenging about these conversations, they said, "How do we spark curiosity without overwhelming or causing harm by not having a chance to fully *unpack* a challenging topic?" "How do we address insensitive comments?" As a group we grappled with a few examples. By designing training to leave space for ambiguity, facilitators came to realize that scaffolding learning in a controlled manner requires listening to the students with empathy and then connecting them with a supplementary source that furthers their understanding.

At the end of our discussion, we touched upon the importance of leaving students with things to wonder about. For example, as facilitators of a student art learning experience, we don't need to give a history lesson about all of globalization, we just need to spark a curiosity using the specific stories the objects tell. At the end of a training a facilitator shared, "The museum is a great place to get things to wonder about!" Other docents nodded in agreement, signaling to me some progress toward reimagining the museum space for curiosity and student voice.

CHAPTER 24

Critical Conversations in Conservative Communities

Kelly Beach and Dianna Montano, with Connie Stewart

In our increasingly divided society, curricula and pedagogies in public schools have become the topic of political as well as academic debate. Some states have endeavored to limit what can be taught. State standards are evaluated through a politically liberal or conservative lens (Brudin, 2022). Many art teachers wonder whether they should address topics of race or gender in their classrooms because of the politically charged climate. To avoid potential issues with administration or parents and guardians, art teachers sometimes opt for lessons on forms and skills without personal or cultural meaning. At the same time, students are affected by current events and are bringing questions to their art teachers for a response (Strain, 2022).

Kelly Beach and Dianna Montano structure their classrooms to meet the needs of all their students. Both teach in Colorado districts where school board members won seats using highly conservative platforms (Meltzer, 2021). Kelly teaches middle school using the Teaching for Artistic Behavior (2021) approach. The space he structures for students allows them to see the art classroom as their studio. The critical conversations addressed in his classroom are ones the students themselves bring up. His role is to guide them in tools and techniques that allow them to explore their ideas and tell their stories.

One way he lets all his students know that the space is a safe environment for them is to display a large rainbow flag signifying LGBTQIA+ Pride. The symbol lets his students know their various identities and stories are welcome. He cultivates an inclusive community by the relationships that develop around artmaking. If a student wants help with a skill or technique, such as wheel throwing, he may suggest they work with a student who has developed the skill, intentionally pairing students who might be from different backgrounds. Friendships that might not otherwise be formed develop through making art together.

Dianna Montano teaches elementary art using a teacher-directed approach to encourage student agency and story in artmaking. She teaches in a Colorado district where the term Critical Race Theory (a legal study of the role of race in institutional policy) has been misused to discuss classroom practices, often resulting in fear and uncertainty for teachers. Dianna has for many years drawn upon her own family's Día de Los Muertos traditions to teach her students about Mexican American culture. After recent elections she feared that the lesson would be seen as expressing Critical Race Theory. She did not allow her concerns to stop her from organizing an important learning activity. She obtained administration support with parental involvement and now hosts a schoolwide Dia de Los Muertos celebration annually. Each student is encouraged to bring a photo of a family member who has passed on so that they can make art honoring them. Dianna did not stop offering an activity that was important to her and beneficial to her students because of current political discussions. Instead of provoking a backlash, as she feared, her celebration was featured in the district newsletter.

Both Kelly and Dianna teach from their own backgrounds and convictions. They are sensitive to differences in their communities and have obtained administrative support for their work. They create environments where critical conversations emerge from student artmaking. In 1934 John Dewey said, "Civilization is uncivil because human beings are divided into non-communicating sects, races, nations, classes and cliques" (Dewey, 1934, p. 336). Dianna and Kelly break down barriers by offering opportunities to make and share art. Shared artmaking experiences provide opportunities for social interaction and cooperation (Lawton, 2019). Teachers can create mutually supportive classroom communities, acknowledging their own and their students' multilayered identities, and showing students how to make art relevant to their lives. Kelly and Dianna are examples of how teachers within currently highly charged political environments can use the power of artmaking to help students combat the human tendency to divide ourselves.

REFERENCES

Brudin, J. (2022, June 9). State school board members grapple with new social studies standards as Colorado lawmakers say they're 'boldly thwarting' the law. *CPR News.* https://www.cpr.org/2022/06/09/state-school-board-members-grapple-with-new-social-studies-standards-as-colorado-lawmakers-say-theyre-boldly-thwarting-the-law/

Dewey, J. (1934). *Art as experience.* Berkley Publishing Group.

Lawton, P. H. (2019). At the crossroads of intersecting ideologies: Community-based art education, community engagement, and social practice art. *Studies in Art Education, 60*(3), 203–218. DOI-10.1080 00393541.2019.1639486.pdf

Meltzer, E. (2021, November 8). *Colorado's school board races reflected state's shifting political ground.* Chalkbeat Colorado. https://co.chalkbeat.org/2021/11/8/22771201/colorado-school-board-races-election-results-conservative-slate-teachers-union

Strain, D. (2022, August 2). As schools become political battlegrounds, one educator sees room for hope. *CU Boulder Today.* https://www.colorado.edu/today/2022/08/02/schools-become-political-battlegrounds-one-educator-sees-room-hope

Teaching for Artistic Behavior, Inc. (2021). https://teachingforartisticbehavior.org/

CHAPTER 25

Facilitating Dialogue About Loss and Grief in the Gallery

Harrison Orr and Carissa DiCindio

Museum educators can facilitate dialogue between program participants and works of art in a way that promotes vulnerability, reflection, and interpersonal connections. We are museum professionals at different points of our careers who have bonded over similar experiences of loss and grief. We share a desire to connect with museum visitors over this common experience through both viewing and making art, as well as through conversation. In this chapter we will reflect on an activity we facilitated in 2019, what we would have done differently, and tools for trauma-informed practice in museums.

Harrison facilitated the Fall 2019 season of Stay Gold, an intergenerational LGBTQIA+ arts program, at the Museum of Contemporary Art Tucson. He invited Carissa, an assistant professor at the University of Arizona, to cofacilitate a gallery activity with him on the first day of the 10-week program. On display was a body of work by Ali Silverstein titled *The Fantastical Reconstruction of the Epine GY7: Chapter 1: The Fragments*. Through the two-dimensional recreation of artifacts, Silverstein documented the aftermath of the 1948 shipwreck of the *Epine GY7*. The wreck occurred off the west coast of Iceland and, over time, the rusted debris of the wreckage washed ashore on a black pebbled beach. Silverstein presented her artifacts along with videos and redacted texts created during a period of immense grief after her boyfriend, Cole, passed away unexpectedly in 2009. In the year that followed his death, she traveled with his cremated remains to Iceland, among other places that held significance to both of them. She saw the remnants of the ship wreckage for herself and created art in the form of full-size rubbings of the artifacts. Silverstein worked in a variety of mediums to create a space in which visitors could interact with her representations of shapes and objects that hold memories of lives lost. Throughout the process, she saw herself as an archaeologist, unearthing artifacts connected to her grieving process as well as the shipwreck (Shook, 2019). She intertwined the two unrelated events through a sense of exploration driven by grief.

Through video, text, and objects, the exhibition encouraged visitors to explore an experience shared by all people at some point, creating a cathartic and thought-provoking environment. The loss of loved ones and the grief that comes afterward are commonplace in our lives. Grieving is a process that connects us all, but is rarely discussed, especially in education settings such as classrooms and museums (Rogers, 2020). Through themes of spirituality, time, and body, among others, artists have addressed the fleeting nature of life (Robertson & McDaniel, 2010). Contemporary art is uniquely positioned as a conduit of dialogue about grief; with access to art forms and technologies unavailable to their predecessors, contemporary artists are able to engage viewers with the same tools that are present in their daily lives. Silverstein's work captures the beauty of life and the transformative experience of grief through a combination of traditional and contemporary mediums.

To deepen museum visitors' engagement with the artwork, we designed a gallery activity that encouraged building connections and openings for vulnerability. Before this session, we asked Stay Gold participants to bring to class an object that held meaning for them. After viewing Silverstein's work, some participants volunteered to share the stories of their objects with the group. One participant brought an item her deceased mother had given her long ago. Another brought a watch that had been gifted to them. We then led participants in a meditative exercise in which they were to examine their objects not through sight, but through touch. We stressed the importance of the shape and texture of the objects to make a connection to the tactile nature of Silverstein's work. We then invited participants to create a small mixed-media piece inspired by their objects using tissue paper and drawing tools in the galleries. Upon completion, participants placed their artworks on the floor to share. We discussed similarities and differences between the pieces and found that the majority of participants chose to depict their objects through abstract shapes and colors. Although we invited participants to share the stories they connected to these objects, many participants were reserved and did not offer much about either their objects or their artwork.

Since this gallery activity, we have reflected on ways in which we could have provided participants with a more meaningful opportunity to explore vulnerability, death, grief, and identity through their own objects as well as those on display in the gallery. Since neither of us is a counselor or therapist, we were unsure how to go about incorporating these potentially sensitive topics into our discussion and activity, especially on the first day of the 10-week program. With over 2 years to reflect on the activity, coupled with new professional and personal experiences, we have considered ways in which we can better incorporate difficult conversations into our gallery practices.

Certain questions remained with us after this facilitation experience. How do we interact with objects and the memory of people that those objects hold? How can shared experiences of grief become a part of museum education? Robinson (2021) writes of the power of objects to spark strong emotional responses and how museums "can provide space to consider death and grieving" (p. 147). Incorporating opportunities in gallery teaching to share experiences and emotions related to loss and grief can open possibilities for how we engage with works of art and each other in the museum. This type of programming may create deeper connections between participants that builds a stronger sense of community. At the same time, participants need the space and flexibility to share and engage as much as they are comfortable.

We also considered our own comfort level in leading this type of activity, finding that more preparation in trauma-aware art museum education (T-AAME) would have given us tools to feel more confident in designing and implementing this type of programming (Armstrong et al., 2021). T-AAME practitioners distinguish between clinical art therapy in museum settings and incorporating trauma-aware practices into museum teaching. Museum educators not qualified in clinical practices can still use trauma-aware approaches to design programming that is welcoming, safe, and validates the experiences of participants (Armstrong et al., 2021, p. 457). T-AAME asks museum educators to be attentive to the needs of museum visitors who may carry their trauma with them in the gallery, utilizing a responsive format that values participants as human beings and is mindful of trauma. This framework offers openings for personal response, building connections, and multiple ways to engage with works of art. These practices take into account how gallery activities and dialogues focused on personal experiences and social justice issues can trigger trauma unbeknownst to the educator.

In this first session, we were concerned about the potential to instigate trauma or alienate new participants who might not be comfortable sharing such experiences. At the same time, our facilitated dialogue and activity remained on a surface level, without openings for willing participants to explore memories further. In hindsight, we see this as a missed opportunity. The activity would have been better suited for a later class, once participants had a chance to become acquainted with one another and the space. We could have worked our way up to our intended goal through writing prompts, artmaking, and dialogue that took place over weeks rather than minutes. Participants could have chosen the aspect of the installation they wanted to explore, with grief and loss as one of the options, and integrated this theme into their own art making.

In revisiting this activity, especially after the collective loss and shared experiences of COVID-19, we see the potential for a program that creates openings for exploration and human connection. By incorporating flexibility and more time into the structure of the program, participants could have examined multiple access points to this body of work and shared ideas and experiences with one another. We believe that this experimentation would have been a powerful way to connect to the artist's work and to dive further into how personal connections and experiences (including loss and grief) can be a critical component of an art museum program.

REFERENCES

Armstrong, J., Evans, L., Legari, S., Tulgan Ostheimer, R., Palamara, A., & Whiskers, E. (2021). Weaving trauma awareness into museum education. *Journal of Museum Education 46*(4), 454–466. DOI: 10.1080/10598650.2021.1981045

Robertson, J., & McDaniel, C. (2010). *Themes of contemporary art: Visual art after 1980* (2nd ed.). Oxford University Press.

Robinson, C. (2021). Museums and emotions. *Journal of Museum Education, 46*(2), 147–149.

Rogers, A. (2020). Death and grieving: Art history and emotional literacy in the classroom. *Art Education, 73*(2), 57–62. DOI: 10.1080/00043125.2019.1695483

Shook, D. (2019, November 15). No, you cannot have the whole truth: A conversation with Ali Silverstein. *Los Angeles Review of Books.* https://lareviewofbooks.org/article/no-you-cannot-have-the-whole-truth-a-conversation-with-ali-silverstein/

CHAPTER 26

How Superficial Themes in the Art Classroom Can Erase the Narrative of Marginalized Students and Communities

Ketal Patel

Dialogue and questioning are key in my work to engage in intentional learning with preservice teachers. This chapter reports on a narrative inquiry conducted with preservice art educators as we explored various approaches to meaning-making in the art classroom (Clandinin & Connelly, 2000; McNiff, 2007). I focus on the ways preservice positionality is explored and how dialogic work (Clandinin, 2020; Pushor & Clandinin, 2009) is employed. If education students fail to center the voices and lived experiences of their future preK–12 students, how will justice be done and erasure defied? The dialogues are composites of voices from preservice educators in their first experiences in the program at a large university in the Midwest.

I am inspired by the late bell hooks (1994) and her text, *Teaching to Transgress: Education as a Practice of Freedom.* hooks (1994) uses dialogue in her own writing to frame the thinking she has in response to the work of Paulo Freire, which "afforded me an intimacy—a familiarity" (hooks, 1994, p. 45). Similarly, the dialogues presented in this chapter reflect the "intimacy and familiarity" I experience as an art teacher who teaches future art teachers. This dialogic approach with narrative inquiry helps provide context and voice to frame the very human-centered and future-oriented work we engage in as art educators.

One of our students' first courses explores curriculum and pedagogy of visual art education. The course is founded on participatory dialogue and exploring how art educators engage in meaning-making with students. At the start of our semester, we discuss these ideas and students brainstorm central foci and relevant themes they hope to teach when they engage with their own future preK–12 students.

Through these initial dialogues, students express a desire to explore a variety of concepts in their role as future art educators. They begin with generic terms like *community* or try to focus their themes to a particular medium they are strong at. Every semester we have students who propose *trauma* as a theme they wish to interrogate with their future students. The preservice art teachers share well-intentioned voice and stories about how they were able to use art to address their own trauma and how they wish to create safe spaces for their future students to do so. The following dialogue is part of a conversation I had with a preservice teacher in the curriculum course and shows how I used questioning to help them move from the personal to think more broadly about the topic:

Preservice Student: I just want to teach students about trauma through art and artmaking.

Me: Why is this a theme you think your future students want to explore in art?

Preservice Student: I just remember my own art classes as a place in the school where I could express my emotions and deal with pain through art.

Me: How do we think about concepts like generational trauma? Or the trauma of marginalized and racialized groups in the United States or globally?

Preservice Student: I haven't thought about those issues when I think about trauma as a theme, I just remember my art classes in high school and how I felt. I haven't investigated what trauma might mean for a particular race or ethnicity.

Preservice teachers' personal experiences and interests are important starting points in curriculum development, but dialogue and questioning are necessary for future teachers to interrogate their curriculum development process.

I support my students through questioning and encourage them to reflectively and intentionally interrogate their initial concepts for the future art classrooms they will lead.

I designed an activity to help preservice teachers engage in a participatory dialogue exploring the themes they propose. I offered a series of questions to guide their reflections on the ideas, positionality, and processes we need to consider as designers of intentional learning. This process is designed to move away from stating superficial themes and toward more intentional thinking about whose ideas are valued in a visual art classroom and whose issues may instead be marginalized or erased.

The students begin by asking themselves and each other the following questions:

- What races, ethnicities, genders, sexual orientations, disabilities, and other identities are present or not present in this future classroom of preK–12 students?
- What is the relevance of the curriculum theme(s) you identified to the student profile you have identified?
- What information do you have or need about the students to engage with the theme you have proposed? And what are potential directions your future students could take to interpret the theme you proposed in the art classroom?
- Who and what are some of the artists, artworks, and visual culture examples connect with the theme you have identified?
- As the students engage in these dialogues, they are reflective of their own pre K–12 experiences, their field experiences, and the research and courses in the licensure program. Students respond with a range of answers to the previously stated questions:

Preservice Student 1: I never imagined my future classroom from the lens of my students, I always picture some of the schools and art rooms I experienced in high school. Thinking about the various identities in the art classroom is a very different way to imagine the future.

Preservice student 2: I always thought curriculum design should be about what I thought was important or the visual art standards. I haven't really thought about what my future students care about.

Me: What changes in your curriculum ideas when we imagine art and teaching art by centering the students and people we will work with, versus the mediums we want to teach or units we will create?

Preservice student 1: It makes me question whose values are centered in curriculum and themes? Is it my values as a future art teacher? Or is it the values of my future students in an elementary or high school?

Preservice student 2: I also think about the way I would need to build relationships and meet my future students to build ideas with them versus for them.

As preservice students begin dialoguing the questions, they begin to explore what may or may not exist in contemporary schooling. Students will often bring up their field experience sites and begin to ask questions about how or why they do or don't see various diverse identities in their sites. They begin to question if the theme they outlined is something they have assumed is valuable for students but that they themselves may need to further interrogate. Engagement in our 2 year licensure program involves work in multiple field sites with art educators and students from various schools. Seeing preK–12 visual arts classes in action moves their dialogues away from theoretical populations in schools to real sites that in some cases are very different from their own educational backgrounds.

For preservice students who said, "I just want to teach about art and trauma," the questions helped prompt generative dialogue about what trauma can mean to various groups. They encouraged the students to think about *why* they wanted to create a curriculum about a theme and question why it is relevant for the future students they will teach. Declaring connections between art and trauma cannot simply be a hopeful attempt to engage students in surface-level meaning-making, but must recognize that there are entire communities and marginalized groups whose trauma is never addressed or is even erased in historical and contemporary society. Questioning helps the preservice teachers to think beyond an artmaking activity to the implications of a topic. It also prompts preservice students to engage with each other about their positionality and address the idea that as humans we can admit "we don't know what we don't know." As educators, we can investigate what we don't know with deep inquiry about the concepts that we wish to explore with our students. We should ask ourselves the reflective questions: Is this a concept that supports or harms the students I teach or will teach? How do I center the humanity of my future students when I think about the art education I want to build?

How we move forward from those questions is the empowering act of designing future art education curriculum that centers students and their humanity in learning with and through art. As art educators and future art educators we have a duty to ensure we are not further marginalizing or disenfranchising our students through ill-informed or shallow attempts to explore a theme in art that may not resonate with the students we serve. Using critical questioning in our work can be a starting point to engage in deeper connections and meaning-making with our students and community.

REFERENCES

Clandinin, D. J. (2020). *Journeys in narrative inquiry: The selected works of D. Jean Clandinin*. Routledge.

Clandinin, D. J., & Connelly, F. M. (2000). *Narrative inquiry: Experience and story in qualitative research*. Jossey-Bass.

hooks, b. (1994). *Teaching to transgress: Education as the practice of freedom*. Routledge.

McNiff, J. (2007). My story is my living educational theory. In *Handbook of narrative inquiry: Mapping a methodology* (pp. 308–329). SAGE Publications. https://www.doi.org/10.4135/9781452226552

Pushor, D., & Clandinin, D. (2009). The interconnections between narrative inquiry and action research. In S. Noffke & B. Somekh (Eds.), *The SAGE handbook of educational action research* (pp. 290–300). SAGE Publications. https://www.doi.org/10.4135/9780857021021

CHAPTER 27

Problematizing Conversations

Creating Art to Engage in Difficult Discussions

William Estrada

Each of us are precious. We, together, must break every cycle that makes us forget this.

—adrienne maree brown, 2020, p. 77

Early on in my teaching career I realized the classroom could be a space where we could practice building the places I could only imagine learning in as a young person. Over the last two decades I have been a teaching artist at Telpochcalli Elementary in Chicago's Little Village neighborhood, a predominantly Mexican American community, where we are encouraged by the administration to create learning environments that celebrate students' culture and language. In my own teaching and artistic practice, I am dedicated to existing in spaces where we can celebrate each other's imperfect experiences and honor everything we are.

EXAMINING POWER IS IMPORTANT

Difficult conversations that examine our layered, complex histories as individuals and as a nation aren't always encouraged in school, creating a disservice to the students we teach. This has taught me, as Ayers (2017) suggests:

> Our work is explicit and intentional in its focus on changing both individuals and the collective conditions of our lives—classrooms, neighborhoods, cities, nation, and larger world. This requires us to include a serious critical examination of *power* as it relates to race, class, gender, sexual orientation, and disability. (p. 62)

Over many years, through both generative and harmful experiences with the students I work with, I realized that creating democratic learning environments is much harder than I had anticipated. We must actively work toward healing the harm we cause and unlearn harmful behaviors we learned growing up, so we aren't replicating problematic power structures in the classroom. We need to engage in exploring what healing can look like to reach a place that allows us to have difficult conversations.

INTENTIONALITY IS CRITICAL

When encouraged, students generate learning opportunities for educators and each other that expand our understanding of what learning looks like, who owns knowledge, and where learning can take place. By problematizing conversations, I was able to create art to engage in difficult conversations with teachers and students. The artworks include portraits of workers celebrating their invisible labor, tapestries inspired by the Arpillera movement in Chile (Agosin, 2008), illustrations of family traditions inspired by Carmen Lomas Garza, and puppet stories in the socially active tradition of the Bread and Puppet Theatre. Through this work in and with community members, I continue to learn how to engage in difficult conversations through collaborative artmaking.

EMBRACE BRAVE SPACES FOR LEARNING

Brave space is a concept I apply in my work. The definition that guides my practice is from Arao and Clemens (2013), who suggest, "Brave space is an asset to us in our work as social justice facilitators. It has helped us to better prepare participants to interact authentically with one another in challenging dialogues" (p. 149). We can practice engaging in brave spaces, moving out of our comfort zone and embracing difficult conversations that may challenge the way we think. But how to do so? As educators we must model how to be vulnerable, listen with compassion, practice apologizing when we cause harm, and be willing to learn from our students' experiences even when they may be different from ours. We must uplift their voices, stories, experiences, and understandings as ways to analyze and challenge the status quo. Brave spaces can help us focus on developing solutions that aren't reliant on power systems that cause harm to us or others.

THE POSSIBILITY OF THE ART CLASSROOM

The art classroom is the place where we can model how to imagine things we thought were impossible. As an educator, I know students witness a variety of things that aren't forgotten when they enter the classroom. Students are consistently teaching me; as brown (2017) states, "Another part of walking this path has been the practice of humility—enough humility to learn, to be taught, to have teachers" (p. 10). Young people create plenty of opportunities to engage in meaningful learning around difficult subject matter, but we don't always feel comfortable engaging, out of fear of saying the wrong thing or getting in trouble for discussing themes others may find problematic. These are missed opportunities. Art creates opportunities for students to build agency, educators to expand our learning, and both to practice democratic ways to solve problems that affect us all. When cultivated, classrooms have been spaces where difficult conversations take place and where we can address systemic structures that cause inequity.

MOVING FROM THE CLASSROOM TO THE STREETS

In 2014, I began to develop public art projects that moved the conversations I was having with mostly elementary-aged students in school onto the streets of the neighborhood. The intention was to create art with adults while engaging in difficult conversations around race, cultural access, power, representation, and their concerns for the neighborhood. I wanted to center public art projects that invite people who might not necessarily see themselves as artists. One example is the Chicago Neighborhood Family Portrait Project. This is a mobile photo studio engaging people in discussing what effect race, class, and gentrification have on their lives. Participating community members receive a free photograph and are encouraged to share what assets they feel are present in the community. The process of photographing individuals and discussing who represents their communities creates counternarratives to popular media representations of their communities.

The Mobile Street Art Cart is another project meant to function in the street; its design is inspired by ice cream and food vendor carts in Little Village. The project provides people with free art experiences rooted in grassroots organizing on the streets of their neighborhoods. Participants usually hand-screenprint, create buttons, design stickers, paint banners, or put together puppets (see Figure 27.1). I address issues relevant to the community, while the

Figure 27.1. ***Reflect Repeat*** **(hand-screen printed and individually colored poster created at Grabadolandia through the Mobile Street Art Cart Project). (Photograph: William Estrada)**

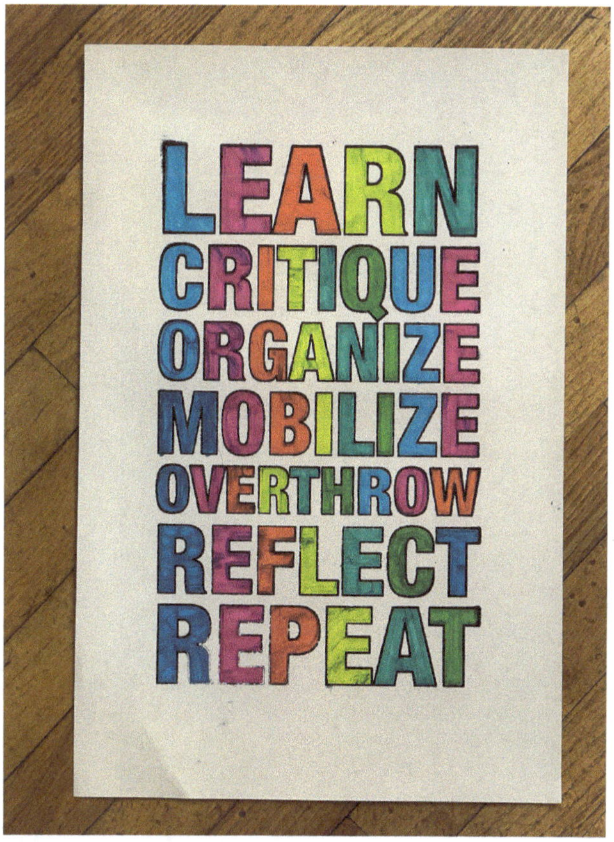

art cart creates a temporary space for difficult discussions that impact our communities, share resources, and build community. The intention is to amplify the creativity that already exists in communities through art-making in the streets.

PRACTICING AND CELEBRATING

Teaching young people in the classroom and adults in the community made it clear that we all need brave spaces to engage in difficult discussions. These conversations challenge all of us to examine our power, our privilege, and the fact that we have so much still to learn. Difficult conversations are part of building healthy democracies. Practicing in as many learning spaces as possible will allow us to begin healing and building spaces that honor the complexities of what makes up our collective story. We can't begin to build just futures if we refuse to engage in difficult discussions, and we can only do that through practice: consistently challenging what we teach; emphasizing complex stories that are often forgotten; inviting people to learn *with* us, instead of from us; creating spaces that celebrate you, me, and the difficult conversations we had to take part in to celebrate each other.

REFERENCES

Agosín, M. (2008). *Tapestries of hope, threads of love: The Arpillera movement in Chile*. Rowman & Littlefield.

Arao, B., & Clemens, K. (2013). From safe spaces to brave spaces: A new way to frame dialogue around diversity and social justice. In L. M. Landreman (Ed.), *The art of effective facilitation: Reflections from social justice educators* (pp. 135–150). Stylus Publishing.

Ayers, W. (2017). Our communities deserve justice! Social justice teaching and community building. In W. Ayers, K. Kumashiro, E. Meiners, T. Quinn, & D. Stovall (Eds.), *Teaching toward democracy: Educators as agents of change* (pp. 59–83). Routledge.

brown, a. m. (2017). *Emergent strategy: Shaping change, changing worlds*. AK Press.

brown, a. m. (2020). *We will not cancel us: And other dreams of transformative justice*. AK Press.

CHAPTER 28

Two Colleagues Talk About Care

Responding to the Emotional State of Our Students

Chris Cain and John Humphrey, with Connie Stewart

Art enables us to find ourselves and lose ourselves at the same time.

—Thomas Merton, 1955

Chris Cain and John Humphrey, two former colleagues at a Denver area high school, discussed care for the lives and emotional states of students within the school setting. Chris is a high school visual arts teacher and John is a middle school social and emotional learning specialist. Key points of their conversation together are summarized here.

ARTMAKING HAS A UNIQUE ROLE IN CARE

Art, through its cathartic nature, gives an opening for care that other subjects in the school may not. Art is a processing tool, a way to question things, and a way to connect to other content areas. A teacher can strategically pick assignments and projects that can encourage dialogue and help students make sense of the world. One example is how Chris Cain uses the work of artist and Disney contractor Jeff Hong (Diao, 2019), who starkly shows Disney characters facing today's real-world problems, or the work of Narsiso Martinez (n.d.), who paints beautifully rendered images of workers in the food industry on produce and Costco boxes. The work the students make in response opens discussions about their lives or social conditions they are concerned about. For a few students, Chris's assignments struck a more personal nerve, and they completed reflective works depicting experiences of anxiety, depression, and suicide. Chris works closely with the trained counselor in his school, who checked in on the students. Before this art assignment she was unaware of the concerns of some of these hurting students.

CARE NEEDS TO BE A SCHOOLWIDE PRIORITY WITH TRAINED COUNSELORS AVAILABLE

Art teachers can work closely with the mental health professional in their school, as Chris does. John points out that in a caring school environment, art teachers are not alone. Teachers, coaches, cafeteria workers, anyone who interacts with students can be the eyes and ears for the trained counselor. They can make the referral to the counselor, but it must be what John calls a "warm handoff," sensitive to the privacy and vulnerability of the student.

AUTONOMY AND HUMILITY

Chris expressed that what he wants most for his kids is autonomy. "I want them to do what they want to do, find the job they want, love the person they want, go where they want." He realizes that there are steps you need to take to achieve autonomy, and the challenges are not equal. John noted that as Chris endeavors to guide students, he shows awareness of his own privilege. Both Chris and John agreed that caring teachers can stop themselves from making comparisons between their own struggles and those of the students with whom they work. They can reserve judgment about their students' choices. John states, "Even if my experience is similar, it is not the same. Our realities are different. Art teachers have big hearts but as educators we need humility. We don't know what our kids are experiencing." They both agree that artmaking and art discussion can be the vehicle for life-sustaining interactions that make change possible.

REFERENCES

Diao, H. (2019). *This artist created unhappy endings to Disney movies, and the result will ruin your childhood.* Bored Panda. https://www.boredpanda.com/unhappily-ever-after-jeff-hong

Martinez, N. (n.d.). *Selected works.* Charlie James Gallery. https://www.cjamesgallery.com/artists/narsiso-martinez

Merton, T. (1955). *No man is an island.* Harcourt Brace.

Part III

INVITING REFLECTIVE STORIES

This section demonstrates the importance of personal narratives and the role of story in affecting change.

Chapter 40: Fifth Dimension Discourse: Afrofuturism and the Creation of Brave Spaces in Art Teaching

Kathy J. Brown and Lauren Cross

Portals for the reimagination of stories

Chapter 41: Start Where You Are

Toya Northington

Concluding thoughts to *Cultivating Critical Conversations in Art Education*; Personal story and social justice

CHAPTER 29

A Not-So-Queer Education

Eli Burke

As a queer/trans person, I never quite felt like I fit into traditional spaces, spending half of the time assessing who to trust and who to avoid. I wondered how my queerness might be received by my instructors. I began my early education with confidence, but by 2nd grade, I learned it would be easier if I could somehow make myself as invisible as possible. Despite that realization, I pushed back throughout much of my K–6 education, standing firm in who I knew myself to be. By the time I entered middle school, puberty hit and I began to retreat into myself and away from the world. School was not a welcoming place, nor was the classroom (Burke, 2019). I barely made it through high school and dropped out of my first year of college. My identity was always present. It took years of working on myself to get to the point where I could learn without the weight of my identity consuming most of my energy in learning environments and other institutional spaces. I still struggle with this. Something occurred during my first year in the PhD program at the University of Arizona, some 40 years since I first began my education, which would change me forever and give me a new perspective on not only how I choose to educate, but also on my relationship with and understanding of my own education.

STAY GOLD: A QUEER PROGRAM

This chapter outlines how the museum program Stay Gold has informed how I approach education, both as a learner and an educator. Stay Gold is an intergenerational LGBTQIA+ arts program that runs at the Museum of Contemporary Art Tucson. Stay Gold intentionally attends to the specific needs of a group of people whose identities are often considered controversial, or not considered at all, especially within classroom spaces. The program aims to intentionally engage and focus on LGBTQIA+ identities and experiences, and also to illustrate how controversy can be embodied. It also begs us to ask ourselves: To whom are we controversial?

When I began my PhD in 2017, I decided I did not want to be the queer student focusing on queer issues. I wanted to dive into the field of art education and see what might lie beyond the issues that affected the queer community and queer learners. I quickly discovered that I cannot separate myself from my research, and that issues around what it means to be queer in the classroom affect everyone, not only those who identify as LGBTQIA+. Every perspective has value in the classroom, even when we disagree.

In the first seminar of my first semester in the PhD program, Issues and Recent Research in Art and Visual Culture Education, Dr. Carissa DiCindio asked the class to create a program that somehow demonstrated a connection to Mapping Q, a program created by Curator of Community Engagement Chelsea Farrar at the University of Arizona Museum of Art (UAMA). Mapping Q invited queer youth into the UAMA to interrogate the museum space from a queer perspective.

Participants explored topics of artmaking, self-care, and harm reduction. During these virtual workshops we learned about LGBTQIA + artists and explore ideas like pride, radical self-care, loss, spirituality, and identity. We learned how to protest the lack of positive representations of queer, BIPOC, and disabled bodies in visual culture through art making (Farrar, 2020). I previously worked with Mapping Q in a collaboration between UAMA, the Tucson Museum of Art, and the Museum of Contemporary Art Tucson (MOCA), where I was then employed as the education director.

As my classmates and I began to brainstorm what type of workshops we might create, I recalled an experience I had working with a group of LGBTQIA+ seniors in the Latona Project, created by Becky Black and David Romero, two PhD students in Art and Visual Culture Education. This was a "collaborative community outreach project developed to examine the issues of changing LGBTQI senior identity within art museums" (Black & Romero, 2016, para. 1). I was invited as a teaching artist to facilitate the studio portion of the program. I had never worked with the 55+ LGBTQIA+ community before, and as I got to know the participants I became deeply affected by their stories.

The program invited LGBTQIA+ seniors into the UAMA to tour the galleries, ultimately ending in front of a 16th-century hope chest. Participants were invited to reflect on the meaning of the hope chest and how it intersected with their own lived experiences. Being unable, historically, to marry legally, LGBTQIA+ people were not afforded this rite of passage celebrated by most in the past. Ending our tour in front of this object opened a space for participants to share their feelings in relation to it. Sharing their stories connected to the concept of the hope chest allowed them to connect and empathize with one another on a much deeper level than before. Their experiences were not silenced or shunned, but welcomed, explored, and validated.

In attending to the unique experiences of this group through the UAMA collection, I recognized that there was a need for programs that provided opportunities for participants to speak their stories, be vulnerable, and connect through shared experiences. The Latona Project fostered meaningful connections within the group where growth, healing, and self-expression were emphasized. Museums and classrooms alike are meant to be spaces where ideas and knowledge can be shared openly and where the exchange of ideas and perspectives can be examined, challenged, and discovered. Art can be a powerful tool to create these spaces because it can be consumed and interpreted subjectively, allowing us to glean multiple meanings and connect despite our differences. It provides the opportunity to better understand and learn from one another.

Inspired by Mapping Q and the Latona Project, the class determined that a series of workshops for the intergenerational LGBTQIA+ community would be our focus. We decided to call the program Stay Gold, inspired by the Robert Frost poem, "Nothing Gold Can Stay," and the film *The Outsiders*. We immediately reached out to LGBTQIA+ community groups and began promoting. Within a short time we were able to enroll 16 participants ranging in ages 15–70. We focused on bookmaking and zines as an activity. All materials were provided, and the program was offered at no cost.

The energy in the classroom during this program was different from other classroom spaces I had been in. During the first Stay Gold meeting, I realized it was the first time I had been in a learning environment with only other queer people and allies. I no longer had to ask myself, "Would they accept and respect me if they knew the truth?" We could all learn and create without the weight of the heteronormative world pressing down on us. The first Stay Gold program was only a few sessions, but showed that people yearned for queer connection outside of their own generations (Burke & DiCindio, 2019).

As queer people, whether younger, older, or in between, many of us have experienced rejection and discrimination due to our status as LGBTQIA+. This can often come from our families of origin, and even within accepting families of origin we can still feel like outsiders simply because who we are does not fit into the heteronormative model that society imposes on us, and that many of our families subscribe to. For this reason, many queer people seek to create chosen families, where the way we live our lives can be reflected back to us through our shared experiences as queer people. Often these chosen families are within our own generations. Stay Gold, then, offered the possibility of creating chosen families across generations.

ACKNOWLEDGING CONTROVERSY

We all embody controversy on some level. When we refuse to acknowledge controversial topics in the classroom, we fail to recognize and value all of our students. Who are we teaching for? Everyone has unique needs as a learner and unique experiences in the world, yet we seem to only center certain needs and experiences in the classroom. Our personal stories have the power to cultivate empathy through vulnerability. Creating a *brave space* means creating a space where students can be vulnerable without the fear of being ridiculed or othered. Brave spaces have no center and no margin. There are ways to attend to the needs of our students, either overtly or through hidden curriculum, which allow for all to feel heard, valued, and validated. When we avoid certain topics, we send the message to students that who they are, and often where they come from, is not relevant, important, or powerful. Instead we began with creating the space to connect through who we are, where we have been, and what we have experienced. Our stories matter, every single one.

REFERENCES

Black, B., & Romero, D. (2016). *Latona Project*. University of Arizona Museum of Art. https://artmuseum.arizona.edu/events/event/latona-project-lgbtqi-senior-identity-art-museum

Burke, E. (2019). Turning the tide: Reframing how we acknowledge and support transgender and gender nonconforming learners in educational spaces. *Art Education, 72*(2),48–50. doi:10.1080/00043125.2019.1559667

Burke, E., & DiCindio, C. (2019). Staying Gold: How a group of university students created intergenerational connections through art museum programming and community collaboration. *International Journal of Lifelong Learning in Art Education, 2,* Article 7. https://scholarscompass.vcu.edu/ijllae/vol2/iss1/7

Farrar, C. (2020). *Mapping Q*. University of Arizona Museum of Art. https://artmuseum.arizona.edu/mapping-q

CHAPTER 30

Story as Pedagogy

Narrative Co-Inquiry With Teachers, Students, and Communities

Pamela Harris Lawton

My practice as an artist-educator-researcher relies on narratives—visual, written, oral, and performed—as a means of transforming teaching and learning, providing both teachers and learners with pathways to see themselves and their worlds in the art education curriculum. I believe that examining life experience is key to developing empathetic, reflexive educators, responsible and socially engaged citizens, and advocates for social justice ideals.

The narratives of life experience are central to how one learns and makes meaning, as I wrote in 2008:

> Through sharing life stories members of a group find common experiences that link them, creating a sense of belonging. Sharing narratives constitutes a form of social interaction, whereby we recognize ourselves in the stories of others, providing a transition from personal identity (I) to collective identity (We). (Lawton, 2008, p. 38)

Many qualitative research methodologies, such as narrative inquiry, life history research, portraiture, and arts-based research, rely on storytelling.

In this chapter I will reference specific teaching approaches from my practice and examine how I use the concept of *Artstories* to establish empathy, develop community, overcome adversity, celebrate diversity, and stimulate the desire to learn and unlearn through critical self-reflection. Much of my work with art teachers, both preservice and in-service, takes place in community settings working with learners across the lifespan in a nonhierarchical, intergenerational, and reciprocal teaching and learning relationship. Art is the medium of both making and learning, which we connect to a big idea common to the group. For example, during a large collaborative woodcut project, a few of the students and community members had experience with relief printmaking, but none had worked on a large woodcut. This provided opportunities to learn, improve, and apply new art skills through conversation while working together to envision the big idea of *freedom*.

BUILDING TRUST THROUGH CO-INQUIRY

Educators often ask me how I manage to get participants of varying ages and backgrounds to collaborate and build trust. My response is: Narrative co-inquiry—stories that are oral, visual, written, and performed. One of the first exercises I do with students and community members is an identity journey map. This simple one-page visual asks participants to reflect upon their "life journey" (Ferreira & Ferreira, 1997, p. 50) up to the current moment, and what led them to this space. It is not meant to be comprehensive, but a reflection on key moments connected to their interest in teaching and/or participating in a community-based art education experience. I ask participants to include only what they feel comfortable sharing. It always surprises me how deeply personal many of these stories are, and I greatly appreciate the participants' willingness to be vulnerable within a group of strangers. I also share my journey, as too often educators expect students to be open but are unwilling to share their own vulnerability.

As a follow-up to this exercise, and to expand upon participants' budding knowledge of and trust in one another, I give an altered book reflective journal assignment with a series of prompts. I encourage them to alter a book rather than use a sketchbook because often the stories presented in the book inspire innovative ways of visually reflecting upon personal and shared experience (see Figure 30.1). This also allays anxieties some feel when faced with a blank page.

Figure 30.1. Amy Keenan-Amago, altered book pages

If participants are open to it, I encourage them to respond to the reflections in one another's books, creating both intimate and communal conversations about the work we are doing together.

CLOSING REFLECTIONS

"Story is education in its most holistic form, a kind of education that honors the knowledge of [life experience and] previous generations" (Huber et al., 2013, p. 215). Through narrative inquiry we can find convergences and connections to others through our stories. Story as a form of pedagogy has tremendous potential for understanding, appreciating, and bridging diverse people and perspectives. "Imagining pedagogy through the transcendent power of story, we see how much difference, openness, and place matter" (Huber, et al, 2013, p. 216). For almost 20 years I have used storytelling as a teaching and learning tool in classrooms and communities with great success.

REFERENCES

Ferreira, E. C., & Ferreira, J. C. (1997). *Making sense of the media: A handbook of popular education techniques.* Monthly Review Press.

Huber, J., Caine, V., Huber, M., & Steeves, P. (2013). Narrative inquiry as pedagogy in education: The extraordinary potential of living, telling, retelling, and reliving stories of experience. *Review of Research in Education, 37*(1), 212–242.

Lawton, P. H. (2008). *Artstories: Narrative construction in intergenerational and transformative learning.* VDM Verlag.

CHAPTER 31

Generating LGBTQ+ Community Through Dialogue

Adam J. Greteman, Nic M. Weststrate, and Karen Morris

"We wonder if you could start by telling us about your interest in joining *The LGBTQ+ Intergenerational Dialogue Project.*" This is the question we ask every interested younger person as we recruit participants into the project. In reply, we have heard with few exceptions that a key reason young LGBTQ+ folks are interested is because they don't know any older LGBTQ+ individuals, a few even noting that they didn't really even know "old gay people existed." Russell and Bohan (2005) observed:

> In [LGBTQ+] communities/families, contact between youths and elders are not an intrinsic element of social systems, as is true in most biological families and in most other communities that face oppression by virtue of their members' identity (racial, ethnic, or religious communities). Rather, LGBT[Q+] interactions tend to be age segregated. (p. 2)

"Any contacts across generations," they continued, "must be arranged with the explicit intent of creating cross-generational interaction" (p. 2). The LGBTQ+ Intergenerational Dialogue Project takes up this explicit need by creating space and time for such intergenerational contact through dialogue.

Bringing together LGBTQ+ folks across generations is not simple; there are few models available that engage in creating sustained, longer-term possibilities for such contact (see Burke et al., 2021, for an exception). We ourselves recognized this challenge in founding the project. We suspected then that it would take years to find and create the conditions that would allow the creation of a community rooted within the diverse realities that make up LGBTQ+ communities. Community could not be assumed just because everyone identified as LGBTQ+. As Fendler (2006) argued, "Assumptions about community are dangerous when they function to perpetuate existing inequities and censor possibilities for differences" (p. 306). Put differently, while the acronym *LGBTQ+* appears inclusive and "queer" is used as an umbrella term, differences reveal themselves within and between the letters. The tensions within LGBTQ+ communities due to gender, race, disability, class, age, and other intersecting differences require careful and complex dialogue to unpack deeper, more complicated histories and generate intergenerational community.

We, a gay educational philosopher, a gay developmental psychologist, and a lesbian anthropologist, cofounded the LGBTQ+ Intergenerational Dialogue Project with a large LGBTQ+ community center in the Midwest in the fall of 2019. Since then, the project has brought together racially, socioeconomically, spiritually, and gender diverse cohorts of LGBTQ+ younger (18–26 years old) and older (60–82 years old) adults for dialogues, storytelling, collaborative artmaking, and shared meals. The community-led research project was designed to respond to the needs of two vulnerable populations—LGBTQ+ college students and LGBTQ+ older adults—for intergenerational connection that could help participants to see one another as knowledgeable subjects, cultivate knowledge of LGBTQ+ cultures, and generate community through dialogue and artmaking. The project is built on an understanding that participants will be present for one academic year and are welcome to continue in different forms as the project expands to create alumni opportunities.

In this chapter we offer insights on the role of dialogue across LGBTQ+ generations. We look at three moments where different forms of dialogue emerged. These include a moment of dialogue as conversation, dialogue as debate, and a failed dialogue. Each is offered to show the possibilities and pitfalls of dialogue within the context of this community-led, collaborative art project.

GENERATING COMMUNITY THROUGH DIALOGUE

Dialogue, while often a keyword within education, is more an exception than a rule. Schools and universities in the 2020s are under various forms of pressure that are at odds with dialogue. This includes concerns about "cancel culture" that contribute to self-censorship from both students and teachers, legislation banning the teaching of "controversial topics," and the continued banning of particular books, to name a few. A key educational problem is "finding ways to involve schools in creating and maintaining conditions in which inclusive, democratic, and open-ended dialogue can thrive" (Burbules, 1993, p. 151). Such work cannot merely rely on rhetorical flourishes that praise the work of dialogue, but rather requires attention to the everyday, rather ordinary experiences of being in relationship with others in dynamic educational spaces. Schools and university classes are often age-segregated, with the teacher being the sole individual from a different generation; our project challenges this age segregation by bringing together school and community for a sustained educational experience involving individuals across generations.

Conversation as Dialogue

The need for and possibilities of such sustained dialogues have been evidenced time and again through this project, despite its challenges. The need for such dialogue is often captured in and through conversation. For instance, when Emerald, a 22-year-old nonbinary artist, expressed:

> Through our conversations I feel like my own perspective on my queer identity has evolved a lot . . . 'cause at the very beginning I was very clear . . . like, my name cannot be associated with this project. I was so scared of being somehow outed through this. Now I'm like, if I was outed through this freaking awesome research study, I'd be so proud. . . . Because this is so important.

A month earlier, Danie, a 69-year-old transgender woman, told a reporter for a local LGBTQ+ newspaper how through the project she had learned that she is still a relevant force and source of knowledge for youth:

> The young people [in the project], right from the very start, have left no doubt that I, as well as the other elders, have something of value that they want. It is wonderful to be sought after and welcomed by youth members. These beautiful young people want to hear from us. They are desperate for it.

Each of these comments draws upon the work of dialogue as conversation. Dialogue, as we have come to understand it, is not a monolithic thing, but rather takes different forms. One of these forms has been conversation. Central to conversation as dialogue are, as Burbules (1993) argues, two characteristics, "a generally cooperative, tolerant spirit, and a direction toward mutual understanding" (p. 112). Understanding becomes central to this form of dialogue, as participants gain insight into a range of lived experiences that are part of the emerging community. As we see with Emerald and Danie, conversations across generations prompt further understanding of one's own self as well as others.

Debate as Dialogue

Emerald's and Danie's comments came during reflection and may not account for conflicts and tensions that are part of dialogue. While we seek to gain understanding with and of one another in conversation, understanding does not always come. Nor is dialogue always and only about understanding the other. There are other lessons to learn from one another through dialogue, including the opportunity to debate different perspectives about issues related to LGBTQ+ politics—including, for instance, the use of the word "queer." While our younger participants are by and large comfortable with and often use "queer" as an identity, elder participants are often more hesitant toward the use of *queer*.

In one of the first meetings of the project an elder, cisgender gay White man, almost immediately expressed his dismay at the word *queer*, narrating his experiences coming of age in 1960s New York City and the danger of being called "queer." Quickly upon his contribution, an impromptu debate took place where different sides were taken about and around the use of "queer." A young participant talked about the importance of *queer* to their sense of self coming of age in the 2010s, and how not being able to use the word queer would be impossible to imagine. This debate as it unfolded was not about winning, but rather about unpacking the different sides that people in the room had around a rather contested and complex term. Dialogue as debate, as Burbules (1993) argued, "does not have any necessary aim toward agreement or the reconciliation of differences" (p. 119). As that debate came to a close, the participants, including the authors, recognized that the different positions and needs of participants could not necessarily be reconciled, but could become part of the larger dialogues. This debate, as well, prompted renaming the project, which was originally called the Queer Intergenerational Dialogue Project. Through debate, the need to be mindful of terms and their historical, material, and educational impact was made manifest on the ground.

Failed Dialogue

While our above examples show debate and conversation as dialogue "at their best," we do not want to romanticize dialogue or argue that dialogue is easy or always leads to such positive experiences. Generating community involves, inevitably, failure and exclusion. The everyday realities and histories of trauma of our and our participants' lives come into play and illustrate the difficulty and effectiveness of dialogue in whatever form it takes. How do we generate community with members of a broad community that has encountered multiple forms of oppression and trauma, without those realities being reproduced?

We have learned we need to acknowledge each year the complications of coming together as an intergenerational group of people who bring with us our histories within LGBTQ+ communities. Recognizing these difficult realities is vital, so that the dialogues do not reproduce histories of exclusion. In the 3rd year of the project, while we were working to create community guidelines for dialogue, an argument erupted between elders that rendered many of the younger participants silent. This argument started when an elder cisgender White lesbian commented that she was tired of hearing "White gay men" talk, triggering for her a history of White cisgender gay men dominating conversations. Given that this was the first conversation and we had just met everyone, this comment hit some nerves (for better and for worse). A transgender woman of color followed up by saying a similar claim could be made about cisgender White lesbians. With those two statements, a heated argument ensued between elders that brought to the surface both past histories and present realities about privilege, access, and more.

This argument persisted for approximately 15 minutes before the facilitators stepped in because of time. In stepping in, we reminded ourselves and participants that such an argument is inevitably part of our work in taking seriously the radical potential of sustained LGBTQ+ intergenerational contact. A sustained dialogue project would allow us to unpack these challenging moments and the histories they implicate—if we were able to parlay the argument into a dialogue. In the days following, we, the authors, had numerous emails and calls with the main elders who were arguing, as well as with several elders who were unsure the space was right for them. This, we felt, was necessary reparative work, particularly at the beginning stage of getting to know one another. However, a certain amount of damage was already done. This was, for us, a key moment of failure; but as Burbules (1993) reminds us, "Exploring the possibilities of dialogue also makes us become aware of *limits*" (p. 146). In this moment that would return in various ways throughout the 3rd year, we learned about the limits of our own facilitation skills, and also the need to balance the needs of the group with the needs of individual participants.

For instance, two of the argumentative elders would, due to their continued negativity, be asked to leave the project, which showed us not just the limits of dialogue, but also the limits of community. Drawing on Fendler (2006),

> It is dangerous to celebrate and promote community building as if it were unproblematic. Instead it would behoove researchers to keep constant vigil and continually challenge the ways community constructs inclusions and exclusions simultaneously. (p. 315)

Generating community with and through dialogue is not, we have learned, for the faint of heart, because of this need for vigilance and for recognition that inclusion is always in question. Dialogue comes in many forms—debate and conversation, to name two—but veers off track when argument enters the fray and people talk over one another. Yet, at the same time, generating community through dialogue, including respecting the inevitability of argument, opens up possibilities and forms of understanding that are sorely needed across and within LGBTQ+ generations.

CONCLUDING THOUGHTS: "I DON'T KNOW ANY OLD GAY PEOPLE"

We started this chapter with our opening question. Responses to that question taught us that many young people have had little to no contact with LGBTQ+ elders. We were first struck by these responses. Yet once this initial shock wore off and a conversation ensued, a realization occurred that the young folks were gesturing—whether they realized it or not—toward long-standing problems impacting LGBTQ+ life. This includes a reality that LGBTQ+ cultures are often (problematically) youth-focused, causing elders to become invisible and excluded from the ever-changing landscape of LGBTQ+ life and media portrayals. Second, in the aftermath of the AIDS epidemic, a large population of LGBTQ+ folks were lost due to governmental, scientific, educational, and social neglect. Yet this genocidal loss is largely devoid in the general public's imaginary, much less in school curriculum. Third, schools, a key site of intergenerational contact, have historically regulated the presence of LGBTQ+ teachers, making it uncommon for most youth to grow up having had a LGBTQ+ teacher, or even professor (Jennings 2015). A central challenge of these legacies, captured in the young participants' responses about not knowing "old gay people," is at its foundation institutional. How do we, LGBTQ+ people, have contact with other generations when institutions have at best only regulated such contact, but at worst contributed to the exclusion and death of LGBTQ+ people?

The denial of contact across generations is not unique to our current moment. Generation after generation of LGBTQ+ people have been and continue to be denied access to LGBTQ+ histories and knowledges, a reality confirmed in 2022 with Florida's passage of the so-called "Don't Say Gay" bill. With the LGBTQ+ Intergenerational Dialogue Project we are developing ways for generating intergenerational LGBTQ+ communities that recognize and share their knowledges and experiences. Generating such intentional community requires staying with the challenges that emerge as generations meet for sustained dialogues. As we explored here, such dialogues can take many forms, including conversation and debate, which themselves can create conflict and moments of failure. Yet each is essential to this process. Such dialogues, to be sure, do not create a monolithic understanding of LGBTQ+ lives that eliminates differences. "There is no reason to assume," as Burbules (1993) contends, "that dialogue across differences involves either the eliminating of those differences or imposing one individual's or group's views on others" (p. 114). Rather, sustained dialogues allow for differences to be named and seen for what they contribute to the rich tapestry of LGBTQ+ life that is never one thing, but a multitude of possibilities.

REFERENCES

Burbules, N. (1993). *Dialogue in teaching: Theory and practice.* Teachers College Press.

Burke, E., Orr, H., & DiCindio, C. (2021). Stay Gold: An intergenerational LGBTQIA+ arts program. In B. Bobick & C. DiCindio (Eds.), *Engaging communities through civic engagement in art museum education* (pp. 269–289). IGI Global.

Fendler, L. (2006). Others and the problem of community. *Curriculum Inquiry, 36*(3), 303–326.

Jennings, K. (Ed.). (2015). *One in ten in the new millennium: LGBT educators speak out about what's gotten better . . . and what hasn't.* Beacon Press.

Russell, G. M., & Bohan, J. S. (2005). The gay generation gap: Communicating across the LGBT generational divide. *Angles: The Policy Journal of The Institute for Gay and Lesbian Strategic Studies, 8*(1), 1–8.

CHAPTER 32

Power Play in the Art Critique

Kerry Downey and Aparna Sarkar

This article considers how power relations underlie art discussions, focusing on the different but interlocking experiences of student and teacher in the critique space. For the student, vulnerability often arises from the mix of sharing intensely personal experiences through their art while harboring anxieties. Am I *good enough*, how can I be *better*, or will I be misunderstood? Meanwhile, teachers can feel pressure to make good use of their own knowledge and experience to *produce* a "successful artist."

Kerry and Aparna met in 2019, when Kerry taught Aparna's graduate-level critique class in painting. Aparna is a 30-year-old, Indian American, queer, first-generation painter teacher living in Brooklyn, New York. Kerry is a 40-something, white, genderqueer artist based in Kingston, New York. Both have been art students and teachers in varying contexts and institutions. What follows is a reflection on an ongoing dialogue sharing their experiences of critique, guided by the question: How can teachers and students work together toward a more mutual dialogue that pushes against relationships of power and knowledge production as defined by historically white institutions?

> *Aparna:* In one of our first studio visits, I asked you to tell me what was "working" about my paintings and what was not—and immediately felt embarrassed. You started the visit asking what kind of feedback I wanted; I was destabilized by that question and my answer was wrapped up in professorial and grad school expectations. At the time, I was comforted by a hierarchy in which the teacher sees farther along the ideal path of my work and tells me what to do next in their "expert," art-historical and formal framework. I was also anxious to receive reassurance of my artistic worth. The kind of feedback that I sought prioritizes a professor's ability to make fast judgments, pass along advice, and champion a particular approach to meaning-making. The actual reading of the work, what the viewer experiences and what meaning they make of it, gets sidelined. And this model gets reproduced as we become teachers with our students and peers in other artists' studios.

In that studio visit, we ended up discussing: What are my goals in making work, and what can critique offer? I began to think of the potential function of the critique as a place to reflect back to the artist what their work is doing, unlocking possibilities for where they can go next.

Then, when I visited your studio after grad school, you asked me to respond "yes" or "no" to each of your prints based on a gut feeling. It was a blast; our common vocabulary and values, the inversion of the professor–student power dynamic, and being physically outside of the institution allowed *this* mode of quick response to be a shorthand for intuition in its relationship to taste. Friends give each other visceral feedback all the time—responding Yes, No, Yes is a kind of love language. It's an embodied response to work, requiring the viewer to be attuned to their mental/physical presence and to be vulnerable without self-editing.

> *Kerry:* Totally. Art school can overly institutionalize these kinds of exchanges, effectively shutting down our intuition instead of building trust in it. It's so much fun to be in artist studios, and then when we get into "group crits," it can feel so intense. There is an artistry to both; in one-on-one visits, I know I can sometimes come on strong, beginning with a barrage of questions. In looking at your work, I was

excited to learn about your intentions, to gain more context.

Yet as a "professor," and particularly in critiques, I often feel the pressure to perform my knowledge, to have all the answers. As part of my own inculturation into white supremacy culture (Okun, 2022), there have been many times I've played the expert, offered advice on how their work could "improve" instead of sharing my experience or what was coming up for me in the work. My own survival as a queer, nonbinary artist and teacher has required that I learn to talk the fancy art talk, to act like a know-it-all. It's all a bit performative.

I want dialogues in art to be driven by curiosity and openness, where we are inside a sacred and unruly experience that exceeds many rational or preexisting notions of what it means for a work to improve. I want language to be psychedelic. But then it can feel disorienting to mess with the improvement model, or taboo to be playful with this game that pretends to have rules but is constantly shifting. It can feel dangerous if I refuse to play into the paternalism of teacher-knows-best or the consumer model wherein the student says, "What am I paying for if you don't have the *answer*?!" But, to me, this is the point of teaching art—to engage in the limits of sense, to make meaning *together*.

Aparna: Right, that space of play—of openness and curiosity—is addicting, and something I aspire to find in all conversations. Of course, there are many reasons not every student in a critique or discussion can speak from that place. The educational institution has a power structure, so some voices are valued over others. As a woman of color in primarily white institutions, I have seen, heard, and felt how whiteness obstructs vulnerability in critiques. I have friends and students of color whose work was met with silence from their White peers and professors (Sherrid, 2016). When I was a peer or teaching assistant in such critiques, I rushed to fill the void—but then my own ability to engage with the work was partially distracted by this aim. When I was the only non-White person in class critiques, I felt a bodily shift toward hypervigilance; I became more aware of my movements, words, volume—sometimes eager to detach what I said from how I was feeling, to literally close myself off from physical experience in the space and therefore the work.

I have been a student and teacher in primarily white institutions as they began bringing in more of us BIPOC students and faculty. I notice heightened conflict in the growing pains of these institutional shifts. Faculty butt heads over denial of systemic issues and the existence of one right way to run the institution or department; students grapple with privilege and discrimination as BIPOC numbers grow, but slowly. This stuff also leaks into the atmosphere of group critiques, making it harder for everyone to locate the patience and focus needed to be present in the critique. So if you ask me how to create those spaces of curiosity and openness, I'll say that it's not always possible—sometimes, more change and more time are needed.

Kerry: Wow, yes to all of this! I'm really hearing your experience of hypervigilance, and how much is felt on a bodily level and what a pressure cooker these experiences can be for students of color inside institutions coming to terms with our racism. As a white professor, I have felt on eggshells and feared causing harm. When I experience the limits of my own knowledge, particularly as a white person working with students of color, I notice anxiety and heat rising in my body. Then I notice the strong desire to overcompensate for this, to then overperform my authority. It is a dangerous and frustrating pattern. Menakem talks about the lifelong somatic work of unlearning white-body supremacy (Menakem, 2017). This means finding ways to cope with the deep discomfort in my body, pause, take breaths. In urgency culture, whiteness seeks quick fixes and Band-aids so that we can move on, so that we can go back to being "productive" and "effective."

What you're saying about whiteness obstructing vulnerability is really profound to me. It is hard for us white teachers to stay inside of the uncertainty, and it's common to project our insecurities onto students of color rather than lose control or lose power. On the flip side, if I move into fragility, I will take up all the space in the room. So I'm always reflecting on what is my own work in this, separate from students, what is coming up in a group or with a particular work. With art, it is a given that there is a lot of powerful psychological stuff being passed between us.

I wonder what's been most supportive in discussions of your work?

> *Aparna:* The most helpful art conversations always have a quality of slowness; the dialogue isn't rushed, there's no to-do list. Professors and peers pause to let in and reflect on their experience of the work, translating into language how they feel and why.

Some of the best group critiques are ones in which the professor/facilitator observes aloud the relational dynamics playing out in the room, including who is talking more or less, how people are physically spaced, and what kinds of observations are being made about the work. I also appreciate discussions of critique goals and expectations as a precursor to the actual critique. There are many exciting formats that structurally destabilize the critique; still, a conversation of why we make things and what we want from the experience of sharing the work feels most important as a baseline. It's also something we sometimes take for granted within an institution, assuming common ground that's not there. Such a conversation encourages artists to think about their value systems and what critique can offer when it doesn't default to white supremacy culture: How does artwork impact and change us? Asking these questions is hard, and at its best, rigorous and specific.

> *Kerry:* I love what you're saying. And I know there are so many models and resources out there—guides to facilitation, critique models, radical vocabularies that move beyond pure formalism, and exercises that engage more of our senses, more of the experiential encounter with art. Art teachers, especially white folks, can do more of this kind of destabilizing work, or decolonizing. I've tried, with some success, to invite students to reflect on goals in advance of receiving feedback or to play around with format. It's a lot more work than just free-form riffing.

Sometimes, when trying to dismantle hierarchy, or decenter whiteness, I've only reinforced it. As a white teacher earnestly contending with racism, the stakes feel and are high, and mistakes can feel unbearable. I have to notice what I'm doing, reflect, and communicate back even when I'm feeling the most disjointed—and inevitably it gets messy. Sometimes my queer shame gets activated, which actually helps me connect back to my work as an artist; I'm reminded that all this is a *practice*. Art hones our perceptions and our intuitions in a world that wants to relentlessly reduce us to nameable and consumable outcomes.

The perfectionistic progress narratives that we have applied to art we have also applied to ourselves. For many of us queer artists, it's a part of what we do, to crack open the possibilities—to be committed to the work, to be accountable to the community and to be inside of grace and humor and experimentation.

> *Aparna:* Yes! Queerness invites us to experience these parts of ourselves on a physical level, producing forms of embodied knowledge that do an important kind of resistance work (Ahmed, 2006). Queerness bridged a gap between your whiteness and my POC experience; it was central to most of our conversations. I had studio visits with a few South Asian artists who read my work first from that shared cultural identity. Within institutions, I've felt limited by conversations about identity, but I've also felt it as an entry point that establishes trust and mutuality.

REFERENCES

Ahmed, S. (2006). *Queer phenomenology: Orientations, objects, others*. Duke University Press.

Menakem, R. (2017). *My grandmother's hands: Racialized trauma and the pathway to mending our hearts and bodies*. Central Recovery Press.

Okun, T. (2022). *What is white supremacy culture?* https://www.whitesupremacyculture.info/what-is-it.html

Okum, T. (2022). *White supremacy culture characteristics* https://www.whitesupremacyculture.info/characteristics.html

Sherrid, E. (2016). *The room of silence* [Video]. Vimeo. https://vimeo.com/161259012

CHAPTER 33

Negotiating White Privilege in a Visual Culture Intervention

Lisa Novak and Breckon Chastain

Reflecting on an interventionist art project for a visual culture and diversity art education course at a university in the Southeast, this chapter is cowritten by a student (Breckon Chastain) and her instructor (Lisa Novak), showing their perspectives on a term project intended to slyly guide local residents into learning about the interrelations between student facilities and the displacement of communities of color. Initially conceptualized by one of the art education faculty, the *Art and Society: Visual Culture, Diversity, and Pedagogy* course critically explores the role of visual culture studies in schools, museums, and communities, and examines the practices of contemporary artists of color who work with and through visual culture toward social justice.

Lisa: Teaching this course remotely for the first time during the height of COVID-19, I adapted some of its initial content, adding lessons on Indigenous artists including Kent Monkman and Wendy Red Star, sharing texts by Judith Butler and Jack Halberstam, discussing the history of art education at boarding schools, introducing the counternarrative work of artist Alexandra Bell, and asking students to watch documentaries including *Disclosure: Trans Lives on Screen* (Feder, 2020) and *United in Anger: A History of Act Up* (Hubbard, 2012). In a predominantly White and middle-class environment where many students admitted that they had not confronted and challenged dominant discourses before attending university, I felt it was necessary to acknowledge the importance of facing our past and confronting our present head-on in a historically accurate and nonromanticized fashion. However, I made it clear that throughout the term, we were in processes of (un)learning *together,* and that it was OK for students to not yet *know* how to speak of or address the ways in which white supremacy and heteronormativity shape everyday life and visual culture.

As a White person from Europe who had only recently moved to the United States, I found the course an opportunity to learn from my students, who through personal stories and research for course projects taught me about life in my new home. This was particularly true for the project Breckon developed with her peers, which brought to light the community displacement that had taken place to make way for student housing in our college town, where "slaves were instrumental in clearing land and building campus infrastructure" (Inwood & Martin, 2008, p. 389). Although the concepts of race and class "loom over contemporary social relations and understandings" throughout the racialized and privileged landscapes of this university (Inwood & Martin, 2008, p. 375), the project provided an alternative history of our campus and community, prompting conversations beyond our classroom.

A STUDENT NEGOTIATES HER WHITE PRIVILEGE

Breckon: In my junior year at a university in the Southeastern United States, I signed up for an art education course titled *Art and Society: Visual Culture, Diversity, and Pedagogy.*

As a graphic design major, I was excited to analyze contemporary art practices, and to participate in critical discussion on topics that are not always highlighted in the usual graphic design coursework. The course projects were in-depth and engaging, with intensive discussions about topics including the forced assimilation and exploitation of Indigenous people, local houselessness, and LGBTQIA+ visibility in art. For our final assignment we were tasked to create a visual culture intervention project that was concerned with one of the topics of the course, and which required some form of public interaction. Not much of an extrovert, I became nervous at the inevitability of "public interaction" and what that could entail, and in the end my group and I decided to develop a project highlighting how the construction of student housing has contributed to the displacement of communities of color in this Southern college town. Through a lengthy process of research, conversations with local experts, and surveys, we discovered the extent to which white supremacy motivated mass displacements in the area. Drawing on the concept of guerilla activism (Abujbara et al., 2017; Boyd & Mitchell, 2012), I used my design knowledge to create a series of three "advertisements"—including one promising free pizza. Each flyer included a QR code which led to a brightly colored webpage confronting the viewer with information about three different sites of community displacement. Once finalized, our plan was to post the flyers on the buildings that had replaced bustling and thriving communities, hoping to lure occupants into scanning the QR code. However, knowing that I had to tack the flyers up in person made me anxious.

Fearing punishment from the university or local authorities, I researched the legality of posting flyers on private property. I grew up in a small, conservative town where progressive acts of activism are not socially sanctioned and, sometimes, can cost you your job. I was terrified of the repercussions my group members and I could face for hanging up our flyers without approval. I emailed my professor in a panic; she calmed me and reminded me of something I failed to consider: As a White woman, I faced minimal risk of being perceived to engage in some sort of criminal activity. The most I would probably get was a slap on the wrist. But years of being taught to follow rules, to be obedient, made it difficult to accept this reality. I was so scared of what my family, who largely oppose movements like Black Lives Matter and critical race theory (Bell, 1980; Crenshaw, 1988; Crenshaw et al., 1995; Delgado & Stefancic, 2012; Harris, 1993; Kraehe et al., 2018; Ladson-Billings & Tate, 1995; Lawrence, 1987; Lynn & Dixson, 2013; Valdes et al., 2002) might think of me addressing white supremacy at my Southern liberal arts college. After Lisa walked me through the possible consequences, she still insisted that it was my choice whether to implement the intervention or not. We went through with it, posting flyers all over the three buildings that had the largest cases of displacement, hoping to bring awareness to the practices of a university we all attend.

I was able to confront my fears and accept how my whiteness protected me from severe consequences. But what if a student of color were asked to engage in an assignment that required this level of public activism? My white privilege allows me to absorb consequences and participate in civil disobedience without the threat of real punishment. Through this project I learned how to investigate local histories, instigate acts of social activism, speak intelligently about current issues, and, most importantly, I realized how my positionality as a white woman from the South impacts my ability to participate in civil disobedience in more than one way.

AN ONGOING PROCESS OF (UN)LEARNING

Lisa: Breckon's reluctance to be disobedient or break the law for the sake of a course assignment was justified, but as a form of activism and memory work, this educational project opened important conversations about how whiteness functions like a protective shield, providing unearned advantages and special provision in daily life (McIntosh, 1988). While the intention of Breckon's project was to provide the student population with often untold local stories of oppression and the QR codes were scanned more than two dozen times, the greatest value was found in the resulting interpersonal reflections. The discussions that followed led to some of the most fruitful moments of collective (un)learning of the term, reiterated the importance of considering the subjectivities of everyone in the room, and reminded us to leave space for students to resist components of, or whole, assignments. After all, the assignment outline that I provided to students that term was written from the comfort and perspective of a White person, whose movements seldom cause suspicion, and whose unearned privilege makes it possible to overlook how activism-as-assignment may be risky and dangerous for BIPOC+ students.

As we met to reflect on this course, with Breckon now having graduated and the displacement of communities of color becoming an ever more prevalent topic in our town, these conversations continue to shape our being-in-the-world. While the project led Breckon to address her whiteness and her production as an obedient and docile student (Foucault, 1977), I continue to challenge myself to (re)consider how my own whiteness affects the designs of my assignments and curricula, which not only attend to a critical multiculturalism (Acuff, 2013; 2015; 2018), but strive to create a safe space for *everyone* inside and outside the classroom.

REFERENCES

Abujbara, J., Boyd, A., Mitchell, D., & Taminato, M. (Eds.). (2017) *Beautiful rising: Creative resistance from the Global South.* OR Books.

Acuff, J. B. (2013). Discursive underground: Re-transcribing the history of art education using critical multicultural education. *Visual Inquiry: Learning & Teaching Art, 2*(3), 219–231.

Acuff, J. B. (2015). Failure to operationalize: Investing in critical multicultural art education. *Journal of Social Theory in Art Education, 35*, 30–43.

Acuff, J. B. (2018). 'Being' a critical multicultural pedagogue in the art education classroom. *Critical Studies in Education*, 59(1), 35–53,

Bell, D. A. (1980). Brown v. Board of Education and the interest-convergence dilemma. *Harvard Law Review, 93*(3), 518–533.

Boyd, A., & Mitchell, D. (Eds.) (2012). *Beautiful trouble: A toolbox for revolution.* OR Books.

Crenshaw, K. W. (1988). Race, reform, and retrenchment: Transformation and legitimation in antidiscrimination law. *Harvard Law Review, 101*(7), 1331–1387

Crenshaw, K. W., Gotanda, N., Peller, G., & Thomas, K. (Eds.). (1995). *Critical race theory: The key writings that formed the movement.* New Press.

Delgado, R., & Stefancic, J. (2012). *Critical race theory: An introduction* (2nd ed.) NYU Press.

Feder, S. (Director). (2020) *Disclosure: Trans lives on screen* [Film]. Field of Vision; Bow and Arrow Entertainment; Level Forward.

Foucault, M. (1977). *Discipline and punish: The birth of the prison.* Vintage.

Harris, C. I. (1993) Whiteness as property. *Harvard Law Review, 106*(8), 1710–1791.

Hubbard, J. (Director). (2012) *United in anger: A history of Act Up* [Film]. Jim Hubbard; Sarah Schulman.

Inwood, J., & Martin, D. G. (2008) Whitewash: White privilege and racialized landscapes at the University of Georgia. *Social & Cultural Geography, 9*(4), 373–395.

Kraehe, A. M., Gaztambide-Fernández, R., & Carpenter, B. S. II. (2018). *The Palgrave handbook of race and the arts in education.* Springer International Publishing.

Ladson-Billings, G., & Tate, W. F. IV (1995). Toward a critical race theory of education. *Teachers College Record, 97*(1), 47–68.

Lawrence, C. R. III. (1987). The id, the ego, and equal protection: Reckoning with unconscious racism. *Stanford Law Review*, 39(2), 317–388.

Lynn, M., & Dixson, A. D. (Eds). (2021). *Handbook of critical race theory in education.* Routledge.

McIntosh, P. (1988). White privilege and male privilege: A personal account of coming to see correspondences through work in women's studies. In *On privilege, fraudulence, and teaching as learning: Selected essays 1981–2019.* Routledge.

Valdes, F., Culp, J. M., & Harris, A. P. (Eds.). (2002). *Crossroads, directions, and a new critical race theory.* Temple University Press.

CHAPTER 34

Critical Conversations in Art History

The State of the Field From Students' Perspectives

Rebecka Black, Aiyana Cady-Alviar, Damaria Moye, and Denise Zubizarreta

Undergraduate art history pedagogy is not always part of art education discourse (Black, 2018). Perhaps it is because for over a century, art historians have deemed object research as the focus of our critical conversations rather than our pedagogical practices. As such, the emphasis of pedagogical research in art history remains focused on what art history educators see as the critical conversations in their classrooms, rather than what our students see as necessary. More immediately, we see conflicts arising among art historians with respect to timely questions of representation of Black, Indigenous, and non-Western artists, as well as of women and gender-nonconforming artists.

This omission is a missed opportunity to engage with honest student feedback in a cultural moment when student activism in the United States is at a peak (Buller, 2021). In this chapter the authors reflect on the critical conversations had, and not had, in their art history courses.

FORMAT

The authors, two current undergraduates, one alum, and one art history professor, have worked together from 2019 to 2022 at an art and design college in Colorado. The three student authors self-identify as women of color. The professor, Rebecka Black, who identifies as White, has worked with all three, either as their instructor or academic mentor. For this essay, Black asked each student to consider this question: "What are the critical conversations you have had or not had in your art history classes?" Their reflections were surprising, considering how the field of art history has progressed in teaching strategies and representation—but maybe not as much as we think.

STUDENT REFLECTIONS

Cady-Alviar: The most pressing conversations in art history are tied to the continued exclusion of non-Western and Indigenous visual culture. I experienced three mandatory Western art history classes to complete the undergraduate program. In contrast, non-Western art history was an elective class, consolidating many, but not even all, global visual cultures into just one course. Unlike three courses for Western art, which gave space for multiple Western voices, the non-Western course had to simplify all non-Western voices throughout history according to the term schedule. For a course so rich with fascinating history and creative inspiration, it was surprising and upsetting, especially as an artist of color, that this course was considered nonessential by the college to complete an undergraduate degree.

By promoting honest education about non-Western/Indigenous visual culture, educators can, in our opinions, actively battle cultural appropriation. Rather than just offering an elective class, non-Western art should be a course learning outcome in all art history classes, Western and non-Western, to engage students in controversial discussions about cultural appropriation. Object and content appropriation are destructive to the preservation of culture because it removes the context from a symbol or concept that is deeply rooted in a people's traditions or belief systems (Young, 2005). When students learn to engage with global visual culture outside of their immediate communities, rather than just memorize it, and are given the tools to grapple with issues of cultural appropriation, it can help prevent distortion of object heritage while spreading awareness of the culture's traditions and knowledge. Having direct conversations about the problematic dichotomy of Western and non-Western (Appiah, 2016), and issues like appropriation, also promotes curiosity and exploration through the student's entire college experience. Educating students in an issues-inclusive manner, Western and non-Western, could help promote awareness of the underrepresented throughout students' communities.

Moye: Racial injustice, queer erasure, and inequity are not new to our 21st century. What differs from humanity historically and currently, in my view, is that students do not idly stand by (Buller, 2021); many of us speak out. These same critical conversations should also be taking place in art history courses, so that we artists have the opportunity to understand the world from different perspectives and with a sense of empathy for others. One experience I had in an art history class that helped me understand the importance of discussing tough topics was, surprisingly, in a required group presentation. I can attest to this as one of my most memorable and effective experiences in an art history course.

The assignment asked us to present to classmates about a feminist scholarly article. Essentially, we were assigned to facilitate a space for the whole class to share our experiences, opinions, and reactions to the controversial article. Not only did I gain valuable perspectives from my own group's conversations, I retained more knowledge from the group presentation series than class lectures (Sowell, 1993). The overall engagement of my classmates was more than I was used to; the article caused people to be upset and openly disagree with one another. However, the assignment parameters set the tone for our presentations to be a safe space for us to be honest and have important, and for some, deeply personal conversations related to feminist art history. The assignment forced me to talk, listen, and empathize with my classmates, giving me new and unexpected perspectives. Art history teachers need to be unapologetic in their desire to expand student mindsets, and teach students how to have such difficult conversations, because the only thing scarier than a critical conversation is willful ignorance.

Zubizarreta: Art history has ingrained in students the basic knowledge of "the greats": Michelangelo, Picasso, Da Vinci, and on rare occasions, Frida Kahlo. This model perpetuates the "one size fits all" version of art history. Though colleges have been investing in diversity efforts and expanding to a global curriculum, some art historians I have worked with have not implemented those principles into course content. Based on my experience, I was more likely to hear about accused murderer Carl Andre than to hear about his wife, Ana Mendieta. Mendieta, the Cuban American artist, and her work are more relevant to my interests, what I am learning in my studio courses, and also to my identity as a Puerto Rican and Cuban American woman. The majority of our student population identifies as female, yet I know of more male artists of the past than I do female or other underrepresented gender identity, past or contemporary.

Talking more directly about representation matters. Why people are or are not represented in art history can help explain how historically elitist power structures still exist. But those structures do not have to be maintained in art history, because art is where humanity has always stretched the conversation about important cultural, religious, and political ideas (Therieau, 2021). It is not only the continued omission of women and global minorities from art history lessons, despite decades of slow change, it is also the lack of representation in art historians. The majority of art history instructors I have had have been White women. However, when I have had an art history teacher of color, the same Western-focused course content was still delivered. It is past time that representation, in curriculum development and instruction, is deemed a critical conversation of art history, not just in the "what" that is taught, but also by whom.

THE IMPORTANCE OF SCHOLARLY DISCOURSE WITH STUDENTS

The issues of representation and inclusion in art history are not new. However, discussions with the student authors here highlight a new issue for art historians to consider—the increase in student activism (Buller, 2021) across American college campuses. If we choose to address it, art historians can no longer rely on past progress or what *we* see as critical conversations. The student authors writing in this article want to learn how to seriously engage with difficult topics and controversial ideas in art history; they want conversation beyond basic obligatory inclusion. Ultimately, from the authors' experiences, the most pressing critical conversation in art history is that we should not rest on our laurels. Instead, we need to listen, then model and engage in difficult, honest, and scholarly discourse *with* our students (Black, 2018).

REFERENCES

Appiah, K. A. (2016, November 9). There is no such thing as western civilization. *The Guardian*. https://www.theguardian.com/world/2016/nov/09/western-civilisation-appiah-reith-lecture

Black, R. A. (2018). Column for Caucus of Social Theory in Art Education. *NAEA News, 60*(1), 24.

Buller, R. E. (2021). Activism, art, and design: Bringing social justice to life in the higher education curriculum. *Art Education, 74*(1), 30–39.

Sowell, J. E. (1993). A learning cycle approach to art history in the classroom. *Art Education, 46*(2), 20.

Therieau, L. (2021, February 15). Representation: The missing backbone of a stellar arts education. *IPaintMyMind*. https://ipaintmymind.org/blog/representation-the-missing-backbone-of-a-stellar-arts-education/

Young, J. O. (2005). Profound offense and cultural appropriation. *The Journal of Aesthetics and Art Criticism, 63*(2), 135–146. http://www.jstor.org/stable/3700467

CHAPTER 35

Opening a Conversation About Adoption Through the Artwork of JooYoung Choi

Borim Song

Adoption is a topic that is rarely discussed in the art classroom. Greenway (2014) claimed that the issue of adoption is almost absent in the visual art field. My review of art education literature corroborated this assertion. Related sources were, in fact, scarce. However, I was able to find three Korean adoptee artists active in the international art scene: Megan Rye, Lisa Wool-Rim Sjöblom,[1] and JooYoung Choi. This chapter introduces JooYoung Choi and examines how Choi's work was used in my discussions of the issue of child adoption with my students at a Southeastern public university. Inspired by art educators who emphasized sharing their own stories of challenges and hardships (Chin, 2015; Rolling, 2010), this essay also includes a story of my overcoming feelings of guilt. With these two components, this account aims to highlight teaching strategies that are helpful in facilitating conversations about difficult social issues through contemporary art.

PERSONAL ENCOUNTERS AND CONNECTIONS

I am a Korean American art educator who left South Korea 23 years ago. I have encountered many Aha! moments in my crosscultural journey while striving to flourish as an art educator in the United States. JooYoung Choi was also born in Seoul, South Korea, and immigrated to the United States in 1982 by way of adoption (Choi, n.d.). Across the genres of painting, sculpture, video, animation, music, and installation art, Choi has documented the interconnecting narratives of an expansive fictional land she titled *The Cosmic Womb* (see Figure 35.1). She introduces herself as "a multidisciplinary world builder" who creates work that "merges the autobiographic with the fantastic into a visual form" (Choi, n.d., para. 3). The Cosmic Womb is an imaginary planet filled with many colorful characters representing different emotions and stories that Choi created with the use of media including drawings, paintings, puppets, painted structures, performances, and videos.

Choi reminds me of my old friend, Mary, one of the first friends I made in New York City. "Mary" and the names of all students included in this chapter are pseudonyms. Mary was an adoptee from South Korea. She was raised by a German-American mother and had several siblings also adopted from Korea and China. We both were in our mid-20s when I met her. As a young adult, I felt that Mary was still going through the identity crisis I had experienced in my teenage years. Mary often felt lost regarding her identity. Not knowing about her roots challenged her beliefs about herself. Listening to her share about her inner and outer struggles, I kept feeling guilty. We both were born in 1973, when South Korea still struggled with severe poverty caused by the Korean War. Due to this devastating situation, many babies were adopted by American and European parents. The fact that my home country did not fully embrace her felt as if it was my own fault. I felt ignorant, selfish, and useless because I could not help with her identity crisis. Exploring Choi's artwork gave me a flashback of these memories and feelings. I realized this was a timely opportunity for me, thinking, "At that time, I was young and did not know what to do. But now, as a professional educator and confident researcher, I can face this issue and work on it together with my students." Choi does not present the issue of adoption in her artwork as explicitly as Megan Rye and Lisa Wool-Rim Sjöblom do. However, audiences can see the connection with adoption through the images and messages in her artwork.

Figure 35.1. JooYoung Choi, *Like a Bolt Out of the Blue, Faith Steps in and Sees You Through* (installation variation with new additions, installed at the Crow Museum of Asian Art, Dallas, Texas, 2022). Photo: Jacqueline Chao. Used with the artist's permission.

STUDENTS' RESPONSES TO THE ARTWORK- THE BODY OF WORK: THE COSMIC WOMB, AND IMAGINARY FRIENDS

My two classes of 45 undergraduate students explored Choi's work and crafted reflections. Eva described her as an "artist whose purpose it is to evoke emotion and drive to a more connected world through visualizations of pop art and culture that lead to a better understanding of the self and its needs and fears" (personal communication, March 14, 2022). This student noticed that every facet of Choi's work is carefully presented to adhere to a certain purpose through symbols. Many students acknowledged the labor-intensiveness of her artwork. Alex mentioned "how much time and effort she seems to put into it," and also reflected, "She took a lot of her childhood pain and turned it into characters that show others that it is okay to feel feelings" (personal communication, March 16, 2022).

The students focused on feelings and their relation to imaginary friends in the Cosmic Womb. For example, Choi's character Bernadette eats bad feelings. Beth noted that Bernadette "helps her friends deal with their feelings of depression and hopelessness" (personal communication, March 17, 2022). In some students' view, Choi encourages others to pull feelings and ideas from their younger selves and to tap into the imagination that they had in childhood to deal with their everyday adult lives. Others thought the viewers could share their feelings by *adopting* imaginary friends living in the Cosmic Womb. Several students also reported that they were moved by some impactful messages delivered through Choi's work. One of them is, "Have faith for you have always been loved." Eva interpreted this message as, "This is me, learn what I am about and use the information to learn to be with yourself and others in a positive way. Be creative. Be You!" (personal communication, March 14, 2022).

The Issue of Adoption Explored

Many students agreed that Choi's artwork could be a helpful resource for starting a discussion about adoption in the secondary art classroom. According to Beth, Choi's art practice is a "journey to self-love and acceptance" (personal communication, March 17, 2022).

Olivia stated that Choi's artwork can help students deepen their understanding of adoption because it illustrates that "although a person might not live with their biological parents, they should have faith because they were always loved and that even though a person is adopted, they can still find a place in this world" (personal communication, March 17, 2022). Emily explained how class discussions about adoption could be facilitated:

> I think the conversation would rather be about discovering one's self, and then maybe a secondary conversation would be about how the adoption process could lead to people attempting to try to find one's self, or similar to Choi, how she tried to collide her worlds of meeting her biological mother and her adopted world. (personal communication, March 15, 2022)

Beyond Stereotypes and Preconceptions

While some students expressed that they felt the topic was familiar, most students confessed that they did not know much about adoption, so they needed careful, in-depth approaches to this theme when applying it to their future classroom practice, to avoid adhering to stereotypes and misconceptions. In addition, students' reflections showed there was a certain oversimplified approach in examining the two families (birth parents and adoptive parents) and two cultural backgrounds (Korean and American). Amy warned about possible narrow-mindedness:

> Adoption is a very touchy subject in schools and with students, so making sure to have a good perspective on the subject is key to being a good teacher and what better way to know more about adoption through art than with an artist who uses her art to depict her childhood through adoption and two families. (personal communication, March 15, 2022)

Debbie shared a possible instructional strategy to incorporate these two different families and cultures:

> This can lead to how a child may be from one place and then move to another but still keep things from their original place of origin. I think first recognizing that there are two different influences for the piece is a good segue into a classroom conversation. (personal communication, March 16, 2022)

Like Debbie, many students endeavored to connect their thoughts and responses to lesson planning and classroom activity design.

The Need for Support Systems

In class discussions, one student pinpointed the concept of "a support system." In her view, the Cosmic Womb created by Choi is a kind of support system for all children who are unique in their own search for belonging.[2] Based on this approach, we can formulate some suggestions for telling stories of childhood adoption through Choi's artwork in classrooms. First, focus on the universal messages Choi purposefully conveys. A message like "failing just means you are trying hard" is relevant for everyone. Second, encourage students to revisit their identities, interests, and cultures and reaffirm the uniqueness of themselves and others. Choi's motto, "Have faith for you have always been loved," helps students embrace their unique qualities, respect others' characteristics and life values, and accept differences. Last, highlight the power of visual art as a creative tool for initiating in-depth conversations about adoption. Choi's colorful and unique paintings, animations, and sculptures deliver inspiring messages that verbal or written communication cannot.

In addition, based on the class conversations shared above, it is evident that the students' responses and reflections went far beyond the topic of adoption and were expanded toward diverse family and personal situations. Also, each adoptee has different experiences within their family. Therefore, incorporating flexibility and conceptual fluidity will be critical for teachers who want to facilitate art-based discussions about diverse social issues. I invite fellow art educators to select a social issue that resonates with them based on their life histories. When exploring this issue through the filter of visual art, the discussion can involve a process of revisiting the past, healing wounds, and growing. This will help foster more confident educators who can help build a supportive community where everyone feels loved and understood.

NOTES

1. Recently, Bae (2022a, 2022b) published two articles about the work of Lisa Wool-Rim Sjöblom, who explained the theme she constantly examines is "the loneliness of transracial adoptees" (2022b, p. 171).
2. The artist JooYoung comments about the absence of the topic of adoption in the visual art field:

> Lastly it's funny how the idea of adoption isn't seen as part of the visual art discussion but so many great characters or people in paintings are adopted, like Jesus, Moses, and many Greek and Roman gods—then in modern current media, I mean Spider-Man was adopted, Superman was adopted, I would have to guess at least half of all the great superheroes and characters in popular visual fiction didn't grow up with their birth parents—like Harry Potter or Dorothy from the Wizard of Oz.

REFERENCES

Bae, J. (2022a). Anti-Asian racism in the time of COVID-19: The work of Lisa Wool-Rim Sjöblom. *Studies in Art Education, 63*(1), 69–76.

Bae, J. (2022b). An interview with Lisa Wool-Rim Sjöblom: Teaching and learning difficult knowledge with comics and graphic novels, *Studies in Art Education, 63*(2), 169–175.

Chin, C. (2015). Failure to be a "real American"? → Challenging failure: An impetus to shape scholarship and teaching. *The Journal of Social Theory in Art Education, 35*, 10–29.

Choi, J. (n.d.). *About.* https://www.jooyoungchoi.com/about

Greenway, K. (2014). Absence: Adoption in art. *Journal of the Motherhood Initiative, 5*(1), 127–147.

Rolling, J. H. (2010). Art education at the turn of the tide: The utility of narrative in curriculum-making and education research. *Art Education, 63*(3), 6–12.

ACKNOWLEDGMENT

I dedicate this essay to my friend Mary and two students, Olivia and Kate. I am also truly grateful to JooYoung Choi for her support for the chapter writing process.

CHAPTER 36

Art and Compassionate Dialogue

Finding and Giving Voice Through Intuitive Knowing and Artistic Research

Rébecca Bourgault and Catherine Rosamond

In her work on creativity and its power to awaken and manifest empathy and compassion, Cain (2019) remarks that the arts offer a unique ability to allow deep meanings to be given forms and to foster supportive conversations through empathy.

We witnessed this enactment as professors of art education with in-service art teachers engaged in graduate arts research, and we believe that these benefits could be transferred to K–12 environments. Indeed, we recognized that a holistic approach to inquiry through the arts opened possibilities for examining layered and intersected identities that encouraged reflexivity, self-compassion, and empathy-building. Students developed a guiding research question based on a personal interest or shared cultural concern and investigated its ramifications through literature and the artistic work of others. They often reach for what Anderson and Braud (2011) refer to as the "fault lines" (p. 25) of their lived history, as "these topics seem to mark places in [students'] psyches or the culture at large that burn brightly. In turn, the findings of their studies tend to illuminate this realm of human struggle for us all" (p. 26). In our teaching at the college level, we have observed that the confidence to talk about personal fears, anxieties, and culturally difficult subjects, especially if they directly affect them, comes with time. Trust and empathy seem to be best built by having students engage in conversation in the intimacy of pairs, then move on to small groups before they build the confidence to discuss with a large class.

Intuitive inquiry, a method articulated by Anderson and Braud (2011) through the lens of transpersonal psychology, has become a theoretical framework that best describes how we interpret personal research investigations of our art teacher-researchers. Life stories "prompt changes in the ways they feel and think about the topic, themselves, others, and the world" (p. 1). The intuitive process in arts research happens over time through candid conversations between the teacher/facilitator and the student, regardless of who comes up with the "Aha!" moments that push the inquiry in a meaningful direction. What follows are critical themes and topics that art teacher-researchers explored.

GENDER AND SOCIOCULTURAL EXPECTATIONS

Understanding that classroom discussions support the development of empathy and compassion by acknowledging the feelings of oneself and others (Barton & Garvis, 2019), some art teachers in our course opted to investigate how conversations on topics such as gender roles and expectations could be examined through artmaking. Based on their understanding that art can be a practice in communication, their artistic production focused on the pressures that cultural conformity and the need for social acceptance placed on their students. Reflecting on their own positionalities and perspectives, their research revealed compassionate insights, further informing their abilities to support K–12 students in their struggles to manage family and community pressures.

For example, one teacher suggested using zines and comics, which can portray gender, race, and class differences and offer a platform for marginalized voices. The text of the zines and comics can combine with the visuals to spur conversation about the students' search for an identity beyond cultural stereotypes. It is evident that "stereotypes are problematic because they create self-fulfilling prophecies in which both men and women accept these descriptions and syndromes as part of their daily lives"

Figure 36.1. T. Chaves, *Accept Yourself* (mixed media, 2019).

(Garcia, 1997, p. 93). During adolescence gender roles are expected to be questioned. However, not every cultural group in a classroom responds to the calls for independence or for conformity with the same sense of freedom and individual agency that is assumed by mainstream American culture. Feelings of powerlessness, fear, and anxiety are made tangible through art, enabling peer sharing, and empathy (see Figure 36.1).

PLACE IDENTITY

Two Asian American art teachers who lived in multiple countries as they grew up engaged in arts research that explored and questioned their identities. Their transient lives were repeatedly disrupted, as they felt uprooted from communities and friends in places that they called "home" for a short time. It is unclear if the social psychologist Proshansky (1978) included the diasporic experiences of immigrants and others who relocated to the United States when he constructed the *place-identity* theory, which states that the development and formation of identity are intrinsically connected to geographical places. Contemporary followers (Grey & O'Toole, 2020) of the place-identity theory focus heavily on the socially constructed nature of the meaning of geographical places by tying the identity of a person making sense of *who* they are to *where* they are.

Where are you from? is a seemingly innocuous question, but it is value-laden with the assumption that people's identity is strongly tied to a specific place. In their research, the art teachers grappled with their sense of belonging because they could not answer this question. One of the ways they found solace and support was through the works of contemporary artists such as Do Ho Suh, Mohamad Hafez, and Zaria, who speak of loss, displacement, diasporic experiences, and homesickness for a home that no longer exists. As if communicating with these contemporary artists, the art teachers created paintings, collages, and photographs through their research that negotiated the layers of their identities, which seemed to shift between prominence and fading over time and places. They constructed and unapologetically told stories of who they were through visual art by gathering building blocks of memories and experiences from the multiple places in which they lived. Their work was a reminder of the complex relationship between place and identity that should always be considered in conversations about students' uprooted pasts.

Ideas were first explored through personal study and arts research, which they enjoyed for its calming solace. Art teachers found their engagement with subsequent artmaking cathartic, as it let them see their own traumas clearly and made possible the sharing of their stories. Vitale (2017) proposed that memories from traumatic experiences are stored as nonverbal and abstract. Using metaphors and images through artmaking helps the artists step outside themselves, see events through a different perspective, and understand their experience through sharing and verbalizing it for others. Teaching art to students who have experienced trauma can result in a similar sharing that facilitates compassionate conversations with peers and teachers.

CULTIVATING COMPASSIONATE DIALOGUES

In this chapter we related our experience mentoring graduate students/art teachers who, through their research projects, examined issues related to their lives, and cultivated the self-awareness and confidence necessary to carry over in the complex world inhabited by their own students, whose voices must be nurtured through empathy and resilience. Guided by principles of intuitive inquiry, a holistic approach to research that nurtures self-compassion and compassion for others, these art teachers explored experiences of personal and social saliency, cultivating a dialogue with their peers and their instructors, as their processes, reflections, and artwork shed light on our divided yet also shared social conditions. The outcome of their research served to "illuminate this realm of human struggles for us all" (Anderson, 2011, p. 26) and taught us how the use of artistic processes as pedagogical strategies has the potential to enable liberating conversations in the classroom.

REFERENCES

Anderson, R., & Braud, W. (2011). *Transforming self and others through research: Transpersonal research methods and skills for the human sciences and humanities.* State University of New York Press.

Barton, G., & Garvis, S. (2019). Theorizing compassion and empathy in educational contexts: What are compassion and empathy and why are they important? In G. Barton & S. Garvis (Eds.), *Compassion and empathy in educational contexts* (pp. 3–14). Palgrave Macmillan.

Cain, M. (2019). But it wouldn't be me: Exploring empathy and compassion for self and others through creative processes. In G. Barton & S. Garvis (Eds.), *Compassion and empathy in educational contexts* (pp. 39–57). Palgrave Macmillan.

Garcia, A. M. (Ed.) (1997). *Chicana feminist thought: The basic historical writings*. Vol. 1. Routledge.

Grey, C., & O'Toole, M. (2020). The placing of identity and the identification of place: "Place-Identity" in community lifeboating. *Journal of Management Inquiry, 29*(2), 206–219. https://doi.org/10.1177/1056492618768696

Proshansky, H. M. (1978). The city and self-identity. *Environment and Behavior, 10*(2), 147–169. https://doi.org/10.1177/0013916578102002

Vitale, A. (2017, June 07). *Using art to revisit trauma helps us put it in the past.* ArtsHub. https://www.artshub.co.uk/news-article/features/performing-arts/agata-vitale/using-art-to-revisit-trauma-helps-us-put-it-in-the-past-253869

CHAPTER 37

Questioning White Privilege Through Contemporary Art

Donalyn Heise and Alisse Guerra

This chapter describes a way of examining white privilege and white fragility using the thought-provoking work of Kathy Barnes-Lou.

Using inquiry prompts focused on observation, interpretation, and personalization, we offer ways to engage learners in dialogue about the ways we can combat our own complicity in white supremacy, and work toward meaningful change for a more just society.

Contemporary art is a powerful tool to bring awareness of social issues and promote critical conversations to help us better understand our world. It provides an avenue to question and dismantle racism and unjust systems. In today's divisive political landscape, facilitating meaningful discussions of race, social justice, and privilege is essential to help all students grow in empathy, teach important democratic discussion skills, and examine existing racial bias. But how can art educators prepare for, initiate, and facilitate critical conversations with productive exchange of ideas while avoiding negative outcomes?

CONSIDERATIONS FOR FACILITATING CRITICAL CONVERSATIONS

- Be clear about your educational goal before facilitating potentially contentious conversations.
- Use contemporary art as a starting point for fostering civil dialogue, not as an approach to solve or come to consensus on an issue.
- Offer all students an opportunity to think and reflect, then share perspectives with the goal of increased understanding and empathy.
- Establish positive rapport with students before attempting to engage in difficult conversations.
- Reflect on your own racial identity in order to identify what privileges you benefit from and how this might affect your teaching.
- Create and enforce class guidelines for productive dialogue that include acceptance of differing perspectives, active listening, and respectful discussion for the purpose of understanding.
- Finally, model respect and compassion as you facilitate critical conversations.

FRAMING WHITE PRIVILEGE

Have students look at *White Privilege Helped Me Escape 201 Poplar*, by Kathy Barnes-Lou (see Figure 37.1). (201 Poplar is the address of the Shelby County Criminal Justice Center in Memphis, Tennessee.) The image is part of the series *Framing White Privilege*, featuring collaborative participants photographed in specifically chosen locations to bring awareness to often unseen privileges. The final digitally manipulated photographs were displayed on the floor rather than the wall (Barnes-Lou, 2022).

Guiding Questions for Facilitators

- How can art stimulate critical conversations about unjust societal issues?
- What is privilege? In what ways do we experience privilege in our lives?
- How can contemporary art communicate what is important to us?

Observation Prompts

- What do you see? What else do you see?
- Describe this work of art for someone who does not have access to it, providing as many details as you can.

Figure 37.1. Kathy Barnes-Lou, *White Privilege Helped Me Escape 201 Poplar* (digitally altered photograph, 2022).

Interpretation Prompts

- What's happening in this photograph? What do you see that makes you think that?
- This artwork is titled ***White Privilege Helped Me Escape 201 Poplar,*** and is part of the artist's larger body of work, ***Framing White Privilege***. The artist is a White female from Memphis, Tennessee. What do you think 201 Poplar refers to?
- Does knowing the title change your first impression of the art?
- How does the artist convey white privilege?
- Is it okay for a White artist to speak about racial issues? Why or why not?

Personalization Prompts

Sue (2003) defines white privilege as the unearned advantages given to white people. The following prompts help all students better understand privilege.

- Have you ever experienced advantages/ opportunities that you felt were unearned?
- Have you ever lost opportunities unjustly?
- Do you have a personal story to tell?
  - » How can you visually communicate your story through art?
  - » What media will you use?

Awareness is often the first step in creating a more just society. Art can bring awareness of issues that are important to us. In a recent discussion, students demonstrated opposing views regarding White artists speaking about racial issues. When dialogue became tense, the teacher remained calm, operated as facilitator, asked clarifying questions in a nonjudgmental tone, and reminded students of the importance of being respectful. Students exhibited acceptance of differing perspectives, often using the phrase "I never thought of it that way." They left energized and motivated to explore ways to use their own art to foster awareness of important issues.

CLOSE LOOKING, QUESTIONING, AND ENGAGING IN CIVIL DIALOGUE

Examining the art of Kathy Barnes-Lou provides learners an opportunity to confront, question, and dismantle white privilege, specifically considering the justice system. The prompts provide a starting point for facilitating critical conversations that can be expanded and adapted to any contemporary art. Through close looking, questioning, and engaging in civil dialogue, learners can examine themselves and their world, imagine new realities, and begin to build a more just society.

REFERENCES

Barnes-Lou, K. (2022). *Artist statement.* https://kathybarneslou.wordpress.com/

Sue, D. W. (2003). *Overcoming our racism: The journey to liberation.* Jossey-Bass.

CHAPTER 38

Investigations of Racism Through a Hexagon Project in an Online College Art Methods Course

JaeHan Bae

I have led non-art major general education preservice teachers since Fall 2017 to create hexagon art projects researching historical or current events that they find interesting and know little about, and contemporary artists of color whose socially relevant work inspires them. The Hexagon Project utilizes the hexagon as a symbol for the interconnectedness and mutual dependency found in complex relationships, similar to human bonds (The Hexagon Project, n.d.). As a stand-alone shape, it signifies light and life, but when combined, it transforms into a magnificent and endlessly expandable architectural feature. The multiplication of hexagons enhances their strength, creating an unending network of connections (The Hexagon Project, n.d.).

I teach in a university in Wisconsin, where most students are first-generation college attendees and over 90% are White. I implemented the Hexagon Project in response to my growing awareness of anti-Asian hostility and broader racist acts in the United States. The Hexagon Project (2022) that now exists as a nonprofit aimed at encouraging peaceful coexistence through examinations of social justice issues began as an assignment in the art methods course I teach for general education preservice teachers (pre-K through 9th grade). Students who take this course gain basic art knowledge and pedagogical applications for their future classrooms. The intended learning outcome of the Hexagon Project was to help preservice teachers explore the complexity of historical and contemporary racial issues through research and art creation. Moreover, I hoped to engage them in a critical reckoning that would cultivate their ability to become more informed, participatory adult citizens and reflective human beings.

I presented the Hexagon Project guidelines and requirements in synchronous online presentations and provided three worksheets designed to guide the students through the project, whose final outcome would be similarly sized, hexagonally-shaped paintings or drawings. Since this was an online art course, each student was instructed to take pictures of their hexagons to insert in their PowerPoint file, which then was posted on our online course platform. I had 18 to 24 students per year and divided them into teams of three or four. Midway through the project, each team met online to share and critique their work on the three worksheets. These worksheets directed each student to investigate personally compelling race-related historical or current events that they knew little about, research at least two contemporary artists of color whose socially relevant work inspired visual and conceptual references in their hexagon, and create initial sketches for their final hexagon project.

STUDENT SAMPLE

One example of an assignment outcome was Mackenzie's hexagon (Figure 38.1), which she created in response to the May 2020 death of George Floyd in Minneapolis, near her hometown of Red Wing, Minnesota. She explained that George Floyd was a 46-year-old African American man who was killed during an arrest for allegedly passing a counterfeit $20 bill for a pack of cigarettes. A White police officer named Derek Chauvin knelt on Floyd's neck for 8 minutes and 46 seconds, during which Floyd pleaded for his life. After his death, major protests quickly spread across the United States and over 60 countries.

Mackenzie described how Floyd's death and the protests that followed made her significantly more aware of racial injustice in the United States. She chose the artwork of a young, Christian, African

Figure 38.1. Mackenzie's final hexagons (left) and Worksheet 3 thumbnails (right) on the death of George Floyd. Courtesy of the artist.

American contemporary artist named Danielle Coke for her project. A positive influencer with over a million followers, Coke has created many illustrations that have become popular symbols in the Black Lives Matter movement. In her social media, Coke's art utilizes many bright colors and includes many powerful and hopeful quotes.

As seen in Figure 38.1, Mackenzie created three hexagons representing the death of George Floyd and systemic racism in the United States. One hexagon (upper left) has a purple sign in the middle that says, "Love lives here." A minimal and effective piece, it has echoes of Coke's recent illustration of Ahmaud Arbery, with a quote by U.S. Vice President Kamala Harris, "Exercising while Black should not be a death sentence" (Gehl, 2020, para. 6). Another hexagon (middle right) is a portrait of George Floyd without facial features, meant to convey that his death symbolizes an individual tragedy as well the far-reaching tragedy of systemic racism (Kraehe & Acuff, 2021). The hexagon at the bottom shows the growth of trees over time and the phrase, "Let's grow together." The brown trees and green grass represent the growth of a new system celebrating antiracism, equity, diversity, and inclusion. Mackenzie sought to convey a message about the continuing need for activism and love, both necessary for changing and healing our divided nation.

REFLECTIVE THOUGHTS

Through this hexagon project, general education preservice teachers gained knowledge about race and injustice, as well as about contemporary artists who have actively responded to social justice issues in the

United States. The project gave them the space to think deeply about the social issues behind their topic and talk about why they were important to them. Prior to the project, for example, Mackenzie had been aware of George Floyd's death and the subsequent protests and riots, but in creating her hexagons she went beyond her newly gained knowledge to express many strong emotions in her hexagons. She remembered her concern for police officers and firefighters who were friends and family, along with friends participating in the Black Lives Matter protests. She realized that learning more about George Floyd's death increased her empathy for those affected by racial injustice in the past and present. During a whole-group online discussion, many students shared that the Hexagon Project helped them see how they might lead children or young adults to investigate and process such difficult topics and knowledge—without relying only on words. The experience of creating their own hexagons had motivated them to do something similar with their students in the future.

As future educators, preservice teachers must address the history of race and current race-related conditions in the United States despite possible hesitations. In my own teaching, the Hexagon Project creates a safe space where teachers and students can respond to feelings about new knowledge of historical and current-day racism. As art educators, we have the opportunity—and the responsibility—to encourage our preservice teachers to educate and prepare themselves for guiding their own students toward lifelong learning and civic engagement. The Hexagon Project is one way to use art and history to cultivate this understanding and promote change for a more equitable and just future.

REFERENCES

Gehl, N. (2020). *4 artists showing that Black Lives Matter*. The Art of Education University. https://theartofeducation.edu/2020/07/31/4-artists-showing-that-black-lives-matter/

The Hexagon Project. (2022). About. Retrieved January 7, 2022, from https://hexagonproject.org/about/

Kraehe, A. M., & Acuff, J. B. (2021). *Race and art education*. Davis.

CHAPTER 39

Giving Voice to the Story of Migration

Naomi Lifschitz-Grant, Allison Ellis, and Catherine Holmes

Birds are not the only things that migrate.

—Student's response to *The Walk* (2022)

One of the most significant issues facing our world is migration. Refugees seek peaceful and secure countries to call home across the globe. In 2022 alone, refugees are escaping violence all over the world. Contemporary artists are addressing these concerns and shedding light on asylum seekers' stories. For example, Amir Nizar Zuabi, artist director of *The Walk*, documents the journey of Little Amal, a 12-foot-tall puppet representing a 9-year-old Syrian refugee (see Figure 39.1). She trudges 5,000 miles across eight countries from Turkey to England in search of her mother. Zuabi said, "As artists, we felt this is an issue we had to engage with . . . I'm happy we've touched hearts. I hope we also touched minds" (Marshall et al., 2021, para. 55).

Another artist, Rafael Lozano Hemmer, highlights issues of migration with a participatory installation at the U.S./Mexico border. Lozano-Hemmer's *Border Tuner* uses sound, light, and human interaction to unite participants, sometimes even joining loved ones separated for years. Searchlights break through invisible barriers in the night sky, and human voices build a bridge as participants share their stories. The requisite for human interaction highlights the need for coexistence and collaboration. Empathetic connections created through public works are rippling across the globe.

In this chapter, we explore the incorporation of contemporary art to confront issues such as migration and how it can help to promote critical discourse in the classroom. Through this practice, students can be inspired to tell their own family's stories and experiences of migration, thereby encouraging a community of empathy.

THE MIGRATION ART LESSON THROUGH CONTEMPORARY ART

Critical discourse about contemporary art, including art that confronts migration, in art classrooms can help to create an environment where students and instructors can be open about their experiences, allowing them to reflect on their lives, families, and communities. Sharing in a safe space can help build a community of empathy in the classroom as the students and instructor gain new insights from an increased understanding of others' diverse experiences. While this can be a rewarding experience for educators and students, careful planning is required to reduce the chances of harm to vulnerable or marginalized groups like immigrants and children in foster care.

Regarding migration, Amir Nizar Zuabi, artist director of *The Walk*, draws audiences to build human connections and empathy as one experiences Little Amal's personification of the refugee journey. Through Little Amal, students can explore ideas of identity, heritage, and transition through interactive conversations and the creation of artwork.

Preparation for the Lesson

Preliminary questions that students can respond to in writing can provide them with a starting point for reflection. This also allows students to respond privately and helps instructors learn about the experiences of the learners before engaging in open discussion in the classroom. Once the comments are received, teachers can read through the materials to find connections between students' experiences. What are

Figure 39.1. ***Little Amal in New York City*** **(2022). (Photograph: Naomi Lifschitz-Grant)**

the common themes? How are they different? What methods would you use to build bridges between different backgrounds? Determine how you would make the discussions safe for everyone.

Some Sample Pre-Questions

We use the word "migrate" or "migration" in the broad sense of the word: moving from one place to another. Families migrate due to numerous circumstances.

1. What comes to mind when you think of migration?
2. What is a refugee? What is an immigrant?
3. Have you or your family moved from a different place(s)?
4. What world events, if any, have affected your family?

Building Connections at Home

In order to build connections and find commonalities with others, it is helpful to look inward. Students can interview a family member to gain insight into their family's stories. Teachers should be mindful that some students, such as those who were part of the adoption or foster care system, may not have a close relative to interview, and that students with little to no knowledge of their ancestry may find these questions uncomfortable. Teachers can provide alternative opportunities for vulnerable students to share aspects of themselves (i.e., favorite foods, personal styles, music, activities, etc.).

Some Sample Homework Interview Questions

1. Where were you born/where did you grow up?
2. How did our family come to live there/here?
3. Where are our ancestors originally from?
4. What circumstances affected our family?
5. Does our family have special ways of celebrating (clothes, traditions, recipes, etc.)?
6. How is the world different today compared to when you were younger?

Artmaking Experience

Puppets are a great storytelling source. Students can combine cardboard shapes (big pieces for the body, long skinny pieces for legs and arms, and little squares for the head) and collage materials (fabric, yarn, beads, papers, buttons, etc.) for details to create figures that will represent themselves or a family member (see Figure 39.2).

Sharing Stories

Presentation of students' puppets can be another opportunity to incorporate a contemporary artwork, such as Rafael Lozano-Hemmer's *Border Tuner.* For example, students can share their puppets' journeys while a lighting crew shines a spotlight on their puppets. One's migration story might be uncomfortable to share with peers, but within a safe and trusting classroom environment, students might be inclined to share their family's journey, an aspect of their family heritage, or their own journey.

Teacher Reflection

Reflecting after the lesson is an important part of growing to become a better educator. Below are a few questions to start the process:

Figure 39.2. *Journey from Mexico*, 2022, 5th-grade student's puppet.

1. What surprised you?
2. What did you learn about your students?
3. What do you think your students learned about each other?
4. How did this project foster a community of empathy?
5. What connections were built?
6. How would you improve on this lesson for future classes?

CONCLUDING THOUGHTS

Incorporating contemporary artists as a starting point in one's lessons can be a powerful tool to encourage active engagement and share stories that will build connections and empathy in a classroom environment. Learning about others' experiences can help in dispelling judgments and stereotypes and bring out one's humanity. In addition to teacher reflections, it is important to give time for students to reflect on this process as well. Their comments can guide the instructor in revising the lesson in the future to support learners, promote dialogue, and give voice to challenging topics such as migration.

REFERENCES

Marshall, A., Gall, C., & Povoledo, E. (2021, November 11). Four months, 5,000 miles: A refugee puppet looks for a home. *The New York Times*. https://www.nytimes.com/2021/11/10/theater/little-amal-the-walk.html

The Walk. (2022). https://www.walkwithamal.org

CHAPTER 40

Fifth Dimension Discourse

Afrofuturism and the Creation of Brave Spaces in Art Teaching

Kathy J. Brown and Lauren Cross

In this resource chapter, (we) two African American tenure-track arts professors operationalize what we gleaned from curating an ongoing cyber conversation entitled *The 2044 Series: Anti-racist Praxis as Futurist Art and Design Pedagogy.* The series was created in response to the summer of 2020 and informed by Bennett Capers's (2019) speculative legal fiction article, *Afrofuturism, Critical Race Theory, and Policing in the Year 2044,* which employed Afrofuturism and critical race theory (CRT) as a lens for reimagining policing in the year 2044, when the United States is proposed to be a majority-minority country. Capers (2019) describes Afrofuturism as more than "melding black culture and technology," but, more importantly, representative of key themes, including

> the insistence that people of color in fact have a future, and a commitment to disrupting racial, sexual, and economic hierarchies and categories. Subsidiary themes include foregrounding alienation and envisioning reclamation. (p. 11)

The series explored Afrofuturism and critical race theory as strategies towards antiracist pedagogy and methods of reframing art and design education.

The virtual panel discussions grew out of our own racialized experiences of being Black in academia colliding with the historic, recurrent uprisings of 2020. Moreover, as teaching artists we had intentions of "troubling the waters," as the African American adage says (Work, 1902), by amplifying the voices of other BIPOC thought leaders and creatives. We sought to reimagine facets of our own Black Womanist border crossings while expanding applications of antiracist pedagogy and engaging in unapologetic critical dialogic encounters to catalyze change. Furthermore, we aimed to foreground Afrofuturism as a multifaceted necessary framework for this practice.

Recorded and disseminated in Fall 2021 and Spring 2022, all six sessions of the *2044 Series* (Onstead Institute, 2021, 2022, various dates) are currently available on YouTube and archived in the UNT Libraries' Scholarly Works repository. Each panel was framed by three to four guiding questions, asking our guests to consider the ways in which their arts research, artmaking, curating, and teaching reimagined new themes, stories, and ideas through an Afrofuturist and antiracist lens.

As a result of engaging critically with guest artists, scholars, and educators, we found ourselves transformed as online participant-observers (Carspecken,1996). We believe that each panelist sparked opportunities for new cultural (re)learning; therefore, we carefully and reverentially investigate the key themes from this public pedagogic project and offer them as portals that reimagine the stories our students can tell. We are convinced that the fruit of these conversations will encourage other scholars, artists, and educators to create brave spaces for their own students, while reinventing and re-creating stories that will empower future perspectives. As we reflect on these six virtual conversations, we do not attempt to assert that there is one distinct pathway to an Afrofuturist praxis, but offer our analysis as entry points, strategies, modalities, and exemplars. Our goal is to de-limit, unbound, and declassify how Afrofuturism and antiracism can unfold in pedagogy and praxis.

ANTI-RACIST PEDAGOGY IN ART EDUCATION: K-12/HIGHER EDUCATION

> Afrofuturism co-opts stories.
>
> —Dr. James Haywood Rolling Jr.

Our first panel, entitled *Anti-racist Pedagogy in Art Education: K-12/Higher Education,* featured art education scholars Drs. Joni Boyd Acuff and James Haywood Rolling. Offering an introductory definition of Afrofuturism, Rolling posited that "Afrofuturist narratives harbor significant implications for anti-racist pedagogies . . . [and inspire] the proliferation of new stories of origin" [12:20–12:30] to spark the imaginations of our students. He also reviewed the antiracist strategies and interventions he outlined in his *Black Lives Matter Open Letter,* which was sent to art educators through the National Art Education Association (Rolling, 2020).

Acuff problematized the deracialization of art curricula as a method for de-siloing students' lived experiences. She also championed the importance of *visual racial literacy*[1] for art educators, which develops cultural competences for understanding the contexts of Afrofuturism before they utilize visual artists like Laulo Senbanjo, Wengechi Mutu, and Jemeel Ammon with their students.

Reflecting on these important conversations, we believe that art educators thinking of using Afrofuturism as a tool to inspire students to (re)imagine new worlds would benefit from the following portals for teacher reflection and future student learning:

- Afrofuturism and antiracist pedagogy are both rooted in storytelling, allowing students to retell their own stories and reimagine the future.
- *Systemic racism.* Racism is by nature systemic, so therefore "systemic racism" is a redundant term. Systems are created to establish and maintain order, then replicated, and thus systemic racism mutates, especially when ignored.
- Teaching Afrofuturism requires research to understand visual racial literacy and cultural knowledge of diverse communities.

ANTIRACIST PEDAGOGY IN DESIGN

In our second panel, entitled *Anti-racist Pedagogy in Design,* designers and scholars Drs. Tameka Ellington, Cheryl D. Holmes Miller, and Terresa Moses, MFA, discussed the intersection of antiracism, erasure, historiographies, determinism, design education, and decolonization, each offering her own description of praxis and recommendations. Ellington, a fashion designer and academic, discussed stereotypes in race and representation, the psychological and sociological legacies of Black hair and cultural appropriation, and antiracist approaches to fashion illustration through artist Malik Shabazz's (2021) drawing instruction book, *How to Draw Black People.* Miller, a well-known design historian, encouraged future BIPOC designers and students to create their own aesthetic, to evangelize one's truth through the decolonization of design histories, and to advocate for diversity in design. Moses, an assistant professor and cocreator of the Racism Untaught toolkit, demonstrated specific ways that her work and research serve to help educators reimagine, re-create, and redesign curriculum to encourage social change. Moses, whose work centers Black women, posited that antiracist pedagogy should call out patriarchy and hegemony. From this talk about how design educators and students can transform design aesthetics, we offer the following portals that might inspire students to bring their whole selves into image-making and dismantle pervasive, oppressive ideas within the field:

- Introduce Afrofuturism as a method for allowing designers to visually respond to racial and cultural appropriation.
- Encourage students to celebrate their own Black aesthetics within design practice, and reclaim African-centered design.
- Teach design through a decolonized lens; highlight, include, and reclaim Black and Indigenous contributions within design history.
- Encourage BIPOC student designers to create their own platforms.

ANTIRACIST PEDAGOGY IN ART AND MUSEUMS

> Culturally specific museums embody racial justice, amidst a universalist and nationalist museum context.
>
> —Stephanie Johnson-Cunningham

Our last live-recorded session, *Anti-racist Pedagogy in Art and Museums,* featured two panelists, museum educator and entrepreneur Stephanie Johnson-Cunningham and curator and professor Dr. Kelli Morgan. During our discussion of anti-Blackness within the museum world, Morgan highlighted her Black feminist approach to curating American art by centering Black community narratives and perspectives in the curation of exhibitions and interpretation of art. She suggested that museums ask the surrounding community what their needs are and engage them as partners. Johnson-Cunningham asks predominantly White institutions seeking to become antiracist to consult long-standing Black cultural institutions because they have been doing the work for many years. Alongside celebrating Black cultural institutions as a model for antiracist museums, her organization Museum Hue (https://www.museumhue.com/) provides tours and maps of cultural institutions that model antiracist practices. From this panel, we offer the following portals to art and museum educators mentoring future museum professionals entering the field: Museums should

- Foster relationships with diverse communities and find ways to engage their voices.
- Value the contributions of identity-centered museums because they are doing antiracist pedagogy work.
- Encourage museum leaders, staff, and educators to foster a sense of belonging for all museum visitors.
- Care for the experiences of the BIPOC museum workers in your museum.

VISUAL NARRATIVES: ANTIRACIST PEDAGOGY IN ART AND DESIGN

The U.S. is a design project.

—Wesley Taylor, MFA

Our first prerecorded session, *Visual Narratives: Anti-racist Pedagogy in Art and Design,* featured art historian and curator Dr. Bridget Cooks, design researcher and professor Omari Souza, and design justice advocate and professor Wesley Taylor. Our discussion began with Cooks and the history of willful exclusion of BIPOC people from the art-historical canon alongside absences of critical scholarship on Black artists and Black feminist art histories. She echoed Johnson-Cunningham from the previous panel and called on the viewers to visit both predominantly White and Black-centered museum spaces and observe the differences, nuances, and values of each institution.

Souza called for alternatives to the design canon, because graphic images perpetuate systemic oppression. He envisioned BIPOC designers and artists as agents, capable of disrupting classification and harmful visual and textual language. Beyond designers and artists, Taylor suggested that educators have the power to ask students to critically reflect on what they value in order to unpack racist systems. He also advocated for designers and artists to create their own Artist Manifestos to foreground their messages; doing so, he suggested, would reverse-engineer how artists become famous, refine the conversations that happen in museums, and reclaim authority through social media and grassroots efforts by taking the power from art world elites. Lastly, he described the United States as an iterative design project built on subjugation and constant revision, moving toward becoming a speculative venture. From this panel we encourage art educators to encourage their students not to be afraid to change narratives and see through these portals for transformative learning:

- Acknowledge the impact of oppression, especially in our respective fields.
- Employ the scholarship of white allies in the field doing antiracist scholarship and practice.
- Teach speculative design and storytelling to help combat systems.
- Introduce students to new art spaces that affirm the Black experience, and create programs illuminating the Black aesthetic in design and visual culture.
- Research Afrofuturist artists such as Titus Kaphar, Noah Purifoy, Cauleen Smith, and David Huffman.

CURATING CULTURE: ANTIRACIST PEDAGOGY IN VISUAL ART

Afrofuturism centers on honoring black bodies and legacies and Reimaging/Counternarrative of tropes of African Representation.

—Stephen Hamilton

Our *Curating Culture: Anti-racist Pedagogy in Visual Art* panel featured Afrofuturist strategist and curator Ingrid LaFleur and visual artist and PhD candidate Stephen Hamilton. LaFleur applies liberatory, Afrofuturist strategies to various endeavors—politics, curating art exhibitions, and building Black entrepreneurs and creating new destinies. Her praxis resists colonial narratives and engages with emerging technologies.

As an artist, Stephen Hamilton's scholarly research-based visual storytelling foregrounds precolonial Africa. For example, in his Founder's Project, Hamilton worked with Boston-area high school students and reframed them in his painted portraits as diasporic royalty. Moreover, he taught the students traditional West African cultural crafts of weaving and dyeing (Acuff, 2020). From this panel we offer these portals of affirmation, which are important for inspiring confidence in our students:

- Understand how to affirmatively engage students of color by recognizing, encouraging, and empowering their visual histories and stories.
- Liberate the Black mind and body from the colonial gaze, through developing cultural competencies and unpacking our own biases.
- Highlight precolonial Africa in addition to contemporary Africa in our art curricula.

REIMAGINING ART: ANTIRACIST PEDAGOGY IN ART AND DESIGN

> Being an artist is more of an autobiographical journey.
>
> —Renee Cox

Our final panel, *Reimagining Art: Anti-racist Pedagogy in Art and Design*, featured visual artists Renee Cox and Nathaniel Donnett. Cox, a Black feminist artist and cultural icon, foregrounds Black joy and celebrates culture. Her most recent body of work, entitled *Soul Culture*, is an Afrofuturistic utopian series of animated images or NFTs [NM1], visualizing safe spaces for Black and brown bodies that are "celestial and spacious . . . about imagination and true fantasy" [9:05–10:25]. During her talk, she championed Black ownership, collective consciousness, and representation. Donnett is an artist who engages in community-based work and self-identifies as a "dark imaginarence practitioner," which he defines as "an identity [he] can control" to express his "freedom" [and] "liberation" [45:45]. When considering how other arts educators could use his work in their pedagogy, he suggests: give the students a voice, allow for imagination, and encourage risk-taking. From this panel, we offer the following portals for those teaching emerging artists:

- Renee Cox encouraged emerging artists to be fearless/stop second-guessing, work from the heart, create your own hype machine, maintain focus, and don't be swayed by money.
- When using Cox's work as an artistic exemplar in our own art pedagogical milieus, K–12 or postsecondary art educators can frame her as an example of a liberatory artist whose principles and beliefs are maintained throughout her body of work.
- If an art teacher decides to utilize Donnett's art in their classrooms, he suggested the big ideas of "interconnectivity" [142:18–142:25] to best describe his work, as he aims to engage and connect with individuals and communities. He posits that in order to "activate future, present and past it's about collaboration . . . pulling from the past . . . reshaped to touch as many people as you can without losing your sense of self" [31:00–31:15].
- Emerging artists, stay true to your voice, don't lose your identity.

Our salient takeaways from this work include the need to openly discuss race, foster collaboration and community involvement, foreground BIPOC voices and imagery, decenter whiteness, encourage voice and freedom, resist classification, self-define and liberate imaginations, and think futuristically while encouraging our students to do the same.

NOTE

1. Visual racial literacy is explained in Kraehe & Acuff's (2021) *Race and Art Education*. Kraehe & Acuff reference Guinier (2004, 2009) in their work.

REFERENCES

Acuff, J. B. (2020). Afrofuturism: Reimagining art curricula for Black existence. *Art Education, 73*(3), 13–21.

Capers, I. (2019). Afrofuturism, critical race theory, and policing in the year 2044. *New York University Law Review, 94*(1), 1–60.

Carspecken, P. F. (1996). *Critical ethnography in educational research: A theoretical and practical guide.* Routledge.

Guinier, L. (2004). From racial liberalism to racial literacy: Brown v. Board of Education and the interest-divergence dilemma. *Journal of American History, (91)*1, 92–118.

Guinier, L. (2009, July 30). Race and reality in a front-porch encounter. *The Chronicle of Higher Education.* https://www.chronicle.com/article/race-and-reality-in-a-front-porch-encounter/

Kraehe, A., & Acuff, J. B. (2021). *Race and art education.* Davis Publications.

Onstead Institute. (2021, April 14). *2044 series—Anti-racist pedagogy in art education: K-12/higher education.* https://www.youtube.com/watch?v=oA-3TQN8Wjs

Onstead Institute. (2021, April 19). *2044 series—Anti-racist pedagogy in design.* https://www.youtube.com/watch?v=sg7nTAWF__0

Onstead Institute. (2021, May 5). *2044 series—Antiracist pedagogy in art and museums.* https://www.youtube.com/watch?v=VkkhaxlRFPc

Onstead Institute. (2021, November 18). *2044 series—Visual narratives: Antiracist pedagogy in art & design.* https://www.youtube.com/watch?v=AFZH44IGcJE

Onstead Institute. (2022, January 18). *2044 series—Reimagining art.* https://youtu.be/Goz1pDNkfQg

Onstead Institute. (2022, April 15). *2044 series—Curating culture: Antiracist pedagogy in art & design.* https://www.youtube.com/watch?v=FJDR23CaOIo

Rolling, J. H., Jr. (2020). *Black lives matter: An open letter to art educators on constructing an anti-racist agenda.* NAEA. https://www.arteducators.org/advocacy-policy/articles/692-black-lives-matter

Shabazz, M. (2021) *How to draw Black people.* Shabazz Arts.

Work, F. J. (1902). *New jubilee songs as sung by The Fisk Jubilee Singers.* Fisk University, Nashville, TN.

CHAPTER 41

Start Where You Are

Toya Northington

I am an artist, researcher, social worker, and social entrepreneur. My educational background includes visual arts and design. In art school, I was taught as a painter that I would create art "for art's sake," without expectation of social responsibility. As I participated in the art industry, I realized that the world that art school put me into had not been created for me or people like me. I did not fit the mold of the mostly male artists who are exhibited in major art galleries and (most notably) museums. My introduction to the art world didn't make me bitter; instead, it made me more aware. I began to question the societal bias against women, not just in my career, but also in my personal life, and the lives of other women and girls around me.

I knew my art could no longer be superficial and detached from social responsibility. I knew art had more power than what was provided in the commercial marketplace where many artists like myself find themselves. My art became a platform to both empower women and facilitate healing from the traumas that they and other marginalized groups face in society.

Suddenly my creative practice wasn't fulfilling. I yearned to use that energy for the greater good of my community by using art as a tool for growth, physical and mental healing, self-development, and to spark joy.

To do this, I had to depart from what I was taught academically in art school and become multidisciplined in my approach to arts education and practice. There are great consequences to going against the grain. It meant harsh criticism, a lack of social capital, and the loss of opportunities in some cases. What I have learned since then is that my departure from the norm has been my greatest superpower, allowing me to see past what is or what has been to discover what could be.

CURRENT WORK

Now, my social practice sits at the intersections of art, mental health, and social justice. I have been using art for healing and empowerment and to address trauma for over 10 years, first with teen girls, then with sexual and gender minorities, and now with other marginalized populations.

In 2012, I founded the ArtThrust Teen Girl Empowerment Program in Louisville, Kentucky. ArtThrust utilizes contemporary art education to foster teens' healthy body image, self-acceptance, and leadership abilities. My success with ArtThrust empowered me to extend my outreach to a broader audience to develop another tier of all-encompassing arts education and programming that could be adapted to address more advanced trauma, mental health issues, and physical challenges.

I developed a social work and research practice focusing on mental health and public administration, public health, and organizational leadership. I chose not to practice as an arts educator, social worker, and researcher in a hospital, therapy office, school, or university. Instead, I took my practice to a museum, originally as the Community Outreach Manager, and currently as the Director of Equity, Inclusion, and Belonging at Speed Art Museum. I am not writing this as an extended resume. I am sharing so that you can understand that the path to growth and resistance can be nontraditional and to offer encouragement so you know that radical work and practice can exist in rigid environments.

BARRIERS TO SOCIAL JUSTICE WORK

Some of you are also embedded in institutions with measures for success built around metrics, standardized testing, attendance numbers, or financial goals. Places where marginalized groups such as those with lower socioeconomic status, Black, Brown, and other people of color, and those with disabilities are left out of sight and out of mind during decision-making and planning. These institutions can be intimidating places to do social justice work. You may have a burning desire to be more inclusive in your practice but be unsure how to start or whether you are the right person to lead the cause.

This burning desire is your tipping point to change your practice and to expand your scope of work beyond teaching the elements of art, technical skills, and western-centered, historical context into art lessons to deepen the participants' critical thinking, communication skills, emotional intelligence, and cultural humility. The advantages extend beyond developing well-rounded and knowledgeable art professionals; these transferable skills apply to any profession.

It doesn't matter if you are in a K–12 school, university, museum, community center, or church; there is no perfect place to disrupt the status quo. Institutions are flawed because we live in a flawed society built from systems of inequity. Every place has a challenge. For some it may be a lack of support from leadership or policies impeding change. Others find that lack of resources, low pay, and too high expectations are in the way. My tipping point came 10 years ago; yours may be starting now, while others will eventually follow.

The outrage, grief, and shock that resulted from the killings of George Floyd, Breonna Taylor, and Ahmaud Arbery caused a shift in our collective consciousness as a nation. Those closest to the communities most affected were forever changed. What was once acceptable is no longer enough. People are demanding more from businesses, corporations, art, artists, and museums (Eve, 2021).

The COVID-19 pandemic created a physical and mental health crisis. Grief from the loss of loved ones, opportunities, major milestones, and the sense of safety left children, youth, and adults with depression and other mental and physical health conditions. Arts education embedded with social justice and psychosocial lessons can be avenues to work through those unresolved feelings or ways to experience joy, wonder, and curiosity during challenging times (Chen et al., 2022).

TIPS AND SUGGESTIONS

Build a Support System

I cannot stress this enough. Doing racial or social justice work can be taxing. It requires both the participant and facilitator to be vulnerable and invest in their experience. Stress from administrators or outside pressures can magnify those feelings. Developing a network will provide you with colleagues who are facing similar challenges. Talking through ideas and plans with trusted peers can help expose some of your blind spots and biases.

It took a while, but I eventually found a community of artists, educators, cultural and community organizers, and other change agents who would become both advisors and comrades.

Do No Harm

Enter this work after careful planning and self-reflection. Before incorporating diversity, inclusion, or social justice topics into art lessons or museum tours, consult subject-matter experts. These are people who have both lived experience and practice in the topic. This could help safeguard you from unintentional mistakes and help to grow your support network.

Art education is the foundation to create the next generation of artists, art administrators, museum professionals, nonprofit leaders, and art patrons. People often say that art doesn't save lives, but I disagree. If done well, every profession could be touched by this influence. Similar to math, science, and philosophy, art should be part of the developmental foundation to build communication skills, critical thinking, empathy, and shared understanding of diverse experiences. It can save lives by reducing isolation, building self-confidence, and affirming self and cultural identity, and it can build peer support systems (Stuckey & Nobel, 2010).

REFERENCES

Chen, Y., Zeng, X., Tao, L., Chen, J., & Wang, Y. (2022). The influence of arts engagement on the mental health of isolated college students during the COVID-19 outbreak in China. *Frontiers in Public Health, 10,* 1021642. https://doi.org/10.3389/fpubh.2022.1021642

Eve, E. (2021). *U. S. business moved to combat racism after George Floyd's murder. Here's what still needs to be done.* MarketWatch. https://www.marketwatch.com/story/u-s-business-moved-to-combat-racism-after-george-floyds-murder-heres-what-still-needs-to-be-done-11619985092

Stuckey, H. L., & Nobel, J. (2010). The connection between art, healing, and public health: A review of current literature. *American Journal of Public Health, 100*(2), 254–263. https://doi.org/10.2105/AJPH.2008.156497

Resources That Inspire

This section includes recommended resources provided by the contributors when asked, "What are your 2–3 go-to resources to inform critical conversations?"

BOOKS

Ahmed, S. (2010). Orientations matter. In D. Coole & S. Frost (Eds.), *New materialisms: Ontology, agency, and politics* (pp. 234–257). Duke University Press.

- This chapter explores why orientations, or how our bodies are oriented toward the world, matter in all we do.

Baglieri, S., & Lalvani, P. (2019). *Undoing ableism: Teaching about disability in K–12 classrooms.* Routledge.

- This book gives practical advice and ideas for engaging in critical discourse with K–12 students about media, disability, and anti-ableism.

Baglieri, S., & Shapiro, A. (2017). *Disability studies and the inclusive classroom: Critical practices for embracing diversity in education* (2nd ed.). Routledge.

- This book shows how disability studies theory can be applied to school settings. It provides historical information on the disability rights movement and addresses the impact of the intersection of race, gender, class and/or sexual orientation with disability.

Ballengee Morris, C. & Staikidis, K. (2017). *Transforming our practices: Indigenous art, pedagogies, and philosophies.* Taylor Francis LTD/National Art Education Association.

- This coedited anthology with 29 Indigenous/Non-Indigenous artist/scholars/researchers/teachers presents content on Indigenous studies and art practices for preK–20 levels.

Barrett, T. (2011). *Criticizing art: Understanding the contemporary* (3rd ed.). McGraw-Hill.

- This is one of Barrett's many books that helps us describe, analyze, write about, discuss, and better understand visual art.

Berger, J. (1977). *Ways of seeing.* Penguin Books.

- A text that encourages the importance of ideas and how we see things: "The way we see things is affected by what we know and what we believe" (Berger, 1977, p. 8).

Boyd, A., & Mitchell, D. O. (2016). *Beautiful trouble: A toolbox for revolution.* OR Books.

- Case studies that focus on creative activism and provide tools and tactics for changemakers.

Burbules, N. (1993). *Dialogue in teaching: Theory and practice.* Teachers College Press.

- Burbules offers a philosophical clarification, rationale, types, and rules for dialogue in teaching.

Dewhurst, M. (2018). *Teachers bridging difference: Exploring identity with art.* Harvard Education Press.

- This book details a White art teacher educator's work to move her students beyond surface-level appreciations of other cultures toward meaningful and reciprocal connections across difference. Although it takes place in a university setting, teachers will find useful theories about race and culture applied to practical art projects.

Duckworth, E. (2006). *The having of wonderful ideas* (3rd ed.). Teachers College Press.

- This classic work teaches us that creating situations can cultivate imaginative idea development for students of all ages and that it's at the center of engaged learning.

Ellington, T., & Underwood, J. L. (Eds.). (2020). *Textures: The history and art of Black hair.* Hirmer Publishers.

- Dr. Tameka Ellington & Dr. Joseph Underwood's exhibition catalog *Textures: The History and Art of Black Hair* is a great resource for how art exhibitions highlighting artworks and historical artifacts can reframe historical narratives on Black hair.

Falk, J. H., & Dierking, L. D. (2013). *Museum experience revisited.* Left Coast Press.

- This book examines museum practices from the perspective of visitors, providing valuable insight for museum professionals who wish to foster a visitor-centered experience.

Hammond, Z. L. (2015). *Culturally responsive teaching and the brain*. Corwin Press.

- An innovative approach for designing and implementing culturally responsive instruction.

hooks, b. (2010). *Teaching critical thinking: Practical wisdom*. Routledge.

- This book is like "talking shop" with another educator; an incredibly wise, thoughtful, and personable one, who really understands the layered possibilities of dialogue.

Hubard, O. (2015). *Art museum education: Facilitating gallery experiences*. Palgrave Macmillan.

- This book is a deep dive into the complex work of facilitating dialogue and experiences around works of art, including real-world examples in museums.

Kaba, M., & Hassan, S. (2019). *Fumbling towards repair: A workbook for community accountability facilitators*. Project NIA.

- A useful workbook with tips, lessons, and activities for community facilitators who work to address interpersonal harm and violence.

Kraehe, A. M., & Acuff, J. B. (2021). *Race and art education*. Davis Publications, Inc.

- This recent publication provides a clear, well-organized overview of key concepts around how race operates in art education spaces and suggests strategies for implementing antiracist lesson plans.

Kumashiro, K. (2004). *Against common sense: Teaching and learning towards social justice*. Routledge Falmer.

- This book provides an antioppressive theory for how we learn, arguing that discomfort is part of the process. Kumashiro breaks down complex processes and helps teachers think through how they might turn moments of crisis and failure into opportunities.

Landreman, L. M. (Ed.). (2013). *The art of effective facilitation: Reflections from social justice educators*. Stylus Publishing.

- The contributors share approaches to facilitating discussion, reflection, and action through personal narratives and social justice education.

Lawton, P. H., Walker, M. A., & Green, M. (2019). *Community-based art education across the lifespan: Finding common ground*. Teachers College Press.

- This book is grounded in social justice and includes ways to connect art education classrooms with communities outside the school. It includes curriculum examples, stories, and research frameworks for community-based art education.

Lerman, L., & Borstel, J. (2003). *Critical Response Process: A method for getting useful feedback on anything you make, from dance to dessert*. Liz Lerman Dance Exchange.

- The Critical Response Process aims to deepen dialogue between makers and audiences and between members of a learning community. This book includes a detailed introduction to the process and guidance for facilitators.

Marcuse, H. (2015). *Eros and civilization: A philosophical inquiry into Freud*. Routledge. (Original publication 1955.)

- If you're going to read midcentury socialist theory, this text is emotive, romantic, and concerned with liberation. Marcuse stirs together Marx and Freud to posit a nonrepressive society fueled by love.

Marshall, J. (2019). *Integrating the visual arts across the curriculum: An elementary and middle school guide*. Teachers College Press.

- This book models how to use contemporary art to drive integrated, inquiry-based instruction.

Marshall, J., Stewart, C., & Thulson, A. (2021). *Teaching contemporary art with young people: Themes in art for K–12 classrooms*. Teachers College Press.

- This useful, full-color resource offers educators strategies, new artists, and curriculum ideas to teach with contemporary art and integrate contemporary ideas and methods into the K–12 classroom.

Mayo, C. (2022). *LGBTQ youth and education: Policies and practices* (2nd ed.). Teachers College Press.

- Cris Mayo offers an updated engagement with policies and practices supporting LGBTQ youth in schools.

McIntosh, P. (2019). White privilege and male privilege: A personal account of coming to see correspondences through work in Women's Studies (1988). In *On privilege, fraudulence, and teaching as learning: Selected essays 1981–2019*. Routledge. https://www.collegeart.org/pdf/diversity/white-privilege-and-male-privilege.pdf

- In this text, McIntosh lists 46 ways in which whiteness and white privilege protect from hostility and violence and afford unearned and special provisions in daily life. Although written more than 30 years ago, McIntosh's reflection is a great resource to begin conversations about how white privilege and male privilege shape our everyday life.

Menakem, R. (2017). *My grandmother's hands: Racialized trauma and the pathway to mending our hearts and bodies*. Central Recovery Press.

- This workbook supports readers in examining the damage caused by racism in America from the perspective of trauma and body-centered psychology, and includes a variety of reflective and somatic exercises.

People's Knowledge Editorial Collective. (2016). *People's knowledge and participatory action research: Escaping the white-walled labyrinth.* Practical Action Publishing Ltd.

- This is an open-source text to address the lived experience and expertise of people and communities and centers those voices and ideas.

Pollack, S., & Fusoni, R. (2017). *Moving beyond icebreakers: An innovative approach to group facilitation, learning, and action.* The Center for Teen Empowerment.

- This resource includes tips on facilitating interactive meetings and describes over 300 interactive exercises in detail that support relationship-building, collaboration, and group dynamics.

Quinn, T., Ploof, J., & Hochtritt, L. (Eds.). (2012). *Art and social justice education: Culture as commons.* Routledge.

- A coedited anthology, with essays, resources, and contemporary artist images in color, that focuses on critical, meaningful, and transformative arts education curriculum.

Ramirez-Valles, J. (2016). *Queer aging: The gayby boomers and a new frontier for gerontology.* Oxford University Press.

- Jesus Ramirez-Valles offers insights into one of the first out-and-proud generations of gay men aging into retirement and the lessons they provide younger generations.

Robertson, J., & McDaniel, C. (2010). *Themes of contemporary art: Visual art after 1980* (2nd ed.). Oxford University Press.

- Uses themes like identity, the body, and time to open perspectives into art of the last 40 years. This text is useful for anyone teaching about contemporary art, in either the classroom or the museum.

Simon, N. (2016). *The art of relevance.* Museum 2.0.

- A practical guide for museum professionals who want to better understand the needs of the communities they serve and how museum programming can serve both broad audiences and specific groups.

Sjöblom, L. W-R. (2019). *Palimpsest: Documents from a Korean adoption.* Drawn and Quarterly. https://www.instagram.com/chung.woolrim

- Graphic novel and personal story about adoption.

Song, B. (2023). I don't want to use my cultural identity just to survive in America! In R. Shin, M. Lim, O. Lee, & S. Han (Eds.), *Counternarratives from Asian American art educators: Identities, pedagogies, and practice beyond the Western paradigm.* Routledge.

- This coedited book highlights the narratives and professional identities of Asian art educators and researchers in North America.

Walker, M., & Unterhalter, E. (2007). The capability approach: Its potential for work in education. In M. Walker & E. Unterhalter (Eds.), *Amartya Sen's capability approach and social justice in education.* Palgrave Macmillan. https://doi.org/10.1057/9780230604810_1

- This book brings together conceptual and empirical writing on the theme of applications of Amartya Sen's capability approach for education.

West, A. (2011). *Mapping the intelligence of artistic work: An explorative guide to making, thinking and writing.* Moth Press: Maine College of Art and Design. https://mecastore.square.site/product/mapping-the-intelligence-of-artistic-work/30

- This book is the go-to for MFA students working through thesis ideas, but it is an excellent resource for artist-educators. Using a series of writing and artmaking prompts, the reader develops a conceptual map of their artistic thinking and ideas that hone writing and art skills.

CONFERENCES AND ORGANIZATIONS

The Allied Media Conference https://amc.alliedmedia.org/

- An annual hybrid virtual/in-person conference held in Detroit featuring workshops and speakers emerging from the confluence of art, education, media futures, technology, and design. Always radical, cool and thoughtful. This conference is the best place to see where discourse will be in three years.

The National Art Education Association (NAEA) https://www.arteducators.org

- Founded in 1947, the National Art Education Association is a professional membership organization exclusively for visual arts, design, and media arts education professionals. Their annual spring conference is a professional learning event and offers sessions, workshops, and opportunities designed to inform, inquire, inspire, and create connections.

The National Association for Multicultural Education (NAME) https://nameorg.org/index.php

- NAME is a nonprofit organization that advances and advocates for equity and social justice through multicultural education. They have an annual fall conference that brings together allies, leaders, educators, researchers, and advocates who champion the work of creating a more just, inclusive, and equitable tomorrow.

JOURNAL ARTICLES

Acuff, J. B. (2020) Afrofuturism: Reimagining art curricula for Black existence. *Art Education, 73*(3), 13–21. doi: 10.1080/00043125.2020.1717910

- Dr. Joni Boyd Acuff's article on Afrofuturism gives specific instructions for how art educators can reshape arts curriculum through the practice of visual racial literacy that challenges traditional conventions in art teaching.

Dewhurst, M., & Hendrick, K. (Eds.). (2017). Identifying and transforming racism in museum education. *Journal of Museum Education, 42*(2).

- This issue of the *Journal of Museum Education* was guest-edited by antiracist scholars and museum practitioners Marit Dewhurst and Keonna Hendrick; it contains several articles that can support (museum) educators' antiracist practices.

Garoian, C. R. (2001). Performing the museum. *Studies in Art Education, 42*(3), 234–248.

- In this article, Charles R. Garoian explores the relationship between museums and visitors as a dialogic encounter between the visitors' private narratives and museums' public narratives.

Kretzmann, J., & McKnight, J. P. (1996). Assets-based community development. *National Civic Review, 85*(4), 23–29. doi:10.1002/ncr.4100850405

- This research comes from community development and works to coalesce around an asset-based approach versus deficit foci. It supports mapping the multitude of assets available in any community to build coalition and change initiatives. This can apply to educators, students, and communities as they explore from a lens of the multitude of assets that are present within a site and community.

Marshall, J. (2016). A systems view: The role of art in education. *Art Education, 69*(3), 12–19. doi:10.1080/00043125.2016.1158587

- Describes how 3rd-graders on a field trip used research workbooks to record their observations and experiences.

Marshall, J., & D'Adamo, K. (2011). Art practice as research in the classroom: A new paradigm in art education. *Art Education, 64*(5), 12–18. doi:10.1080/00043125.2011.11519139

- Describes how high school students use research workbooks to inform their artwork.

ONLINE RESOURCES

Anti-Racist Art Teachers https://www.antiracistartteachers.org/artists

- Archive of diverse artists to decolonize your art history.

Antimodular Research. (2022). Rafael Lozano-Hemmer. https://www.lozano-hemmer.com/

- This website is specific to the contemporary artist Rafael Lozano-Hemmer and his artwork and accomplishments.

Antiracist Social and Emotional Learning, Puget Sound Educational Service District https://www.psesd.org/programs-services/learning-teaching-and-family-support-ltfs/enhancing-social-emotional-practices/antiracist-sel

- The website explains what antiracist social and emotional learning is and what actions educators and administrators can take to cultivate SEL (social and emotional learning) for antiracism.

Art Against Racism. https://artagainstracism.org/

- This website features artists who confront racism in their art.

Art21.org

- A website presenting many artist interviews and thought-provoking content about contemporary art.

ArtStories https://www.pamelaspress.com/research-1

- Pamela Harris Lawton shares research about collaborative and intergenerational making and social justice–related art.

Kathy Barnes-Lou—Artist https://kathybarneslou.wordpress.com/

- Artist statement stating how the series "Framing White Privilege" interrogates power, white privilege, and colonialism.

Biewen, J. (Executive Producer). (2017). *Seeing White* [Audio podcast]. Scene on Radio. https://www.sceneonradio.org/seeing-white

- This podcast, which examines whiteness (and is part of a larger series), is an accessible means of learning more about the history and functions of whiteness.

Brave Spaces https://www.ctznwell.org/ctznpodcast/brave-space-not-safe-space-micky-scottbey-jones

- Brave Space/Safe Space: Jones, M.S. (2022, March, 3). CTZNWELL. A call to a different practice that risks mistakes and accountability to each other in truth and love.

Brave Spaces—Poem https://www.grossmont.edu/faculty-staff/participatory-governance/student-success-and-equity/_resources/assets/pdf/brave-space-poem.pdf

- An invitation to brave spaces by Micky ScottBey Jones.

Building Anti-Racist White Educators (BARWE) https://www.barwe215.org/

- Each school year this nonprofit organization puts together a decentralized reading and inquiry series to support teachers as they explore their own racial biases with the goal of improving their own teaching practices. BARWE provides a monthly set of tools for learning, introspection, and having conversations about issues of racism in our schools, classrooms, and communities.

Center for the Study of White American Culture (CSWAC), *Raising anti-racist White children.* https://cswac.org/raising-anti-racist-white-children/

- CSWAC's remote and in-person workshops are terrific resources for parents and teachers interested in their mission, which is "to build an equitable society in the United States by decentering white culture and centering an anti-racist multiracial culture free of white supremacy."

Chalk Talk Resources:
National School Reform Faculty:
https://www.nsrfharmony.org/wp-content/uploads/2017/10/chalk_talk_0.pdf
Project Zero, Harvard GDS:
http://www.pz.harvard.edu/sites/default/files/Chalk%20Talk_1.pdf

- Two takes on a strategy for silently reflecting on questions, considering learning, and generating new ideas.

Danielle Coke—Artist

- You may find Danielle Coke's racial justice graphics and artworks at her social media.

Instagram: www.instagram.com/ohhappydani

Facebook: www.facebook.com/ohhappydani

Twitter: www.twitter.com/ohhappydani

Cooks, B. R. (2022). *The Black Index.* https://www.theblackindex.art/

- Dr. Bridget R. Cooks's *The Black Index* is a great resource for an art exhibition and featured artists that embody Afrofuturist ideas towards challenging traditional categories, definitions, and labels.

Cult of Pedagogy https://www.cultofpedagogy.com/

- Blog, videos, podcast. Jennifer Gonzalez, former ELA teacher, shares practical strategies and ideas, bringing experts to explain, in accessible ways, theories from educational and social psychology. The podcast has covered topics such as suicide prevention, critical race theory, restorative justice, and teaching students with disabilities.

(divorcing) White Supremacy Culture: Coming Home to Who We Really Are https://www.whitesupremacyculture.info/

- Website to identify the principles of WSC, how they show up in workplaces, and antidotes to combat them.

Facing History & Ourselves https://www.facinghistory.org/

- From the website: "Facing History resources address racism, anti-semitism, and prejudice at pivotal moments in history; we help students connect choices made in the past to those they will confront in their own lives." It is an excellent resource for teachers and students and provides resources to place current events in a historical context. It offers webinars and tangible strategies to engage in discussion with students. Two resources we particularly recommend are listed below.

Facing History & Ourselves—Barometer: Taking a Stand on Controversial Issues https://www.facinghistory.org/resource-library/teaching-strategies/barometer-taking-stand-controversial-issues

- This website highlights the work of a nonprofit community arts organization that promotes interdependency and interconnectedness through the arts. It offers useful resources, ideas, and examples.

Facing History & Ourselves—Preparing Students for Difficult Conversations https://www.facinghistory.org/resource-library/preparing-students-difficult-conversations

- Facing History's guide to preparing students for difficult conversations

Hamilton, S. (n.d). *The Founders Project.* https://www.nowandthere.org/foundersproject

- From the website: "*The Founders Project* is a multimedia installation by artist Stephen Hamilton that re-imagines Boston Public School High-School students as the legendary founders of West and West-Central African ethnic groups; specifically, those that are part of the ancestral base of the African diaspora."

Hexagon Project
https://hexagonproject.org/

- This website highlights the work of a nonprofit community arts organization that promotes interdependency and interconnectedness through the arts. It offers useful resources, ideas, and examples.

- Justseeds Artists' Cooperative https://justseeds.org

- A decentralized network of 41 artists committed to social, environmental, and political engagement.

LaFleur, I. (2022). Think like a Afrofuturist. *The Afrofuture Strategies Institute.* www.thinklikeanafrofuturist.com/

- Consultant and educator on Afrofuturist strategies.

LGBTQ Curricular Laws. Movement Advancement Project. https://www.lgbtmap.org/equality-maps/curricular_laws

- Regularly updated interactive U.S. map showing policies related to LGBTQ inclusion in, or exclusion from, school curricula or standards.

Learning for Justice, a project of the Southern Poverty Law Center. (Formerly Teaching for Tolerance.) https://www.learningforjustice.org/

- Pursues the racial justice mission of the SPLC in the education realm. Specific resources we recommend are listed below.

Learning for Justice—Agree/Disagree Statements https://www.learningforjustice.org/classroom-resources/teaching-strategies/close-and-critical-reading/agreedisagree-statements

- A useful reading strategy that challenges students to think critically about what they know about a text, idea, topic, or theme.

Learning for Justice—Critical Practice https://www.learningforjustice.org/frameworks/critical-practices

- Learning for Justice's Critical Practices for Anti-bias Education and applications for the classroom.

Learning for Justice—Social Justice Standards https://www.learningforjustice.org/frameworks/social-justice-standards

- A framework for anti-bias education with anchor standards and age-appropriate outcomes for social justice teaching and learning.

Learning for Justice—Speak Up at School: Respond to Everyday Stereotypes and Bias https://www.learningforjustice.org/sites/default/files/general/speak_up_pocket_card_2up.pdf

- A Teaching for Tolerance pocket guide.

Leslie-Lohman Museum of Art. Queer Art TV https://vimeo.com/leslielohman

- Short videos featuring artwork created by LGBTQ artists or art about LGBTQ+ themes, issues, and people. The museum's website includes virtual exhibitions and a searchable collection database: https://www.leslielohman.org/

Metropolitan Museum of Art. (2021–2023). *Before yesterday we could fly: AfroFuturist period room.* [Exhibition Catalog]. https://www.metmuseum.org/exhibitions/listings/2021/afrofuturist-period-room

- The exhibition catalog for The MET's Afrofuturist Period Room *Before Yesterday We Could Fly* provides further context for the installation featuring works from the museum's collection with other works. The essays situate the Afrofuturist period room within the historical context of other traditional, European period rooms and unpacks the nuances of Afrofuturist narratives and aesthetics that inform the installation.

Middle School Art, High School, College Art Project, Visual Journal, Altered Book Lesson https://www.teacherspayteachers.com/Product/Middle-School-Art-High-School-Art-Project-Visual-Journal-Altered-Book-Lesson-1210913?st=6b907a25795d5453fce849044fed4cde

- This is part of the "Teachers Pay Teachers" curriculum resources site and offers PowerPoints, lessons, and presentations on weekly visual journaling. The resources are developed by and for teachers, are reasonably priced, and are digital resources.

Miller, C. D. H. (2020). From "Black designers: Missing in action" to "Forward in action": 3 essential industry articles. *Print.* https://www.printmag.com/design-inspiration/from-black-designers-missing-in-action-to-forward-in-action-3-essential-industry-articles/

- Series of design articles written by scholar Dr. Cheryl D. Holmes Miller published by *Print* magazine, which helps to chart a new path for Black designers past, present, and future.

Moses, T., & Mercer, L. (2022). Resources. *Racismuntaught.com*

- Resources for the Racism Untaught Toolkit, which helps educators and organizations to help students to engage in antiracist design research.

National Glossary of Terms (compiled by PFLAG) [https://pflag.org/glossary

- Recognizing that there is no universal agreement on definitions, explore evolving terms relevant to gender, gender identity, sexual orientation and beyond.

National Museum of African American History & Culture, Smithsonian https://nmaahc.si.edu/

- A museum focused exclusively on the documentation of African American life, history, and culture. It has lesson plans for educators on pieces in their collection.

National SEED Project https://nationalseedproject.org/

- The National SEED Project (Seeking Educational Equity and Diversity) partners with communities, institutions, and schools to develop leaders who guide their peers in conversational communities to drive personal, institutional, and societal change toward social justice.

Phillips Collection. *Checking in on our biases.* https://drive.google.com/file/d/1hi5fKxv_hEyxMNnfl6taDq50wwC6uaCq/view?usp=sharing

- A checklist of questions developed by Erica Harper, Hilary Katz, and Anne Taylor Brittingham at the Phillips to check on biases while selecting artworks and artists for investigation.

Project Zero, Harvard Graduate School of Education. (2016). Project Zero's thinking routine toolbox. http://www.pz.harvard.edu/thinking-routines

- This website provides many different types of effective and adaptable thinking routines used to scaffold and support student learning across all subject matters.

Quick Write Strategies https://www.oxfordsd.org/cms/lib/MS01001032/Centricity/Domain/18/WICOR%20Strategies%20and%20Summarizations.pdf

- This document provides multiple quick summarizing strategies to utilize in teaching.

Rethinking Schools https://rethinkingschools.org

- Preeminent publisher of social justice education materials, started in 1986 by activists, teachers, and community members in Milwaukee, Wisconsin.

Smithsonian Institution. (n.d.). Educator resources: Learn with the Smithsonian. https://www.si.edu/educators/resources

- Offers educators resources and digital tools that support active engagements in the arts.

Teaching Contemporary Art with Young People https://www.teachingcontemporaryart.com/

- Website that accompanies the book by Marshall, Stewart, and Thulson (2021) with art and artists to support teaching contemporary art in the classroom.

The Walk Productions Limited. (2022). *Little Amal: The Walk.* https://www.walkwithamal.org/about-us/little-amal/

- This website covers "The Walk," the journey of Little Amal, a 12-ft. puppet, in support of refugees searching for family or a new home.

Timm-Bottos, J., & Chainey, R. (2015). *Art hives how-to-guide.* Concordia University. https://arthives.org/sites/arthives.org/files/art_hives_how-to-guide_1.pdf

- This open-source tool kit offers practical information to help institutions and individuals develop and sustain Art Hives, as well as information about the history and theory associated with these spaces.

Michael Vasquez—Artist http://www.michaelvasquez.info/

- An American artist whose work explores identity and the cultivation of community through personal explorations of extended families, social situations, and peer/society pressures.

Woke Kindergarten https://www.wokekindergarten.org/

- A resource for abolitionist early childhood education.

TELEVISION SERIES

Comely, B. (Executive Producer). (2006). *Simon Schama's The Power of Art.* BBC Series. https://www.imdb.com/title/tt0887235/

- Also see the accompanying text, *The Power of Art* (2006) by Schama. These resources are an amazing way to learn the historical and cultural context of eight important Western works from Schama, a thoroughly engaging historian/art critic.

About the Editors and Contributors

ABOUT THE EDITORS

Dr. Connie Stewart (she/her) is a professor emeritus at the University of Northern Colorado, and former area head of art education. Her research activities include classroom applications of contemporary art, transdisciplinary learning, and critical art theory. She is the author of *Teaching Contemporary Art With Young People* (2021) with Julia Marshall and Anne Thulson. She has received two Arts Work grants from the National Endowment of the Arts. Specific research studies center on exploring questions and questioning in instructional practices.

Eli Burke, MFA (he/him) is a senior program manager for design projects and PhD candidate in Art and Visual Culture Education, University of Arizona, Tucson. As the former Education Director at the Museum of Contemporary Art Tucson, Eli provided leadership, direction, and coordination for the museum's education and public programs. Eli is also an artist and received his MFA in Studio Art from the School of the Art Institute of Chicago, where he was a full-tuition Merit Scholarship recipient. His research focus is on the queer imaginary, the LGBTQIA+ community, intergenerational learning, creative aging, contemporary art, and access + equity.

Dr. Lisa Hochtritt (she/her) is director of the Master of Arts in Teaching program at Maryland Institute College of Art (MICA) in Baltimore. She is the co-editor of two Routledge publications: *Makers, Crafters, Educators: Working for Cultural Change* (2019) with Elizabeth Garber and Manisha Sharma, and *Art and Social Justice: Culture as Commons* (2012) with Therese Quinn and John Ploof. She has received awards for her teaching and service including the National Art Education Association (NAEA) Higher Education Art Educator of the Year and the Colorado Art Education Association Art Educator of the Year.

Toya Northington, MSSW (she/her) is an artist, researcher, and social entrepreneur. She holds a Bachelor of Fine Arts degree from Georgia State University and a Master of Science in Social Work from the University of Louisville. Working in mixed media and across disciplines, Toya's works are an act of resistance, pushing back against societal expectations. In 2012, Toya founded an art-based, mental health and social justice organization, ArtThrust, employing art-based, trauma-informed programming to address the psychosocial needs of Black girls and LGBTQ+ youth in Louisville, KY. She is the director of Equity, Inclusion, and Belonging at the Speed Museum.

ABOUT THE FOREWORD AUTHOR

Dr. James Haywood Rolling Jr. is a dual professor of Arts Education and Teaching & Leadership and the codirector of the Lender Center for Social Justice at Syracuse University. A former elementary school art teacher who earned his BFA in art from The Cooper Union, his MFA from Syracuse University, and his doctorate in art education from Teachers College, Columbia University, Dr. Rolling is currently the 37th President of the National Art Education Association.

ABOUT THE CONTRIBUTORS

Michelle Antonisse is a Los Angeles-based artist and educator and Manager of Teen & School Programs at The Museum of Contemporary Art (MOCA). She holds a BA in art history from Bard College and attended the Gerrit Rietveld Academie for conceptual art in Amsterdam. Michelle also runs experimental environmental education workshops under the name "Into the Field." All of these practices explore the intersections between art, science, and critical thinking through reflective practice and student-centered learning.

JaeHan Bae, PhD, is professor of art education in the Department of Art at the University of Wisconsin–Oshkosh. He holds a Doctor of Philosophy degree in art education from the Florida State University in Tallahassee, Florida, and a Master of Education degree in Elementary Fine Arts Education from Daegu National University of Education in Daegu, South Korea. His research interests include Asian critical theory, contemporary art in art education, and preservice teacher education.

Outside of being a husband and father of two amazing girls, ***Kelly Beach*** is an art educator. Through a choice-based art curriculum and the Teaching for Artistic Behavior philosophy, he believes in creating a safe and inclusive learning environment and empowering all students to see themselves as lifelong artists. He was a member of Colorado's State Standard Revision Committee 2021, established Colorado TAB Inc., and cohosts Colorado TAB, Inc.'s annual art conference.

Alice Bebbington (she/her) is the Specialist, K–12 & Community Audiences at the Hammer Museum at UCLA and serves as the President of the Museum Educators of Southern California. She has worked in museum education for over 8 years, including most recently as the Manager, School Programs at The Museum of Contemporary Art, Los Angeles. Throughout her work, Alice sustains a reflective teaching practice and centers learners through inquiry-based, anti-oppressive pedagogies. Alice holds a BA with High Honors in Art History from UC Berkeley.

Mary Kate Bergh is a K–8 art educator at an elementary school in North Philadelphia. Previously, she taught middle school and high school art in Maryland. She has experience teaching a wide variety of art courses, along with a civil discourse class. Mary Kate received her BS in art education in 2013 and received her MEd in art education in 2019 from Kutztown University. She has presented on topics exploring relational pedagogy, student voice, and the power of the visual journal.

Rebecka Black holds a PhD in art history and education from the University of Arizona. Black's art historical and art education research focuses on issues of power and identity. Her research in art education also focuses on pedagogy and student engagement in undergraduate art history courses, particularly related to community-building through socially engaged pedagogy.

Rébecca Bourgault is a visual artist, community art practitioner, and educator. Chair and assistant professor of art education at Boston University, she holds an EdD in art & art education from Teachers College, Columbia University, and an MFA from the University of Calgary. Bourgault's current visual and scholarly research interests include socially engaged art, art in a posthuman world, and hybrid approaches to research-creation and arts research.

Kathy J. Brown, PhD, is a HBCU graduate, former K–8 art teacher, and practicing artist. She is an assistant professor of art education at the University of North Texas and holds a leadership position with the Texas Art Education Association. Her research interests include antiracist pedagogy, social justice in art education, art teacher narratives, cultural epistemologies and visualities, and Afrofuturism. Her chosen methodologies are narrative inquiry, duo/autoethnography, and art-based research.

Aiyana Cady-Alviar holds a BFA in Fine Arts from Rocky Mountain College of Art + Design.

Chris Cain, with a MAT & BFA from University of the Arts in Philadelphia, is a Colorado artist/high school art educator who combines painting, photography, digital technology, collage, and mark making, in no particular order, into mixed media artworks. It's an intuitive process, and the sequence of the media makes no difference. Mentoring artmakers from kindergarten to college over the past 25 years, Chris follows a similar teaching method, passionately focusing on variety for the whole learner.

Breckon Chastain is a graphic designer, illustrator, and painter. She graduated from the University of Georgia with a BFA in Graphic Design and an emphasis track in Cultural Studies. Her personal work centers on print and branding while exploring social and cultural issues/perspectives in design.

Katie Coogan is a visual artist and educator with experience teaching in traditional classroom and museum education settings at the elementary, secondary, and collegiate levels. She received her MEd at the University of Maryland–College Park (UMD) and has since served in the Elementary Education, Arts Integration, and Art Education departments before becoming the PDS coordinator for the UMD Art Education program in 2019. Her personal artwork currently focuses on regeneration, rebirth, and transformation.

Lauren Cross, PhD, is program coordinator and assistant professor of Interdisciplinary Art and Design Studies at the University of North Texas. Cross's research addresses critical multicultural approaches in arts practice, arts entrepreneurship, curatorial studies, museum studies, and art history. Cross is the director of the award-winning documentary *The Skin Quilt Project* (2010), and she has been recognized nationally and internationally for her art practice and community work in museums and galleries across the United States and in Edinburgh, Scotland.

Carissa DiCindio, PhD, is an assistant professor in Art and Visual Culture Education at the University of Arizona. Her teaching and research center on art museum education, with a specific focus on museum–community partnerships, university art museums as spaces for collaboration and innovation, and creating opportunities for dialogue and connection in art museum programming. DiCindio has been in the field of art museum education for almost 20 years.

Libya Doman, a National Board-certified visual art and cultural responsiveness educator, designs and delivers curriculums, workshops, and keynotes to help educators grapple with topics that are often deemed taboo. Ms. Doman is proud to have degrees from Spelman College (an HBCU), Moore College of Art & Design, and Teachers College, Columbia University. In addition to 19 years of K–12 teaching, she has served as mentor, coach, and professor.

Kerry Downey is a genderqueer, interdisciplinary artist and educator based in Kingston, NY. Like their teaching practice, their artwork explores embodied forms of resistance and transformation. Downey holds a BA from Bard College and an MFA from Hunter College. Downey spent over a decade running community-based arts programs at The Museum of Modern Art; they have recently taught at Williams College, Rhode Island School of Design, Parsons/The New School, and Hunter College.

Allison Ellis is an elementary art teacher in Columbus County, North Carolina. She earned her BA in Fine Arts and BS in Biology from the University of North Carolina at Pembroke. She earned her MA in Art Education from the University of North Carolina Pembroke. Prior to being an art teacher, she was a migrant tutor for Columbus County, where she serviced migrant students in English, reading, and mathematics.

Robb Epps, MFA, is an artist and the Martha Beach Endowed Chair at UNC–Pembroke. He has been teaching animation, illustration, and digital art since 2000. His work has appeared in such places as *Animation Magazine*, NBM's *Confessions of a Cereal Eater* comic series, and *Pollyworld: The Polly Pocket Movie*. Robb has served as a textbook reviewer for Cengage Publishing and a subject matter expert for both Pearson Publications and Career Education Corporation.

William Estrada is an arts educator and multidisciplinary artist. His current research is focused on developing community-based and culturally relevant projects that center power structures of race, economy, and cultural access in contested spaces that provide a space to collectively imagine just futures. He is currently a clinical assistant professor at UIC School of Art & Art History and a teaching artist at Telpochcalli Elementary in Chicago, Illinois.

Amy Felder earned her MA from University of Northern Colorado and her BA from College of Charleston. In 2012, she earned her National Board Teaching Certificate with Art/Early and Middle Childhood certification. While Amy is a very committed and dedicated teacher, she is also an artist. Spanning a breadth of mediums including paintings, wall hangings, installation work, and embroidery, her work reflects a contemporary experience of nature and struggle to preserve wilderness.

Adam J. Greteman, PhD (he/him), is an associate professor of Art Education at the School of the Art Institute of Chicago. He is the author of *Sexualities and Genders in Education: Towards Queer Thriving*, which received an Outstanding Book Award from the Society of Professors of Education. He is also a coauthor of both *On Liking the Other: Queer Subjects and Religious Discourses* and *The Pedagogies and Politics of Liking*. Adam is a cofounder of The LGBTQ+ Intergenerational Dialogue Project (www.generationliberation.com)

Kelly M. Gross, PhD, is an assistant professor of Art and Design Education at Northern Illinois University. She is currently working on several research projects that focus on the intersection of art education, special education, and disability studies. Kelly cofounded The Rubber Band Project, a K–5 STEAM nonprofit, which develops project-based learning curricula. Kelly is a former special education teacher and K-8 art teacher who has taught in New Orleans, New York City, and Chicago.

Alisse Guerra is a MA candidate in Art Education at The University of Texas at Austin, investigating how art education can enhance resilience in schools and communities affected by climate disasters. She is an artist, maker, and educator with bachelor's degrees in painting and art history from Louisiana State University.

Donalyn Heise, EdD, is associate professor of Instruction at The University of Texas at Austin with over 30 years of experience teaching art in K–16 school and community settings. Her teaching and research focus on fostering resilience through art for youth who have experienced trauma. Her work has been published in three books, eight book chapters, 20 journal articles, and over 200 juried paper presentations and professional development workshops.

Hannah Heller is a Philly-based art museum educator and has worked at several cultural institutions, including the Whitney Museum of American Art, El Museo del Barrio, and the American Folk Art Museum. She has an EdD in Art & Art Education from Teachers College, Columbia University, and an MA in Museum Education from Tufts University. Her research focuses on blending object-based and antiracist pedagogies and exposing impacts of whiteness in gallery teaching practices.

Amara Higuera (she/ella) is a Los Angeles–based artist and educator. Her artistic practice explores how material and historical conditions manifest and shape our spirits and psychic landscapes. Her teaching practice focuses on anti-oppressive pedagogy that centers the knowledge and experiences learners bring to the classroom. Amara built the foundations for this practice with her coauthors, labor organizing with arts workers, and through a formative liberatory reading group made up of high school teachers.

Catherine Holmes is an elementary art teacher in North Carolina. She earned her BA in Psychology from the University of North Carolina at Chapel Hill and attended the North Carolina Governor's School in Visual Arts. She will obtain her MAT in Art Education from the University of North Carolina at Pembroke in Spring 2023. Her research explores social–emotional learning and empathy through contemporary art and culturally relevant pedagogy in art education.

John Humphrey refers to himself as a "recovering art teacher" with tongue firmly in cheek. He earned a BFA from Rocky Mountain College of Art + Design and a MA in School Counseling and Clinical Mental Health Counseling from the University of Northern Colorado. John served as a 7–12th-grade visual art teacher and now is a middle school social–emotional learning specialist. He combines teaching and academic scholarship with participation in competitive air guitar.

Kimberly Lane is a visual art teacher at The Blake School, a pre-K–12th grade school in Minneapolis, MN. In addition to her teaching, Kim has published two books on talking about art with children. She holds a Bachelor of Arts from the University of Notre Dame and a Master of Arts and a Master of Education from Teachers College, Columbia University.

Pamela Harris Lawton, EdDCTA, MFA, is the Florence Gaskins Harper Endowed Chair in Art Education at Maryland Institute College of Art. Her scholarly research and teaching revolve around visual narrative and intergenerational arts learning in BIPOC communities. Lawton's artwork is grounded in social practice, seeking to illuminate contemporary issues, cultural traditions, and the stories of people impacted by them. In addition to numerous publications, presentations, and exhibitions, Lawton coauthored *Community-Based Art Education Across the Lifespan: Finding Common Ground* (Teachers College Press).

Naomi Lifschitz-Grant, EdD, is an associate professor, Coordinator of Undergraduate Art Education, and Interim Graduate Program Director of Art Education at the University of North Carolina at Pembroke. She earned her doctoral degree in Art and Art Education from Teachers College, Columbia University, where she also obtained an MA in Art Education. Her research explores how the arts can serve as a community-based process to implement school change, particularly in disadvantaged school settings.

Beth Link, PhD, is a visiting assistant professor at the University of North Texas. She received her doctorate in Curriculum and Instruction at the University of Texas at Austin and is a former elementary art teacher. Beth's research applies critical theory on race and whiteness to visual art curriculum, enactment, and teacher-identity formation to understand the complex ways teachers navigate difference and tell stories through art objects.

Ashley Mask, EdD, MFA, is an artist, art museum educator, professor, and researcher-scholar. She is assistant professor of Art and Museum Education at Western Washington University. She previously led the education departments at the Rubin Museum of Art in New York City and the Boulder Museum of Contemporary Art in Boulder, Colorado, and taught at Columbia University, Naropa University, the Metropolitan Museum of Art, and the Brooklyn Museum.

Dianna Montano earned a BFA in Sculpture from Colorado State University and a BA in Art Education at Montana State University. She is an experienced visual arts educator with over 11 years of teaching in the Denver metro area, and during that time earned a MA in Art Education from the University of Northern Colorado. Throughout her career, she has catered to a diverse range of students' needs across the state, including Bishop Machebeuf High School and Aurora Central High School, where she instructed students in one of Colorado's largest refugee populations. Now in Douglas County, Dianna instructs elementary art, and holds a position on the visual arts curriculum council for the district.

Karen Morris, PhD (she/her) is an associate professor of Cultural Anthropology in the Department of Visual & Critical Studies at The School of the Art Institute of Chicago. Her research investigates understandings and enactments of kinship and family, gender and sexuality, and activism and care work within marginalized populations. Karen's work has been published in *City & Society; Anthropology News; International Journal of Qualitative Studies in Education;* and *Studies in Art Education.*

Damaria Moye is a Fashion Design major at Rocky Mountain College of Art + Design.

Lisa Novak, previously based in England, and on the traditional and unceded territory of the xʷməθkʷəy̓əm (Musqueam), Sk̲wx̲wú7mesh (Squamish), and səlilwətaɬ (Tsleil-Waututh) Nations, is an Austrian educator, social practitioner, and doctoral candidate in art education at the University of Georgia. She is the founder of the School of Collaboration and Invention (socai.org), and has facilitated numerous workshops and youth-led arts intensives across Canada and the United States.

Harrison Orr is the Education Manager at the Museum of Contemporary Art Tucson, as well as an adjunct instructor in Art & Visual Culture Education at the University of Arizona. He earned a BFA in Media Arts and an MA in Art & Visual Culture Education at the University of Arizona. His current research interests include intergenerational learning, the experiences of LGBTQIA+ learners and educators, and partnerships between museums and schools.

Ketal Patel is an art educator and the director of the Field Experiences and Licensure Program for the Arts Administration, Education, and Policy department at The Ohio State University. She earned her PhD from OSU developing a participatory action research study with fellow art educators about their practices and intersections with creative placemaking. Her work is grounded in action research and how participatory and narrative inquiry can be used to dismantle and question whose knowledge is valid.

Alice C. Pennisi, EdD is associate professor and Coordinator of Art Education at SUNY Buffalo State. She has been a visual arts, language arts, science, and social studies teacher, and Arts Integration Specialist, in New York City, where she cofounded New Design High School. Her research interests and teaching involve reengagement of secondary students through art curricula centered on social theory, teacher–student curriculum negotiation, as well as cross-disciplinary curriculum design.

Amy Pfeiler-Wunder is professor of Art Education at Kutztown University, where she has served as chair and coordinator of the Master's in Art Education program, and currently as the interim associate dean in the College of Visual and Performing Arts. She received her PhD in Teaching and Learning–Art from the University of Iowa. Prior to joining higher education, she engaged in play and artmaking with pre-K–9th graders in various settings. She is an active member of NAEA, serving in numerous roles, most recently as the chair of the Research Commission. Her work examines the impact of intersectionality on one's professional identity with keen attention to views of the learners and curriculum creation.

Kristin A. Ponden serves as the Middle Level Commissioner on the National Art Education Association's Equity, Diversity, and Inclusion Commission. She has given workshops and presentations and participated in panel discussions on equity and antiracism for a variety of organizations. Kristin was selected as the 2021 Independent School Art Educator of the Year and the 2021 Outstanding Connecticut Art Educator.

Valeska Maria Populoh works as an artist, facilitator, educator, and cultural organizer in Baltimore, Maryland. Embracing a wide array of tactics, from puppetry to participatory performance, Valeska's work is motivated by an interest in healing and repair, in our relationships to each other and to the natural world. Valeska serves on the faculty of the Fiber and First Year Departments at the Maryland Institute College of Art, where she has been teaching since 2008.

Gladys Preciado (she/her) is an art educator who has taught at various art and cultural institutions. She is now a professor of Art History in the art department at Santa Monica College. She implements a liberatory pedagogy based on antiracist, student-centered, and community-engaged practices. Gladys aims to challenge the Eurocentric foundations of art history by teaching a global and intersectional curriculum, one that defies the traditional art historical canon.

Natasha S. Reid, PhD (she/her) is an assistant professor of Art Education in the Department of Curriculum and Instruction at the University of Victoria (2022–present). She was the executive director of the Visual Arts Centre in Montreal (2017–2021) and an assistant professor of Art and Visual Culture Education at the University of Arizona (2013–2016). Using narrative research and arts-based practices, she investigates and activates art spaces and public pedagogical sites as locations for antioppression work.

Erica Richard is Associate Educator, Youth and Family Learning at the Saint Louis Art Museum, where she works to reimagine how the museum engages young people and their grown-ups. Previously, Erica managed the teaching resource website, community showcase program, school field trip offerings, and teacher professional development at the Denver Art Museum. In the classroom, Erica taught art to early childhood, grades 3–5, middle school, and high school. Erica believes art changes people, and people change the world.

Amanda Tobin Ripley is a doctoral student in Arts Administration, Education, and Policy at The Ohio State University. Her work within museums supports the imaginative power of art to foster a shared sense of belonging, responsibility, and humanity. Amanda holds an MEd in Arts in Education from the Harvard Graduate School of Education and a BA in Art History from Oberlin College.

Ariana Robles (she/her) is a Latina museum educator interested in museums as service institutions, focusing on how museum education can be transformed into a reflective and inclusive space for all learners. As museums grapple with their identities as collecting institutions, Ariana is interested in how transparency, care, and collaboration with local communities can redefine the museum's function.

Catherine Rosamond, EdD is the chair of the art education department at the School of Visual Arts (SVA) in New York City. Rosamond obtained her doctorate at Teachers College, Columbia University, and has over 2 decades of experience as an artist educator in museums and community-based organizations. She serves on SVA's DEI task force and the National Art Education Association's (NAEA) ED&I Commission. Her current scholarship interests include arts research, specifically in transdisciplinary investigations that consider non-Western approaches to inquiry.

Nikki Sandschaper taught for 12 years in Denver, Colorado, before entering the sphere of international education. Her first years as a special education teacher and with underresourced communities led to continual reflection on the inclusiveness of her practice. She holds a BFA in Art History and an MA in Art and Design and encourages students to joyfully explore the intellectual experience of artmaking. Her class centers critical thinking through engaging discussions and meaningful studio experiences.

Aparna Sarkar is a queer, first-generation Indian-American painter in Brooklyn, NY. Her paintings collapse the false poles of abstraction & figuration, flatness & perspective, and ornament & utility. Aparna holds an MFA in Painting from the Rhode Island School of Design (2021) and a BA in Mathematics from Pomona College (2014). She teaches art and math at a private K–12 school.

Rebecca Shipe, PhD is an associate professor in Art and Educational Studies at Rhode Island College. Prior to her employment in higher education, she worked as a professional illustrator, served as a Peace Corps volunteer, and taught art for eight years in the Arizona public schools. Her current research interests include arts-based research, international collaborations, and exploring ways that experiences with visual art can promote conflict transformation.

Borim Song is an associate professor at the School of Art and Design of East Carolina University, Greenville, North Carolina. She holds her EdD and EdM from Teachers College, Columbia University in New York City. Her research interests include new technologies for art education, online education practice, contemporary art in K–12 curriculum, and crosscultural and intercultural movements. Song's writings appear in publications in both the United States and Korea.

Kryssi Staikidis is professor of Art Education at Northern Illinois University, and holds a Doctor of Education degree in Art Education from Teachers College, Columbia University and an MFA in Painting from Hunter College. Research interests are Indigenous pedagogy, collaborative ethnography, and arts-based research. Her books include *Transforming Our Practices: Indigenous Art, Pedagogies, and Philosophies* (2017) and *Artistic Mentoring as a Decolonizing Methodology: An Evolving Collaborative Painting Ethnography*, with Pedro Rafael González Chavajay and Paula Nicho Cúmez (2020).

Taylor Michelle Styles is a graduate student at the University of North Carolina–Pembroke, where she is pursuing a master's in art education. She earned her BA from Berea College, where she studied Art and Art Education. As a teaching artist, she collaborates with a variety of schools and programs to assist in developing and instructing art curriculum-based activities.

Julie Toole (she/her/hers) is the 1st–8th-grade art teacher at Baker Demonstration School. This is her 31st year teaching, with 20 of those years in Chicago Public Schools. She is an instructor at the TAB (Teaching for Artistic Behavior) Summer Institute at the Massachusetts College of Art and Design. Julie is a trained SEED (Seeking Educational Equity and Diversity) facilitator and the cofounder and advisor for her middle school GSA (Gender Sexuality Alliance). Julie is a frequent presenter on her equity work and TAB practice.

Margaret Walker received her EdD in Art and Art Education at Teachers College, Columbia University, and is coordinator of the Art Education program at the University of Maryland. She has been an artist and educator in community, school, museum, and university settings in New York, Maryland, and Washington, D.C. She recently coauthored the Teachers College Press book *Community-Based Art Education Across the Lifespan: Finding Common Ground* with Pam Lawton and Melissa Green. Her primary studio work is oil painting.

Nic M. Weststrate, PhD (he/him) is an assistant professor in the department of Educational Psychology and member of the Center for Research on Health and Aging at the University of Illinois Chicago. Nic studies positive aging and intergenerational relationships within the LGBTQIA+ communities. His research has appeared in such journals as *Developmental Psychology, Emerging Adulthood, The Journals of Gerontology: Psychological Sciences, Psychological Inquiry, Journal of Personality,* and *Personality and Social Psychology Review.*

Injeong Yoon-Ramirez, PhD is Endowed Assistant Professor of Art Education, University of Arkansas. Her research, teaching, and community organizing are interconnected around issues of antiracism and anticolonialism. She publishes widely in academic journals and her Routledge book, *Decolonial Arts Praxis: Transnational Pedagogies and Activism* (2023), explores how arts, pedagogy, and activism interplay to radiate decolonial imagination. Dr. Yoon-Ramirez founded Entretejer/Interweave Community School (www.interweavecommunity.com) to offer a critical and creative learning space for working-class immigrant families.

Simona Zappas is the youth programs manager at the Walker Art Center. She facilitates informal learning opportunities and designs public engagement strategies. Earlier, Simona directed WFNU Frogtown Community Radio in Saint Paul, Minnesota. Simona holds a bachelor's degree from Macalester College and a Masters of Education from the University of Minnesota. Simona sits on the board of the Saint Paul

Neighborhood Network and volunteers at Planned Parenthood as an abortion doula.

Denise Zubizarreta "The Vamp DeVille" Zubizarreta is a neurodivergent Puerto Rican + Cuban multidisciplinary creative, researcher, and scholar currently living and working in Arvada, CO with a BFA in Fine Art from the Rocky Mountain College of Art and Design. She currently focuses her writing on arts and culture for both Hyperallergic and Southwest Contemporary. Her mixed media works explore postcolonial theory through blending traditions, memories, and contemporary life to honor, reclaim, and reinvent narratives of the past, present, and future.

Index